God in Flesh and Bones

By

Marcelino Esquilin

ISBN 978-1-960903-09-9 (Digital)

ISBN 978-1-960903-10-5 (Paperback)

ISBN 978-1-960903-11-2 (Hardcover)

Publify Publishing

1412 W. Ave B

Lampasas, TX 76550

publifypublishing@gmail.com

Dedication

This work is dedicated first to my wife, Sofia; then our sons, Erick, Obed, Ian, and Gindy; our daughters, Melody, Lizbeth, Willianie; our grandkids, Eriannie and Nathanial; then to my professor Dr. Ralph D. Curtin who prophesied that I would write books collaborating and bless many.

Finally, to whomever acquires and reads this work, thank you.

Look at [the marks in] My hands and My feet [and see], that it is I Myself. Touch Me and see; a spirit does not have flesh and bones, as you see that I have.

- Luke 24:39

Contents

Prologue

Many people express having difficulty understanding the biblical text and subsequently declare that no one can ever decipher its content. They prefer to tag the biblical literature as worthless, folklore, and/or pious fiction instead of acquiring its sweet spiritual nectar through a thorough study/research of its foundation. The erroneous beliefs about the biblical God and religion (*for Christians and non-Christian alike*) commence not by the content of biblical literature but by opinions resembling old cultural rituals from individuals that invent interpretations by assimilation, not having studied the biblical text in its intimacy, in other words, its literature structure, synthesis of literature, and the spiritual effects its content produces and teaches away from the old gods they used to serve. As we study the biblical content in depth, we must be reminded that theology (*the study of God's word*) is the fuel that ignites our worship and its structure is based upon the shoulders of biblical giants. Not only by the prophets, the psalmist, and the apostles (Jews) who wrote and gave their life and blood establishing the Bible's teaching but by the post-apostles, the fathers of the second to third centuries, and by many men and women throughout the church history who stood up and fought to keep its doctrinal teachings pure. It is by the exposition of giants such as John Wycliffe, John Wesley, John Hus, Martin Luther, John Calvin, Charles H. Spurgeon, and contemporaries such as Vernon McGee, Billy Graham, Millard Erickson, Wayne Gruden, Chuck Missler (*and many others not mentioned*)that observed and follow what was later called systematic theology. By their work and candor, we understand the message of the Bible synthesis in better terms. The truth they followed is the tradition, or theology the *eyewitnesses'* apostles gave us and declared in their writings. These individuals' work and their dedication added to the *Spirit of Truth (whom the Bible says it comes from*) and declared the secrets and mysteries that the Scripture brings to life by the Spirit of the Father. He is the One who guided the preceding believers to the fountains of His living waters, whose waters, in turn, is for everyone to obtain, consume, and enjoy. It is by their theological discernment and inspiration that this book has been arranged to deepen the knowledge of today's twenty-first-century Christians. We are bringing their views for the enrichment of our brothers and sisters in Christ but through a different route.

Our reality according to Scriptures has been created by God, the intellectual architect of His universe, which He also sustains. Therefore, we must look at reality through the eyes of God according to His written word in order to receive a truthful exposition of the life we are living. The biblical text, as Christ explained, takes us back to the reality God meant for us to live. He said, **"Everyone who hears these words of Mine and acts on them, will be like a wise man who built his house upon the rock,"** which we concluded (*in our book* The Apostles Methodology to Interpret Scripture) that the house is our reality and the rock is God's written words (Matt. 7:24 AMP).

First lesson: God's word is immutable/unchangeable. This is how we must observe the biblical text, for it comes from the mind of an *omniscient* BEING. We are His creation, and therefore, we are reading omniscient knowledge from the mind and consciousness of an Omni-God. This is also why scripture says, **"He has also set eternity in the human heart,"** so that we can understand His words (Eccles. 3:11).

Second lesson: Who is God, and can we know Him? Then let us begin to comprehend the purity of the biblical text as the apostle Paul taught Timothy:

> **I urged you [...] so that you may instruct certain individuals not to teach any different doctrines, nor to pay attention to legends (fables, myths) and endless genealogies, which give rise to useless speculation and meaningless arguments rather than advancing God's program of instruction [*redemption*] which is *grounded in faith* [and requires surrendering the entire self to God in absolute trust and confidence].**

Let us advance in God's program, for His covenantal word was created in His terms and His design (1 Tim.1:3–4 AMP). All we must do is to be grounded in it by the faith/hope it produces in us, by the merit of Jesus Christ's priestly works. Paul clearly exhorts to follow the apostolic theology (*tradition*); for it was redacted by God the Holy Spirit, which He heard from God Jesus and the Father, to declare it to us His disciples. Paul also knew and taught the same theology as the other apostles (*he read their work*) that he knew God Jesus had told/taught him and them as he wrote:

> **But the [Holy] Spirit explicitly and unmistakably declares that in later times some will turn away from the faith [*Gospel*] paying attention instead to**

deceitful and seductive spirits and doctrines of demons [misled] by the hypocrisy of liars whose consciences are seared as with a branding iron [leaving them incapable of ethical functioning] [...*no spiritual power*, and] If anyone teaches a different doctrine and does not agree with the sound [doctrine] words of our Lord Jesus Christ, and with the doctrine and teaching which is in agreement with godliness (personal integrity, upright behavior), he is conceited and woefully ignorant [understanding nothing]. He has a morbid interest in controversial questions and disputes about words, which produces envy, quarrels, verbal abuse, and evil suspicions.

God Jesus also taught those days: "**You are all wrong because you know neither the Scriptures [which teach the resurrection] nor the power of God [for He is able to raise the dead]**" (1 Tim. 4:1, 6:3–4; Matt. 22:29). Paul urged on following the apostolic tradition that leads into a godly based living by the power of the anointing that God the Holy Spirit gives, making Him (God's Spirit) the source and power for our Christian living.

Throughout the history of the church, God has called men and women to lift His powerful word (*by the wisdom of God's Spirit*), contributing knowledge and ample understanding to the biblical text. We also have a vast history of women called by God, as were Priscilla, wife of Aquila; Phoebe the deacon; and Junias (*a Greek female name; she was among the apostles*) who also knew Christ (Rom. 16).To name a few contemporaries in our times(search the Internet and read of them at www.cbeinternatinal.org/blogs/10-awesome-women-pastors-history):

- *Jarena Lee (1783–1864): "In 1819, Lee became the first African-American woman authorized to preach in the African Methodist Episcopal Church."*

- *Isabella Baumfree (1797–1883) "was born into slavery in New York. She was repeatedly sold and suffered beatings and separation from her children. After her emancipation, she became a devout Christian and co-founded Kingston Methodist Church."*

- *Antoinette Brown Blackwell (1825–1921) "living in Rochester, New York, began preaching in her Congregational church at the age of nine. She was a schoolteacher for four years, saving money to enroll in Oberlin College, founded by Charles Finney and one of the first American colleges to train women in theology."*

- *Maria Woodworth-Etter (1844–1924): "In 1885, she began preaching and praying for the sick. Her healing meetings drew such crowds that she eventually purchased an 8,000-seat tent. She was pivotal in founding the Assemblies of God church in 1914, and in 1918, she founded what is today Lakeview Church in Indianapolis."*

These and many more have contributed through their harmonized and dedicated life to the study of theology, bringing understanding to what we know as systematic theology. They are mentioned with honor because Scripture teaches, **"Where there is no [wise, intelligent] guidance the people fall [and go off course like a ship without a helm], But in the abundance of [wise and godly] counselors there is victory."** It is in the shoulders of giants as these that we base our understanding of theology that is *"in the multitude of counselors"* (Prov. 11:14).

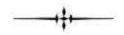

He Became like One of Us

Systematic theology provides the Bible student a guidance, a path of light into understanding what God wants to teach/reveal to us in prime time living. This book's modest Bible study is formed as a collaboration to the vast research done by the giants of biblical truth mentioned. We will not cite their names and teachings but will touch on the biblical discernment and strategies they followed from Scripture to give this book a fresh and vivid aspect of the times we are living in this twenty-first century. The universe in which we are programmed by God to exist in a natural arrangement is our reality, which continues to be His vivid codification. It is said of Him: "*For in him* all things were created [...] through him and for him [...] and *in him* all things hold together," meaning that there is no *Mother Nature* taught by God's written word. This so-called Mother Nature is but a lie, a conjured illusion of dead/sinful men in a rebellious status against the living God and His word (Col. 1:16–17). Scriptures tell us Jesus Christ is the image and substance of the invisible God. It is by Him all things were created, and it is written of Him:

> The Son is the radiance and only expression of the glory of [our awesome] God [reflecting God's Shekinah glory, the Light-being, the brilliant light of the divine], and the exact representation and perfect imprint of His [Father's] essence and upholding and maintaining and propelling all things [the entire physical and spiritual universe] by His powerful word [carrying the universe along to its predetermined goal].

The Bible student bases his life upon this rock, for He became like one of us as those chapters (*1–2*) continue to express (Heb. 1:3). Our life is programmed in all the sense of God's word, and we must accept and walk in its light. There is no free will (*it is also an illusion of the flesh*), for He is the One guiding our lives and all reality naturally (*since before we were created [Jer.1:1]*). What does exist is obedience and disobedience to the knowledge of God's persona, where the last one is known in Scripture as sin (*and darkness follows*), and both are rewarded by their actions. Even our conscience is examined, as God says, **"I am He who searches the minds and hearts [the innermost thoughts, purposes"** and also, **"Not a creature [*person's life*] exists that is concealed from His sight, but all things are open and exposed, and revealed to the eyes of Him with whom we have to give account"** (Rev. 2:23; Heb. 4:13). Therefore, our lives are deciphered by His word (*like a vehicle's manual to a conductor*) for "**_in Him_ we move and live and have our being,**" in Him (Acts 17:28). It is God Himself who reveals His Being through His Word and His Spirit in us (Rom. 8:11). His touch by His word is engaged by a systematic theological format, and she formulates the understanding thereof, as it teaches us God's will and persona. It is written by the vocal words of God:

> **But let the one who boasts, boast in this, that he [*and she*] "understands and knows" Me [and acknowledges Me and honors Me as God and recognizes without any doubt], that I am the Lord who practices loving kindness, justice, and righteousness on the earth, for in these things I delight.**

The LORD wants ardently that we may *know* and *understand* Him (Jer. 9:24 AMP). It is clear that to know and understand the invisible God, it must be through the testimony He has given of His Son (Jesus Christ) in scripture, who is the image and substance of the Father, and He became like one of us. John the apostle said,

> The one who believes in the Son of God [who adheres to, trusts in, and relies confidently on Him as Savior] has the testimony within himself [...] The one who does not believe God [in this way] has made Him [out to be] a liar, because he has not believed in the evidence that God [the Father] has given regarding His Son. (1 John 5:10 AMP)

This is the importance of the Word of God. We must build our house (*reality*) upon this Rock (*His Word*). This is the greatest treasure of the human spirit/soul to reach eternity: God's word and the greatest riches of the universe. Peter mentions that in "**these things even the angels long to look upon,**" and they are spirits (1 Pet. 1:12). Therefore, Scripture's state of itself:

> **All Scripture is God-breathed [given by divine inspiration] and is profitable for instruction, for conviction [of sin], for correction [of error and restoration to obedience], for training in righteousness [learning to live in conformity to God's will, both publicly and privately behaving honorably with personal integrity and moral courage]; so that the man of God may be complete and proficient, outfitted and thoroughly equipped for every good work.**

As theist believers, Scripture creates this understanding that God is a personal God. He is not far from each one of us, and as we acknowledge His Word, He reveals His truth vividly in us (2 Tim. 3:16–17; Acts 17:28).

We must give thanks to all those erudite doctors of words, theologians (*conservative and liberals alike*), for their arguments, lectures, contradictions, and translating the Bible from its original languages, Hebrew, and Greek, into our native languages. We must embrace their systematic theology, for by its topics and subdivisions, we understand the major doctrines of the content in the Bible. They fought in their (*particular*) generations and epochs from those who worked at destroying God's purpose for us and the meaning the word stands for. The word *theology* is a compound word from the Greek language, where *Theo* means "God" and *logy* derives from the word *logos*, meaning "word." Together it means "the word of God," whereas the contemporary meaning is the study of God's word. Therefore, we must acknowledge and state again: "*Theology is the fuel that ignites our worship, for the knowledge of its content provokes us to believe in Him.*" We must seek to understand the true meaning of God's word in all its angles. She gives us the victory over all our enemies, visible and invisible alike, as she directs to realize: "**[For the intent of God is that] through the church the multifaceted wisdom of God [in all its countless aspects] might now be made known,**" and this is not a small statement (Eph. 3:10). Everything starts by the listening of God's word; for she produces the faith that starts as a mustard seed, which grows to become one of the greatest trees on earth (*where birds [heavenly angels] come to rest*), and that we can tell this evil reality, *evil age*, and programmed illusions in our head to "*Stop*, you will not guide me any longer." We have left our worldviews and the gods of our culture and what we believed those gods were. We cannot compare them and their aspects to the God of Abraham, the true and only God. This God is a moral and holy God who calls us to live according to His concept and precepts by His power through His word. Therefore, when He tells us, "**Have I not long ago proclaimed it to you and declared it? And you are My witnesses. Is there a God besides Me? There is no other Rock; I know of none.**" That was to the people of Israel whom He demonstrated His powerful BEING in words and works (Isa. 44:8). He also said,

9

For I am God, and there is no one else; *I am* **God, and there is no one like Me, Declaring the end** *and* **the result from the beginning [***the word of His Prophecy***] and from ancient times the things which have not [yet] been done, Saying, "My purpose will be established,** *and* **I will do all that pleases Me and fulfills My purpose."**

He is an Omni-Being (Isa. 46:9–10). He is telling the whole human race that He looked throughout the vastness of infinity, its dimensions, and so forth and found no other Rock but Him. Then as He tells us to build our house upon this rock (His word), we must take it to heart that He is talking about Himself as our God/Rock. He has given His word, His personal attribute of unchangeableness: **"So will My word be which goes out of My mouth; It will not return to Me void"** and **"My words will not pass away"** (Isa. 55:11; Mark 13:31). This teaches us His word is more than meets the eyes; and we must look at reality through the eyes of God, according to His written word, to live by His authority of truth.

In this book, you will be shown the word of God through a systematic theological approach. It will set your spirit/soul free by the light, which is God, and the presence of His attribute. It is said in the Scriptures to start knowing and understanding His persona. It is from His invisible reality that He reveals Himself to those He has called through His Word. God reveals Himself in three ways: His creation, His saving grace/special revelation (*being born again*), and mainly through His living written word. Therefore, there is no excuse for those who will not accept His terms and design to receive eternal life (Rom. 1:19–20; Eph. 1:13–14; 2 Tim. 3:16). We are confident this work of literature (*Bible study*) will bring a deep understanding of the presences of the God BEING through His Holy Spirit, the Spirit of Truth, which is *the truth constant* in us all.

A Recap of Our First Published Book

In our first published book, *The Apostles Methodology to Interpret Scripture,* we open with this insightful introduction, and we must pick up its tab as an element of repetition to enforce wisdom. We hypothesized that at one time in the biblical tale, a question was asked by a certain man in power: *What is truth?* (John 18:38). There is no reason to speculate that this question is carried with no answer in the back of people's minds. Many today still ask this question in doubt, and there are even those that challenge the statement by declaring, *"There is no truth."* When this challenge is pronounced (in that certainty), it draws from the power of truth in contradiction (*an oxymoron*). This happens because truth is a constant light in the human soul, a foundation from which we draw authority to live life. This *truth constant* is what we are seeking to unfold through the research in this book and in looking at what truth is to a Christian theist believer. We will not look at speculations but at the assertions found in the biblical text; for truth in Scripture is a living being flowing from God's Spirit, the *Spirit of Truth,* where truth's authority becomes the power of salvation to those who embrace its radiance (John 6:63, 14:6; Rev. 4:5). God never intended for any of us to live in darkness; therefore, He reveals Himself to us. *God is Light.* He has no reason to hide His truth as we seek to understand Him and look for answers in the light of things. Truth is light and the basis from where all reality sprouts; and beware, for once it touches your spirit/soul, you will never be the same (1 John 1:5; Heb. 4:12–13).

Then we are directing ourselves to those who have been lit up as a light bulb by the truth of God. We are also seeking to touch those who have not, but in our understanding of the words of Paul, not all people will accept God's terms: **"for not all men have [***are of the***] faith,"** in Christ Jesus (2 Thess. 3:2). Now in the words of an eyewitness (*the apostle John*), we must walk with this light's truth, for he was present as an ocular witness and wrote:

> **That which was from the beginning, which we have heard, which we have seen with our eyes, which we have looked at and our hands have touched—this we proclaim concerning the Word of life. Life appeared; we have seen it and testify to it, and we proclaim to your eternal life, which was with the Father and has appeared to us. We proclaim to you, what we have seen and heard, so that you also may have fellowship with us. And our fellowship is with the Father and with his Son, Jesus Christ. (1 John 1:1–3)**

John uses noun adjectives to speak of Jesus Christ, calling Him the *Word of God*; *the life appeared*; and *the eternal life, which was with the Father*. And this, so that we can have a communion (*as in a family unity*) brought by this new knowledge, which leads us to much more than meets the understanding. We must comprehend that we came from our pagan rituals, worshiping dead gods, being dead ourselves. And it was revealed to us:

> **The idols [of the nation's] are silver and gold, The work of man's hands [*imagination*]. They have mouths, but they cannot speak; they have eyes, but they cannot see; they have ears, but they cannot hear; they have noses, but they cannot smell; they have hands, but they cannot feel; they have feet, but they**

cannot walk; nor can they make a sound with their throats. Those who make [and worship] them will become [*are dead*] like them.

There is a similarity in this with what the apostle's theology teaches us and the way we were before, as a dead thing through spiritism and the worship of dead idols (Ps. 115:4–8). Scripture states of us now:

And you He made alive, who were dead in trespasses and sins, in which you once walked according to the course of this world, according to the prince of the power of the air [*the idols*] the spirit who now works in the sons of disobedience [*who built their house on the sand*] among whom also we all once conducted ourselves in the lusts of our flesh, fulfilling the desires of the flesh and of the mind [*worldviews*] and were by nature children of wrath, just as the others.

You must then think that a dead person cannot spiritually speak, see, hear, move for he is dead. But as you have been called by Christ and now worshiping a living God who brought you to life, your status is that of a living person (Eph. 2:1–3). We can now understand our fallen nature and the condition we once had. Our fallen nature status tells us the story of our life as scripture teaches and what God is saying of it: "**There is none righteous, no, not one; There is none who understands; There is none who seeks after God. They have all turned aside**" (Rom. 3:11–12). Understanding God by His attribute of omniscience/omnipresence means that He had looked at yesterday and today, even tomorrow, and said He found none, not even one, who is righteous. Now man's religions are declaring that they are looking for God; but He tells us by His omniscient/omnipresent conscious stand that, no, that it's not the truth, that not even one is looking for Him, for all have turned aside. Therefore, He said, "**You did not choose Me, but I chose you and appointed you that you should go and bear fruit.**" Those who have been sealed by God's saving grace understand this very well (John 15:16). This is a lot to swallow for those who have not received God's special touch, but it's what Scripture declares. Those of us that have obtained it, we know that the Word is true (*she is spirit and is alive*). If you are interested in reaching the truth, He will not turn you away, but He will reveal Himself to you through His three forms. Christ said, "**And this is the will of Him who sent Me, that everyone who sees the Son and believes in Him may have everlasting life; and I will raise him up at the last day.**" God reveals Himself to us through His Anointed One. Let Him touch you through the faith produced by His living word; but you must listen (*the start*), study (*to grow*), and research (*to mature*) (John 6:40). To understand His word's truth, you must begin by accepting that *in the beginning God created the heavens and the earth*, for this is the dialogue the scripture brings: "**In the beginning God,**" and "**In the end God.**" It is He who wants to reveal Himself to us as we accept His plan of redemption. It is because of *sin* that *death* came, and it is because of sin we cannot see God. He made a way to reveal Himself, and this is through His only begotten Son, who said, "**I am the way, the truth and the light and no one comes to the Father if not through Me**" (John 14:6). It is only through Christ that we can reach God's revelation into eternal life, by the *God of Abraham, Isaac, and Jacob/Israel.*

This introduction is structured to produce a realization (*the light in the spirit/soul*) so that the lector begins to understand the biblical context through *systematic theology* in its topics and researching its subdivisions. Then let us begin by understanding each section, which is what this Bible study is seeking to provide and go from the understanding of one topic to the next in a systematic format so that we can grasp, extracting the sweet nectar of life that Scripture is sharing with us, as we begin living our eternal life in Him, the God BEING, who is Light. We are going to produce in the reader's spirit/soul a path to acquire what Jeremiah and Isaiah mentions—that is, to know and understand God Jesus who now lives in a body of *flesh and bones* (Jer. 9:23–24; Isa. 44:8). We are going to attempt to make you understand who the God is BEING but that according to Scripture, as He discloses Himself in the believers' life through His written word. At the end, we are going to live with Him from everlasting to everlasting in a body of flesh and bones. As our other book explains of repetition, these one-use repetitions to create [infuse] God's word to establish truth. There is also a slight curve between what we are bringing into systematic theology and our take. We are also reminding you that in this work, we are pointing to a path, not a conclusion, and that's what sets this book apart.

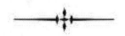

FIRST LESSON

Understanding the Immutable/ Unchangeable Word of God

A mature believer not only gets to learn how Scripture is divided into its testaments, Old and New, but also knows of its forty writers, plus (*redactors* and *Amanuenses*) those who worked and revised the books and letters they wrote. These are the drafted, accepted writings (canon) of the Old and New Testaments: *39 (OT) + 27 (NT) = 66 (in all)*. The disciple distinguishes the doctrines/teaching highlighted, connecting them to the persona of God Jesus. The Old Testament plants the terms designed by God (seed) for our redemption, and the New Testament is the germinated/accomplished terms and designed (*God's promise and oath* [Heb. 6:12–23]), planted, and fulfilled by His Son. The Father said, **"As the heavens are higher than the**

earth, So are My ways higher than your ways And My thoughts higher than your thoughts." He said this with the intention/understanding that He wants us to dislodge ourselves from our reality (*worldviews and philosophies*) and look at reality through His eyes, according to His written word, for He will prove the truth she implies (Isa. 55:9). The knowledge of God is the glory of men: "But [the time is coming when] the earth shall be filled With the knowledge of the glory of the Lord, As the waters cover the sea" (Hab. 2:14; Num. 14:21). The God and Father of our Lord Jesus Christ asked of this from those who would study Him:

> Thus says the Lord, "Let not the one who is wise and skillful boast in his insight; let not the one who is mighty and powerful boast in his strength; let not the one who is rich boast in his [temporal satisfactions and earthly] abundance (*today's scientist, wise and educated men, athletes and/or the rich and famous*); but let the one who boasts boast in this, that he (*and she, would*) understands and knows Me [and acknowledges Me and honors Me as God and recognizes without any doubt], that I am the Lord who practices loving-kindness, justice and righteousness on the earth, for in these things I delight."

And that is in *knowing* and *understanding* Him (Jer. 9:23–24). It is in knowing His persona (by His attributes) and understanding His will (*about redemption*) that God is delighted, and this knowledge comes through His word, which reveals us His persona. God delights in this because this is the way He planned things to be, for the creature called human got dumb blinded by sin. Salvation is in His terms and by His design. When He spoke about creating us, it is said:

He has made everything beautiful and appropriate in its time. He has also planted eternity [a sense of divine purpose] in the human heart [a mysterious longing which nothing under the sun can satisfy, except God]—yet man cannot find out (comprehend, grasp) what God has done (His overall plan) from the beginning to the end.

Sin and death does not let us know and understand God, but He said that it is because of this eternity planted in our hearts by Him that we are able to *understand and know* Him (Eccles. 3:11 AMP). He asked of us to repent—that is, to turn from our worldviews to His word's truth. It's like changing a computer's platform to a different system. Scripture teaches us that we are family of God, but in this existence, we have been destitute and fallen short of the glory of God by sin and death, and now we must live by His power until His promise of redemption happens. In the meantime, as students of His teachings, knowing that faith in Christ makes us His sons and daughters, we are promised a day in which redemption from this fallen nature will come (Rom. 3:23–24). Scripture calls that day the covenant of the permanent, the transformation (1 Thess. 4:13–18; 1 John 3:2; Hos. 6:2).

What Does It Mean to Be a Disciple?

Now the term *disciple* signifies to be a student, an alumnus molded to the image of his master or teacher. In the case of Scripture, God Jesus said, "A disciple is not above his teacher, but everyone who is perfectly trained will be like his teacher." This is the model offered in Scripture—that is, for us to be like Jesus (Luke 6:40). Many believe that once their sins are forgiven, they become disciples of Christ, but they are further off from the truth in Scripture. When a believer is born again (*a term used by God Jesus describing the new birth*), it is like changing a computer's operating system to another operating system, using new programming and applications. A disciple of Christ (*once touched*) seeks to learn, changing his/her reality (*worldview*) to become an apprentice of the Word's biblical terms and become like his/her teacher, who prayers and fasting cannot provide. Only the study of Scripture can make a believer a disciple (*as they leave their old-gods belief and rituals*). The prophet Isaiah was made to write, "**Bind up the testimony, Seal the law among my disciples,**" giving the understanding that a disciple needs to advance to a deeper learning, understanding God's testimony of the Son, and to stop being a child, an immature, and a superficial student of the word (Isa. 8:16; Heb. 5:11–14). The apostle John wrote that the testimony of the Father is about His Son, saying,

> **He who believes in the Son of God has the witness in himself [*Spirit seal (Eph. 4:30)*] he who does not believe God [the Father] has made Him a liar, because he has not believed the testimony that God has given of His Son. And this is the testimony: that God has given us eternal life, and this life is in His Son. He who has the Son has life; he who does not have the Son of God does not have life.**

As you can see, there is a warning for those who do not believe the testimony that God the Father gives about His Son (1 John 5:10–12). This scripture is best understood when you join them with "**the Revelation of Jesus Christ, which God [the Father] gave Him to show His servants.**" God the Father gave the revelation (*testimony*), which an angel confirmed by saying, "**Worship God! For the testimony of Jesus is the spirit of prophecy.**" In other words, the testimony of Christ is everything Moses, the prophets, the psalmist, and the apostles wrote about (*Messiah*) and is what the Father said about His Son; for the Word is Christ-centered (Rev. 1:1, 19:10). We must receive the word of God as the testimony He gives of His Son and open our hearts to it all as truth: *God is Light*. This is how the believer becomes a disciple: studying God's testimony of His Son and changing their platform (*again once touched and sealed*), their worldview to God's word. God Jesus said, "**If you abide in My word, you are My disciples indeed** (*and so there you have it*). **And you shall know the truth, and the truth shall make you free**" and "**It is the Spirit who gives life.** [...and] **The words that I speak to you are spirit, and they are life.**" This is no different than what the prophets and psalmist were declaring, "**O Lord God, You are God, and Your words are truth**" [...and] "**Your word is a lamp to my feet And a light to my path**" (John 8:31, 6:63; 2 Sam. 7:28; Ps. 119:105). Christ Jesus also told them,

> **So everyone who hears these words of Mine and acts on them, will be like a wise man [...] who built his house on the rock. And the rain fell, and the floods and torrents came, and the winds blew and slammed against that house; yet it did not fall, because it had been founded on the rock.**

He implied that the *house* is our reality and the *rock* is His holy word (Matt. 7:24–25). The word becomes life, light, spirit guide, and the power in the believer to move forward. God does not ask us something He can't, then beneficiate, bless, and change us for our best in return. Then by our faith/hope, the disciple submerges in His word. The believer is touched by their faith in

Christ into being born again; and now they can make the decision to become a disciple, seeking to understand what had suddenly happened in their spirit/soul once touched by Christ Spirit of truth, which confirms God's existence and power (2 Cor. 3:17). This is taught in scripture, as it says, "**So faith comes from hearing [what is told], and what is heard comes by the [preaching of the] message concerning Christ.**" The word of God provokes us to believe in Him as we listen to its truth. She clearly explains, "**When you believed, you were marked in him with a seal, the promised Holy Spirit, who is a deposit guaranteeing our inheritance until the redemption,**" that a living and powerful change has happened (Rom. 10:17 AMP; Eph. 1:13–14). This is the power of the word of God, and it is why we declare that the knowledge of theology is the fuel that ignites our worship. God Jesus said about His word testimony: "**You are in error because you do not know the Scriptures or the power of God.**" Scripture is well understood by those who are sealed and born again (*God's power touch*) (Matt. 22:29). The word of God is spirit, is alive, and is truth: "**For the word of God is alive and active. Sharper than any double-edged sword, it penetrates even to dividing soul and spirit, joints and marrow; it judges the thoughts and attitudes of the heart.**" But this is where this mystery (power) starts to unravel, and you must be aware of it every moment (Heb. 4:12). The verse following this one (*which verse numbers and chapters did not exist when they were written*) submerges and entwines itself with God's persona; for there is no break, conjunction, or other type of adhesive. It sounds as if one and the other are the same (*God and the action of His living word*). We read both simultaneously (vs. 12–13), "**Nothing in all creation is hidden from God's sight. Everything is uncovered and laid bare before the eyes of him to whom we must give account,**" See, the unity is like if the spoken written word are God's eyes. Examples of this (*metaphor/simile*) language source is when Jesus said, "**I and the Father are One**" and/or as "**In the beginning [before all-time] was the Word (Christ), and the Word**

was with God, and the Word was God Himself." It is a truth to accept, for it is a God BEING thing, the only God (Heb. 4:13; John 10:30, 1:1 AMP). The disciple can capture this mystery and ponder inside the heart and soul. The seal/fire that as a born-again believer he or she feels/marked as the word touches their inner self is a realization in their spirit/soul. The apostle Paul taught his Gentile disciples, saying,

> The word is near you, in your mouth and in your heart"—that is, the word [the message, the basis] of faith which we preach—because if you acknowledge and confess with your mouth that Jesus is Lord [recognizing His power, authority, and majesty as God], and believe in your heart that God raised Him from the dead [*He now lives in a glorified flesh and bones body*] you will be saved. For with the heart a person believes [in Christ as Savior] resulting in his justification [that is, being made righteous—being freed of the guilt of sin and made acceptable to God]; and with the mouth he acknowledges and confesses [his faith openly], resulting in and confirming [his/her] salvation.

She depends upon God's will and power to do what it was sent to do (Rom. 10:8–10). He also taught, "**God did this so that they would seek him and perhaps reach out for him and find him, though he is not far from any one of us. 'For in him we live and move and have our being.'**" God is a personal God, as Paul was referring to this quality into all humanity as offspring, to become the son of God by His will (Acts 17:27–28; John 1:11–13). God told this to the prophet Isaiah (55:11) for our edification: "**So shall My word be that goes forth from My mouth; It shall not return to Me void, But it shall accomplish what I please [*she has been***

programmed]. **And it shall prosper in the thing for which I sent it.**"
Therefore, God is pending in the reaction the word of His BEING
has upon those who listen. The old spiritual knowledge (*spirit of
the world*) must be detached from us as carnal thoughts. The word
of God dwells in you, for that is how He created us, and we accept
His terms and designs. Your body becomes a temple of the Holy
Spirit, which is the testimony (anointing) of Christ in you. That is
the testimony God the Father speaks of His Son (1 John 5:10–12).
Paul explains it, saying, "**He redeemed us in order that the blessing
given to Abraham might come to the Gentiles through Christ Jesus,
so that by faith we might receive the promise of the Spirit**" (Gal.
3:14; Acts 2:32–33). This is the main topic in Paul's teaching to
the Gentiles as he wrote to the Romans believers: "**And if the Spirit
of him who raised Jesus from the dead (*God the Father*) is living
in you, he who raised Christ from the dead (*God the Father*) will
also give life to your mortal bodies because of his Spirit who lives
in you,**" and God the Holy Spirit works according to God the
Father and Son's words, which they pronounced (Rom. 8:11). The
disciple must understand that the word of God is more than
alphabetic phrases, number values, and graphic letters symbols
producing sounds in the ear and the thoughts. The word of God
provokes a belief in the listener that produces faith, hope, and life
in those who then seek to understand its intentions. She is a
fountain of power, and only through the faith, she produces in the
heart. When we listen to its content, it will activate the City of
Light's power inside our life to guide us further than death. She
explains, "**For this God is our God for ever and ever; he will be
our guide even to the end.**" (*Spanish version says*, "Más allá de la
muerte," *meaning*, "*further than death*.") And this is provoking
the soul/spirit to believe in praise and worship, for we are walking
toward the City of God, City of Light, and its culture (Ps. 48:14).
God Jesus confirmed this by saying, "**I am with you
always [remaining with you perpetually—regardless of
circumstance, and on every occasion (*Heb. 7:25*)], even to the end**

of the age" (Matt. 28:20 AMP). The word of God moves the believer/disciple with a heavenly plan/purpose.

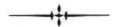

Build Your House upon This Rock

Systematic theology stipulates the teachings and central doctrines of the Bible in its context and arguments, so that the disciple advances, identifying the *ways* (*paths*) and *thoughts* of God. The first lesson that the disciple must ingest and assimilate is that the word of God possesses God's attribute of *unchangeableness*—that is, she is immutable, meaning concrete. She is unchanging, unable to be modified or unmodified, and she does not shift or change as the God who spoke it. He doesn't change. The LORD said, "For I am the Lord, I do not change." This is where in theology the term of God's attribute of unchangeableness derives (Mal. 3:6). God told Moses to write, **"God is not a man, that He should lie, nor a son of man, that He should repent. Has He said, and will He not do it? Or has He spoken and will He not make it good and fulfill it?"** (Num. 23:19). The LORD also proclaims, **"Did I not proclaim this and foretell it long ago? You are my witnesses. Is there any God besides me? No, there is no other Rock; I know not one,"** meaning that He looked throughout dimensions; parallel universe, if there is such things; through the vast space/time and its matter (*biggest macro to smallest micro*), and if there's a place with no space, matter, and time. In other words, He looked everywhere that His Omni-BEING could think of and found no other God, no other BEING like Him (Isa. 44:8). The LORD God also makes a statement that moves us into truth's authority. He said, **"So is my word that goes out from my mouth: It will not return to me empty, [it] will accomplish what**

I desire and achieve the purpose for which I sent it" (Isa. 55:11). This is a most important revelation by God because there are three ways by which the LORD has revealed Himself to humanity: First, through His creation:

> **Because that which is known about God is evident within them [in their inner consciousness], for God made it evident to them. For ever since the creation of the world His invisible attributes, His eternal power and divine nature, have been clearly seen, being understood through His workmanship [all His creation, the wonderful things that He has made], so that they [who fail to believe and trust in Him] are without excuse and without defense. (Rom. 1:19–20 AMP)**

Second, by His special revelation:

> **In Him, you also, when you heard the word of truth, the good news of your salvation, and [as a result] believed in Him, were stamped with the seal of the promised Holy Spirit [the One promised by Christ] as owned *and* protected [by God]. The Spirit is the guarantee [the first installment, the pledge, a foretaste] of our inheritance until the redemption of *God's own* [purchased] possession [His believers], to the praise of His glory. (Eph. 1:13–14)**

We must add that *we are the word* of God *manifested/activated* for "*In Him we move and live and have our being,*" *in* Him (Acts 17:28). Third, God reveals Himself by His Holy Word:

All Scripture is God-breathed [given by divine inspiration] and is profitable for instruction, for conviction [of sin], for correction [of error and restoration to obedience], for training in righteousness [learning to live in conformity to God's will, both publicly and privately behaving honorably with personal integrity and moral courage] [spoken and written]. (2 Tim. 3:16)

It is by His written word we understand His character, and He said, "**God is not a man, that He would lie, Nor a son of man, that He would change His mind; Has He said, and will He not do it? Or has He spoken, and will He not make it good?**" His word provokes us to believe that He is truth and He is Light (Num. 23:19).

It is written about the God BEING, and Christ Jesus is that part of Him (the Word) that "**His word became flesh and walked among us**" (John 1:14). Let's take this word's concept a bit deeper and reason to this next teaching God Jesus said, "**For it is out of the abundance of the heart that the mouth speaks**" (Luke 6:45) and apply it as that the Word/God also comes from the abundance of the God BEING's heart, and He walked among us. To understand the unity of the God BEING as He is the only God that exists, God Jesus said, "**I and the Father are one**" and "**All that belongs to the Father is mine.**" Then He proved it not just by walking on water but by resurrecting from the dead, as He said He would (John 10:17–18, 30, 16:15). It has also been said of God Jesus, "**[He] is the same yesterday, today, and forever,**" and He proved it by getting up from the dead (Heb. 13:8). God does not change, and He has given His written word that same consistency, for they are "*One*" as scripture keeps proving. The LORD wants us to know this:

In the same way God, in His desire to show to the heirs of the promise the unchangeable nature of His purpose, intervened and guaranteed it with an oath (*that oath is that His Son would pay the price for the promised Holy Spirit*) so that by two unchangeable things [His promise and His oath] in which it is impossible for God to lie, we who have fled [to Him] for refuge would have a strong encouragement and indwelling strength to hold tightly to the hope set before us. This hope [this confident assurance] we have as an anchor of the soul [it cannot slip and it cannot break down under whatever pressure bears upon it]—a safe and steadfast hope that enters within the veil [of the heavenly temple, that most Holy Place in which the very presence of God dwells (*in His reality of invisibility*)], where Jesus has entered [in advance] as a forerunner for us (*He has call us into His reality*) having become a High Priest forever according to the order of Melchizedek.

How then will you receive the bearing of His word in you? It is also written, "By God's word the heavens came into being and the earth was formed out of water and by water" and "By the same word the present heavens and earth are reserved," meaning also, all of us in it "for in Him we live and move and exist [that is, in Him we actually have our being]" (2 Pet. 3:5–7; Acts 17:28). We are God's spoken word in physical action, and after He brings us back into life (*in a glorified body*), we will understand God's word in depth, for He is the light, which is the life of humans, as written: "In him was life, and that life was the light of all mankind" (John 1:1–4). This bond of God's word is like the love of a man toward a woman (*and vice versa*). It grows deeper for each other as it matures (Heb. 6:17–23). Jesus Christ, in His ministry, knowing this truth, said, "**Heaven and earth will pass away, but my words will never pass away.**" This is their *adhesive* that ties us onto their Word's heart and soul, and this is the way the Word provokes us to believe as she acts by its authority of truth in us (Mark 13:31). The prophets were also given to write: "**The grass withers and the flowers fall, but the word of our God endures forever.**" The word moves and acts as earth's plants and vegetation flourishing naturally, and the prophet wrote, spoken from God's heart abundance (word): "**For as the rain and snow come down from heaven, And do not return there without watering the earth, Making it bear and sprout, And providing seed to the sower and bread to the eater**" (AMP) and "**So is my word that goes out from my mouth: It will not return to me empty, but will accomplish what I desire and achieve the purpose for which I sent it**" (NKJV). The word is a steady rock, and it works as nature's process (*God's hand*) in vegetation and plants (Isa. 40:8, 55:10–11). God the Father proclaimed through the prophets that His word would never come back to Him empty, and Christ (the Word) confirmed it in His ministry. In this understanding, we know that His word is a Rock, a stronghold: "**My salvation and my honor depend on God; he is my mighty rock, my refuge**" (Ps. 62:7). Therefore, when God Jesus asked us to build our house upon this rock, He meant His words (*as into Himself*), and we must comply, for He was giving a profound teaching.

There are two types of people in this life: those that live their life in randomness and those that plan their steps each day through God's word. Jesus taught this very thing, saying,

> **So is everyone who hears these words of Mine and acts on them; it will be like a wise man [...] who built his house on the rock** [*the Word/persona of God*]. **The rain fell, and the floods and torrents came, and the winds blew and slammed against that house; yet**

it did not fall, because it had been found on the rock
(*His written words*). And everyone who hears these
words of Mine and does not do them, will be like a
foolish (*insipid*) man who built his house (him and
her reality) on the sand [*their own worldviews*]. The
rain fell, and the floods and torrents came, and the
winds blew and slammed against that house; and it
fell—and great and complete was its fall.

This teaching was meant to resonate through the ages because it was God who created us, and it is Him who maintains us together, alive, for **"He is life and life is the light of man"** (Matt. 7:24–27; John 1:4). Now those who built their house upon the sand are those who live in prisons of darkness in their own worldviews and philosophies. Isaiah (14:7), speaking of the evil one, mentions how the devil has no love for his prisoners and wrote, **"That [*the devil*] opened not the house [*trap by their worldviews*] of his prisoners."** Again there are two types of people: those enslaved by sin and those made free by Christ's anointing power (Isa. 14:17). The prophet said of Christ:

> **The Spirit of the Lord God is upon me; because the**
> **Lord anointed me to preach good tidings unto the**
> **meek; he sent me to bind up the brokenhearted, to**
> **proclaim liberty to the captives, and the opening of**
> **the prison to them that are bound.**

This was said by God Jesus, who exposed humanity's prisons of darkness, to open them wide (Isa. 66:1; Luke 4:18). The apostle John speaks about the condition of the people of this world, saying, **"We know [for a fact] that we are of God, and the whole world [around us] lies in the power of the evil one [opposing God**

and His precepts]." The whole world (*without Jesus*) is under the control of the evil one, enslaved by the darkness of sin (1 John 5:19).

In our studies of psychology (*college elective*), people in our society are under the devil's influence (*Christian perspective*) and can be classified by their worldviews and/or cosmovision, giving a glimpse unto what darkness drives them (*as zombies*). These are the prisons in which people away from God's word live. Their mind is entrapped, enslaved in different types of darkness as their house is built upon the sand. There are those standing by the prison's open gate (*door*) who are called *deist*. In general, a deist's stand is a belief on the existence of a god who made the world but ever since has let it run its own course and maybe will bless this or that individual but not all, like the Greek gods, for example. In other words, they believe that God the Creator is not a personal God. Hollywood portraits them as the good guys in all their movies and sitcoms (*using His name in a curse tone*). They are educated, moral, humanistic at heart overall but take revenge on their enemies, becoming good nihilists. For example, they do not accept Christ and His teachings as the Son of Almighty God. At one time, they walked in our Christian ranks, but Scripture best describes them as what God Jesus said:

> **I know your deeds, that you are neither cold (invigorating, refreshing) nor hot (healing, therapeutic); I wish that you were cold or hot. So because you are lukewarm (spiritually useless), and neither hot nor cold, I will vomit you out of My mouth [rejecting you with disgust].**

The verse goes on to say the humanistic reason:

> **Because you say, "I am rich, and have prospered *and* grown wealthy, and have need of nothing," and you do not know that you are wretched and miserable and poor and blind and naked [without hope and in great need].** (Rev. 3:15–17)

John the Apostle ends, explaining to them that they were with us but never were of us. The apostle John writes:

> **They went out from us [seeming at first to be Christians], but they were not really of us [because they were not truly born again and spiritually transformed]; for if they had been of us, they would have remained with us; but they went out [teaching false doctrine], so that it would be clearly shown that none of them are of us.**

Many good folks fall under this category. Without Christ's anointing, their fallen nature (*evil hearts*) fools them into creating false doctrines of human goodness instead of following the apostle's tradition/theology in faith/hope (1 John 2:19 AMP).

Behind the prison gates, these folks are followed by those called *pantheists*. Their worldview does not stipulate an entity as a god, rather natural law, existence, and the universe (*the sum of all the things that were, are, and will be*) as their god. These are like the Hindus, witches, and those that practice spiritism, New Age, and such beliefs that mention their so-called Mother Nature as their god. Then there are those in deeper darkness that are called *existentialists*. They maintain that existence precedes essence, reality is before thought, and will to intelligence. The existentialists are centered in the evaluation of their human condition (*not accepting their fallen nature*) in their liberty, individual responsibility, and their emotions (*which are not objective truth*) and in their own personal significance of human existence. Like the deist, they are self-sufficient, without the need of a deity. They have built their house upon the sand, though they seem to be good human beings, well educated, and ethical. But without the belief of God in Christ, they live in the error of darkness (*spirit of the world and sin*). Then there are also those that, like the last, are well educated, moral, ethical but are in a deeper darkness. They are openly *atheist*. In its more ample form, they live in the total rejection of any entity as a god. They reject the belief of any entity but themselves (*though they deny it*), holding the stand and posture that there is no god, as they oppose any theist aspect of reality. Their core belief runs between the existentialist unto the nihilist belief of atheism.

Now in conclusion of these worldview's dispositions of humanity's mental entrapments, we come to those who are in the deepest region of darkness in the devil's den (*prisons*): the *nihilist*. Their worldview derives from the Latin term *nihil*, or "nothing." They live in total rejection of any moral and/or religious principle as their belief that life has no meaning. Nihilists are people who incline to no law or human authority and accept no belief as an article of faith. They become psychopaths, narcissists, terrorist, antagonist, vile, following their animal instincts and/but are found in any level or positions in our society. They don't believe in social norms and have a hardened and embittered heart toward and against all other human beings.

All these are enslaved prisoners in their mental (spirit/soul) worldviews and have their roots of reality, their house, built upon the sand. They are *people in a trance*, a theme to a future book. Now those that build their house upon the rock (*the word of God*) are called *theist*. Theist comes from the Greek word θεός *theós*,

God. Their stand is best understood by the doctrine that affirms there is a Creator of the universe, who is compromised to the maintaining and governing the cosmogony. In other words, our God is a personal God (*the God of Abraham, Isaac, Jacob/Israel*) to all individuals, His creation. Scripture states of Him:

> It is He who gives to all [people] life and breath and all things [...and] so that they would seek God, if perhaps they might [seek] grasp for Him and find Him, though He is not far from each one of us. For in Him we live and move and exist [that is, in Him we actually have our being].

How can anyone reject this truth in Scripture when our own guts tell us it is the truth (Acts 17:25, 27–28 AMP). Scripture also states,

> For [by Him all things were created in heaven and on earth [...] all things were created and exist through Him [that is, by His activity] and for Him. And He Himself existed and is before all things, and in Him all things hold together. [His is the controlling, cohesive force of the universe].

In other words, there is no *Mother Nature*, as sinful man in darkness have been made to believe (Col. 1:16–17). The word of God teaches us that our God is such, for we (*believers*) have been made reborn by Him (*a perceptive act*) as temples of His Holy Spirit. He chose us from those prisons of darkness, saving us forever, as He paid for our life's eternal disorder and its consequence to the lake of fire (John 15:16). Isaiah wrote the words that Jesus Christ mentions as His own, in releasing people that the evil one have as prisoners, saying, "**The Spirit of the Lord**

God is upon me, Because the Lord has anointed and commissioned me To bring good news to the humble and afflicted; He has sent me to bind up [the wounds of] the brokenhearted, To proclaim release [from confinement and condemnation] to the [physical and spiritual] captives And freedom to prisoners." As you can notice, He opened the prisons of our delusions by choosing each and every one of us from our enslavement of darkness, as we listened to the spoken/written word (Isa. 61:1; John 15:16). The God BEING has redeemed us onto Himself. He paid the price of our eternal disorder.

The information about these worldviews—deist, pantheist, existentialist, atheist, and nihilist—are what, in theology, we understand of the people who built their life, their mental state (*reality*), upon the sand, instead of those who built their house/reality upon the Rock, which is the Word of God. There are even those who state that they believe in God in their own way, but God Jesus said, "**I am the [only] Way [to God] and the [real] Truth and the [real] Life; no one comes to the Father but through Me.**" In other words, God does not believe in you, in your own ways (John 14:6 AMP). In this understanding, we become theist because we believe that our God is a personal God and salvation is on His term and His design. Those who stand in unbelief will share in this contradiction on judgment day: "**Whoever does not believe God [*in His words*] has made him out to be a liar, because they have not believed the testimony [*evidence*] God has given about his Son**" (1 John 5:10). Like a change of computer platform, we have been given the ability to come and change our mindset, deleting the old gods, their doctrines, and personal life teachings to the understanding that the God of Abraham, Isaac, and Jacob/Israel is the only Rock (God BEING) of ages as He has stated, and He found no other God BEING throughout all existence's dimensions and/or that which does not exist. He is who makes existence and every moment of our life (*the here and now reality*), and in Him all things hold together (*we are a moving expression of His word in action, we are His creation*). This is His statement in accord to reality, our house, our consciousness. He is omniscient. In other words, He cannot learn anything new because He knows it all, and when something new happens, it is because He created it or made it to be. This is the why and the how come. Therefore, we must establish His word as the sum of all our past, present, and future existence. It is written, "**For no prophecy was ever made by an act of human will, but men moved by the Holy Spirit spoke from God.**" The word of God is of God. Therefore, we are reminded by the Word, God Jesus (*who is the truth*), saying, "**However, when He, the Spirit of truth, has come, He will guide you into all truth; for He will not speak on His own authority, but whatever He hears He will speak; and He will tell you things to come.**" It is by the touch/power of God that His word comes alive in you (2 Pet. 1:21; John 16:15). God told the prophet Isaiah (46:9–10) to write,

> **I am God, and there is no one like Me, Declaring the end and the result from the beginning** [*for all was established in a divine, heavenly summit before the foundation of the world*]. **And from ancient times the things which have not [yet] been done, saying, "My purpose will be established, And I will do all that pleases Me and fulfills My purpose."**

God's attributes are His, and He does not share His glory with no created creature. The Word of God provokes us to believe in its content and says, "**He [*she*] who does not believe God [*words*] has made Him a liar, because he [*she*] has not believed the testimony that God has given of His Son.**" The whole Scripture is (*Christ centered*) the testimony the Father gives of His Son, and she provokes you to believe in Him (1 John 5:10). Let us enforce this testimony of God about His Son by His *Name.* In the Hebrew language, YHVH is known as the tetragrammaton and by its pictographic format (*Hebrew is three languages in one: pictographic, numeric, and phonetic*). It adds a unique meaning to His name in Hebrew, *Yud-Hey-Vah-Hey,* which also means "*Behold the Hand, Behold the Nail.*" The word of God is the testimony He gives of His Son/Word. Therefore, a theist Bible student believes that all that the prophets, the psalmist, and the apostles wrote in their original draft (*through their many preserved copies, gives us 99.9 percent of its original draft*) is the testimony of Jesus as the angel told John: "**Worship God! For the testimony of Jesus is the spirit of prophecy,**" and so we also have the testimony of the angels clarifying God's truth (Rev. 19:10). This is the testimony God the Father offered us about His Son in the cross of Calvary. He paid for our sins and healed us from the virus of sin evil's disobedience. Then by His love, He offers us forgiveness (*a justice*) by the blood payment of Jesus Christ our King. It is what Scripture testify and Paul preached through the Spirit of truth, saying,

> **Therefore God overlooked and disregarded the former ages of ignorance; but now He commands all people everywhere to repent [that is, to change their old way of thinking (*worldviews*) to regret their past sins, and to seek God's purpose (*anointing*) for their lives], because He has set a day when He will judge the inhabited world in righteousness by a Man whom He has appointed and destined for that task, and He has provided credible proof to everyone by raising Him from the dead. (Acts 17:30–31)**

This is also why a disciple doesn't only know the canon and the order of Scriptures, but as he or she reads the whole Bible, they reach this mature comprehension of it. They begin to see the special characteristics, projecting a better conception of the Bible's content, defined by its *authority, capacity, realization,* and *dependence.*

The Authority of the Word

This can immediately be seen. As this characteristic is grasped by the spirit/soul, we rapidly recognize she is directed into the intentions of the heart. Therefore, scripture let us know:

> **The word of God is living and active and full of power [making it operative, energizing, and effective]. It is sharper than any two-edged sword, penetrating as far as the division of the soul and spirit [the completeness of a person], and of both joints and marrow [the deepest parts of our nature], exposing and judging the very thoughts and intentions of the heart.** (Heb. 4:12 AMP)

It is said and has been written, for it is programmed by God: **"Jesus replied, "It is written and forever remains written, 'Man shall not live by bread alone, but by every word that comes out of the mouth of God,"** and this is because we are God's word activated/manifested into this reality (Matt. 4:4). We must be reminded that in the original written version, Scriptures had no chapters or verse numbers. They were placed afterward for a better understanding of the script. Then we must perceive in its verses the continuity of her content as we read it. Verse 12 of Hebrew 4 is followed by the thought that Scripture is part of God Himself and continues to say without break, **"Nothing in all creation is hidden from God's sight. Everything is uncovered and laid bare before the eyes of him to whom we must give account,"** making a jump, or transition, to God Himself (as the Word is God [John 1:1–4]). It is Him behind His word's authority, and this must be unequivocally captured, for God has given His word, His attribute of immutability or unchangeableness and power (Heb. 4:13 NIV). In this powerful way, the word that He has spoken will not come back to Him empty, but it will do what He orders it to do (*He is omnipotent, and she is backed by that potency*) as He said, **"Heaven and earth will pass away but His word will never pass away."** She is an expression of an Omni-God (Isa. 55:11; Mark 13:31). There is no wonder why we are affected by it: **"For in Him we live and move and exist [that is, in Him we actually have our being]"** (Acts 17:28). By the word of His mouth, He spoke to the elements to become and create what we acknowledge as existence. In that place, God turned and said,

> **"Let there be light,"** and there was light [...then He turn again] **and God said, "Let the water under the sky be gathered to one place, and let dry ground appear"** [...and to the land] **God said, "Let the land produce living creatures according to their kinds: the livestock, the creatures that** move along the ground (including the monkey) **and the wild animals, each according to its kind." And it was so.**

He spoke to the elements, and they produced reality (Gen. 1:3, 9, 24). This recollection is very important to us because when God was going to make man and woman, He looked all around, and then He spoke to Himself, to His divinity, as the I AM, the Word, and the Holy Spirit, the God BEING. And They said, **"Let us make mankind in our image, in our likeness"** [...and] **"So God created mankind in his own image, in the image of God he created them; male and female he created them."** Both the woman is also included as image and likeness of God for the purpose of earth, but soon all born again are going to be the same as members of Christ Jesus's physical body, where there is no male nor female (Gen. 1:26–27; Gal. 3:28). Therefore, we became offspring of God not because of sin (*general grace*) but by His word of authority and power as we believe and receive His Son's testimony. We are made to be (*born again*)as sons and daughters of God (John 1:11–13; 1 John 5:10–12). The word of God becomes encrusted to our being, for we are God's word activated and manifested with the angels in this universe. Scripture teaches us that we are part of this creation in Him, for is in Him and through Him that we subsist. This is in the knowledge of our instincts (*articulation, inclination*), emotions (*commotions, behavior*), and realizations (*substance, purpose*) by which we understand that the Creator is our Potter. Again, scripture states, "**In him we live and move and have our being.**" In Him, *we are* part of His existence (Acts 17:28). God told the prophet Jeremiah (18:1–10) to write:

> **This is the word that came to Jeremiah from the Lord: "Go down to the potter's house, and there I will give you my message." [...] The pot he was shaping from the clay was marred in his hands; so the potter formed it into another pot, shaping it as seemed best to him** [*born again*]. **Then the word of the Lord came to me. He said, "Can I not do with you, Israel** [*as He does to the church*]**, as this potter does?" declares the Lord. "Like clay in the hand of the potter, so are you in my hand." [**...this is His reality, and] **"If it does evil in my sight and does not obey me** (*my Word*)**, then I will reconsider the good I had intended to do for it."**

The reader may say this was told to Israel under another covenant, but the disciple understands that God speaks through His word to all man and woman that have ever existed and accepted His ways. No one can escape God's word, for all things are His, and He makes them stay alive. Paul uses this same metaphor to convey this imagery, saying, **"Will the thing which is formed say to him who formed it, 'Why have you made me like this?' Does the potter not have the right over the clay?"** This was explained in very explicit detail in my first book entitled *The Apostles Methodology to Interpret Scripture* (Rom. 9:20–21). The authority of the word can be sensed in us as the air is felt in our lungs and as our heart beats in every thought, because it was spoken in relation to those made in the image and likeness of God. The word's *authority* is bound legally, permanently over us, bought at the price of blood. The authority of the word moves us forward, making us come alive, for we are an expression and manifestation created by the authority of the word God.

The Capacity of the Word

Moses told the Israelites to read the written scriptures that he gave them. The word has clarity of purpose and the capacity to lead a human person to spiritual heights that he/she does not understand. Moses told them,

> Now this is the command; the statutes and the judgments (precepts) which the Lord your God has commanded me to teach you, so that you might do (follow, obey) them in the land" [...and]. These words, which I am commanding you today, shall be [written] on your heart and mind. You shall teach them diligently to your children [impressing God's precepts on their minds and penetrating their hearts with His truths] and shall speak of them when you sit in your house and when you walk on the road and when you lie down and when you get up. And you

shall bind them as a sign on your hand (forearm), and they shall be used as bands (frontals, frontlets) on your forehead. You shall write them on the doorposts of your house and on your gates. (Deut. 6:1, 6–9 AMP)

The word of God has the capacity to guide a person's life, and this is no different than what God Jesus told us. God Jesus said, "So everyone who hears these words of Mine and acts on them, will be like a wise man [...] who built his house on the rock." The house is our reality, and the rock is God's words (Matt. 7:24). The prophets, as does the psalmist, wrote with the capacity and clarity on what the word has over the human soul:

Blessed [fortunate, prosperous, and favored by God] is the man who does not walk in the counsel of the wicked [following their advice and example], nor stand in the path of sinners, nor sit [down to rest] in the seat of scoffers (ridiculers). But his delight is in the law of the Lord, and on His law [His precepts and teachings] he [habitually] meditates day and night. [...and] The law of the Lord is perfect (flawless), restoring and refreshing the soul; the statutes of the Lord are reliable and trustworthy, making wise the simple. The precepts of the Lord are right, bringing joy to the heart; the commandment of the Lord is pure, enlightening the eyes. The fear of the Lord is clean, enduring forever; the judgments of the Lord are true, they are righteous altogether. (Ps. 1:1–2, 19:7–9 AMP)

God Jesus challenged His listener on what they clearly read of the word, saying, "**Have you not read [in the Scripture] what God said to you**" [...also] "**But Jesus replied to them, 'You are all wrong because you know neither the Scriptures nor the power of God**"—that is, the capacity and authority expressed by it (Matt. 22:31, 29). God Jesus also instructed His audience about the researching scripture and said, "**You search the Scriptures, for in them you think you have eternal life** [*eternal life is Christ Himself*] **and these are they which testify of Me. But you are not willing to come to Me so that you may have life.**" People who listen to their flesh's reasoning cannot get it (John 5:39–40). The apostles also gave instructions on researching scripture for clarity, saying,

> **All Scripture is God-breathed [given by divine inspiration] and is profitable for instruction, for conviction [of sin], for correction [of error and restoration to obedience], for training in righteousness [learning to live in conformity to God's will, both publicly and privately behaving honorably with personal integrity and moral courage]; so that the man of God may be complete and proficient, outfitted and thoroughly equipped for every good work.** (2 Tim. 3:16–17 AMP)

The word of God has the capacity and power to restart the mind and spirit/soul of the believer, and this is like having a new performance computer platform. It is by the authority of truth that God is creating (*a new reality*) in those He saves, and it's not what we have formed through our life experiences (*worldviews*) and/or Hollywood's indoctrination (Eph. 2:10). He dictates what's to come as we live to His pleasure. His word gives us the capacity (power) to overthrow our emotions and behaviors: "**Many plans are in a person's heart, but the advice of the Lord will stand.**" It is

His sovereign right. He is the God BEING, and we are His creation (Prov. 19:21).

The Realization of the Word

As you look at reality through the eyes of God, according to His written word, your reality becomes obscured by the realization of the vivid reality of God; for she illuminates the spirit, mind, and soul of the believer. The *revelation* of God is read from His word through our physical senses, and we react to it for she provokes us to believe in Him producing faith. Now as that provocation reaches the spirit/soul, it becomes *realization of truth* in the believer, which lights us up as a light bulb with a newly acquired wisdom. Scripture gives us the authority of truth to visualize our eternity and make decisions toward our upcoming reward (Heb. 11:6). The creation speaks to us about the glory and power of God (*first revelation*), but it does not tell us about our sins and about forgiveness for salvation. It is only scriptures that speak to us about our sin and fallen condition, and this as we read, applying it, and coming to terms by the realization of truth's authority. The apostle Paul was very explicit when he wrote:

> Because that which is known about God is evident within them [in their inner consciousness], for God made it evident to them. For ever since the creation of the world His invisible attributes, His eternal power and divine nature, have been clearly seen, being understood through His workmanship [all His creation, the wonderful things that He has made] so that they [who fail to believe and trust in Him] are without excuse and without defense

Again, this is a challenge, provoking us, as it makes us realize that there is *no Mother Nature*. It is a lie of sinful man departed from the truth of God (Rom. 1:19–20 AMP). It is God who maintains this reality alive; for Him, through Him, and in Him all things hold together (Col. 1:16–17). When we confess the truth, the word produces in our heart a faith/belief realized by its true authority. It cleanses us by God Jesus's blood from sin and death, then our heart is sealed by God the Holy Spirit as God's special revelation happens. This is the second way in which God reveals Himself to humanity. In the letter to the Ephesians (1:13–14), it is written:

> **In Him, you also, when you heard the word of truth, the good news of your salvation, and [as a result] believed in Him, were stamped with the seal of the promised Holy Spirit [the One promised by Christ] as owned and protected [by God]. The Spirit is the guarantee [the first installment, the pledge, a foretaste] of our inheritance until the redemption of God's own [purchased] possession [His believers], to the praise of His glory.**

This is called saving grace and special revelation, reserved for those who believe. It is a real contact established by God for His chosen. This special revelation is realized, as Paul wrote:

> **But what does it say? "The word is near you, in your mouth and in your heart"—that is, the word [the message, the basis] of faith which we preach— because if you acknowledge and confess with your mouth that Jesus is Lord [recognizing His power, authority, and majesty as God], and believe in your heart that God raised Him from the dead, you will be saved. For with the heart a person believes [in**

Christ as Savior] resulting in his justification [that is, being made righteous—being freed of the guilt of sin and made acceptable to God]; and with the mouth he acknowledges and confesses [his faith openly], resulting in and confirming [his] salvation. For the Scripture says, "Whoever believes in Him [whoever adheres to, trusts in, and relies on Him] will not be disappointed [in his expectations]." For there is no distinction between Jew and Gentile; for the same Lord is Lord over all [of us], and [He is] abounding in riches (blessings) for all who call on Him [in faith and prayer]. For "whoever calls on the name of the Lord [in prayer] will be saved."

And this is a promise of God for whoever adheres to His terms and design of salvation (Rom. 10:8–13). In theology, this is where *sanctification by position* comes from. It is God who says and does the cleansing of us; and therefore, *justification* becomes an act of God and *sanctification* a work of God promised for all believers. The writer of the above verses asks, but **"How will they hear if no one tells them?"** Paul, in all his writings, teaches of the three church columns gluing us together by the activities believers do after being washed save. They are **"to worship, be edified, and evangelize."** Paul taught, **"Having strapped on your feet the gospel of peace in preparation [to face the enemy with firm-footed stability and the readiness produced by the good news],"** which he got from Isaiah as he wrote, **"How beautiful and delightful on the mountains Are the feet of him who brings good news, Who announces peace, Who brings good news of good [things], Who announces salvation"** (Eph. 6:15; Isa. 52:7) We must give/tell others by grace what we received by grace, and that is the Spirit words of the gospel salvation as we realize its value for all mankind. The believer walks in what scripture says of them: "For in Him all the fullness of Deity (the Godhead) dwells in bodily form [completely expressing the divine essence of God]. And in Him you have been made complete [achieving spiritual stature through Christ]." This is sanctification by position, and in Him we are complete (Col. 2:9–10). Scripture statements make us realize this truth, and its authority expresses, "**Christ has now reconciled you [to God] in His physical body through death, in order to present you before the Father** *holy* **and** *blameless* **and beyond** *reproach*" (*sanctification by position*). That is, as you place your belief in His (*faith-producing*) word and be set free by the hope of His return to redeem, it transforms us (Col. 1:22; John 14:1–4).

The Dependence of the Word

Once a person is touched by the power and authority of truth from the gospel (*or God-spell*), he and/or she will never be the same but will live seeking to understand the deeper meaning of these holy words that transformed their inner selves. They will immediately know that the knowledge of theology is the fuel that ignites their worship, for the word provokes us to believe in Him. Therefore, a disciple seeks to acquire more knowledge of the God of Abraham (Rom. 4:22–25). In this statement, we must remember how we the Gentiles have come from worshiping other gods, spirits, entities, and so forth; but now we have come to the true and only God. We have all approached the LORD erroneously using ideas, concepts, premonitions, and notions from the gods of our cultures and their man-made doctrines. We need to *stop*! The believer must understand:

> **You have come to Mount Zion, to the city of the living God, the heavenly Jerusalem. You have come to thousands upon thousands of angels in joyful assembly, to the church of the firstborn, whose**

names are written in heaven. You have come to God,
the Judge of all, to the spirits of the righteous made
perfect, to Jesus the mediator of a new covenant, and
to the sprinkled blood that speaks a better word than
the blood of Abel. (Heb. 12:22–24)

We have come to the only God Creator of heaven and earth
without no spiritual doctrines whatsoever, and our first lesson is
that we must never compare, use, or assimilate those old doctrines
(*spiritism*) with the God of Israel. Jesus of Nazareth (*100 percent
God, 100 percent human*)is an Israelite from the tribe of Judah.
He is their promised Messiah. He is the (*unique/only*) Son of the
invisible Omni-God, and this is how we must begin to know God,
the One who called us from the dead in replacement of those who
did not want to heed the call. The new birth is a new
literary/spiritual platform, and we must eliminate, delete the old
applications and old-gods worship. Even the Leviticus priesthood
order and worship the God BEING in the new priesthood order of
Melchizedek (*through God the Holy Spirit*). God the Father made
us come out of darkness for this purpose:

Giving thanks to the Father, who has qualified us to
share in the inheritance of the saints (God's people)
in the Light. For He has rescued us and has drawn
us to Himself from the dominion of darkness and has
transferred us to the kingdom of His beloved Son, in
whom we have redemption [because of His sacrifice,
resulting in] the forgiveness of our sins [and the
cancellation of sins' penalty]. (Col. 1:12–14 AMP)

At one point, the LORD said, "I am God, and there is no
other; I am God, and there is none like me. I make known the end

from the beginning, from ancient times, what is still to come. I say, 'My purpose will stand, and I will do all that I please.'" This is God's sovereignty, and He is the only omniscient Being (Isa. 46:9–10). Therefore, the knowledge and realization of the word of God becomes an addiction, a dependence to a disciple, and even more when he/she are baptized by God the Holy Spirit with the evidence He gives. When a person comes out of darkness into the powerful light of the kingdom of Christ, he/she desires first of all "**like newborn babies [you should] long for the pure milk of the word** [*ABC of the gospel*] **so that by it you may be nurtured and grow in respect to salvation [its ultimate fulfillment].**" And this is to know what has happened to you once saved, but then move on to deeper things by the Spirit of God as a disciple: "**Things which the eye has not seen and the ear has not heard,**" which He has reserved for those who loves Him (1 Pet. 2:2; 1 Cor. 2:9). It is necessary for a disciple to desire pure milk, but as growth happens, they must digest stronger nourishment. The apostles taught the advance disciple to move on:

> **For though by this time you ought to be teachers [because of the time you have had to learn these truths], you actually need someone to teach you again the elementary principles of God's word [from the beginning], and you have come to be continually in need of milk, not solid food. For everyone who lives on milk is [doctrinally inexperienced and] unskilled in the word of righteousness since he is a spiritual infant. But solid food is for the [spiritually] mature, whose senses are trained by practice to distinguish between what is morally good and what is evil**" [that is, good and evil and/or good from evil]. (Heb. 5:12–14)

The writer of Hebrews continues to teach the outcome of moving ahead (*of the ABC*) in the doctrines of the gospel, saying,

> **Therefore let us get past the elementary stage in the teachings about Christ, advancing on to maturity and perfection and spiritual completeness, [doing this] without laying again a foundation of repentance from dead works and of faith toward God, of teaching about washings (ritual purifications), the laying on of hands, the resurrection of the dead, and eternal judgment. [These are all important matters in which you should have been proficient long ago.] And we will do this [that is, proceed to maturity].**

It is eminent for the disciple to grow in equal balance about his/her salvation (Heb. 6:1–3 AMP). The apostles pointed into a greater insight that the believer/disciple must reach, saying,

> **And we desire for each one of you to show the same diligence [all the way through] so as to realize and enjoy the _full assurance_ of hope until the end, so that you will not be [spiritually] sluggish, but [will instead be] imitators of those who through faith (*understand, there is no merits of works in this faith but a trust/believe in His word*) [lean on God with absolute trust and confidence in Him and in His power] and by patient endurance [even when suffering] are [now] inheriting the promises. [*Then the writer points to something more literary, spiritual.*] For when God made the promise to Abraham, He swore [an oath] by Himself, since He had no one greater by whom to swear, saying, "I will surely bless you and I will surely multiply you." And so, having**

patiently waited, he realized the promise [in the miraculous birth of Isaac, as a pledge of what was to come from God]. Indeed, men swear [an oath] by one greater than themselves, and with them [in all disputes] the oath serves as confirmation [of what has been said] and is an end of the dispute. In the same way God (*the LORD comes to a place, to our level, to teach us something powerful about the faith He expects from us*) in His desire to show to the heirs of the promise the unchangeable nature of His purpose (*He gave His word an attribute of unchangeableness*) intervened and guaranteed it with an oath, so that by two unchangeable things [His promise (*Holy Spirit, Gal. 3:14*) and His oath (the pledge for His Son to make the payment for our salvation, 1 Cor. 6:19–20)] in which it is impossible for God to lie [*He gives us significance*] we who have fled [to Him] for refuge would have strong encouragement and indwelling strength to hold tightly to the hope set before us [*these are the tools Paul taught the disciple to follow: faith, hope, which produces love*]. This hope [this confident assurance] we have as an anchor of the soul [it cannot slip and it cannot break down under whatever pressure bears upon it]—a safe and steadfast hope that enters within the veil [of the heavenly temple, that most Holy Place in which the very presence of God dwells], where Jesus has entered [in advance] as a forerunner for us, having become a High Priest forever according to the order of Melchizedek.

God Jesus now lives in a body like ours but in *flesh and bones*, in God's invisible reality (Heb. 6:11–20). Spiritual maturity happens rapidly if the believer becomes a disciple, deciding to study, research, and learn to know and understand God through His word (Jer. 9:23–24). God's word teaches how to proceed into maturity:

> For this very reason, applying your diligence [to the divine promises, make every effort] in [exercising] your faith to, develop moral excellence, and in moral excellence, knowledge (insight, understanding), and in *your* knowledge, self-control, and in *your* self-control, steadfastness, and in *your* steadfastness, godliness, and in your godliness, brotherly affection, and in your brotherly affection [develop Christian] love [that is, learn to unselfishly seek the best for others and to do things for their benefit]. For as these *qualities* are yours and are increasing [in you as you grow toward spiritual maturity], they will keep you from being useless and unproductive regarding the true knowledge *and* greater understanding of our Lord Jesus Christ. For whoever lacks these *qualities* is blind—shortsighted [closing his spiritual eyes to the truth], having become oblivious to the fact that he was cleansed from his old sins.

God Jesus used the apostle Peter to write these things, which, through his sufferings, he learned to mature faster (2 Pet. 1:5–9). As we study the narration of the New Testament, we also understand that the follow-up letters of Paul (*who suffered more than the other apostles*), his letters to the Thessalonians, were profound in their content as he taught them and spent time with them. We know from the church history studies that Paul spent months in Thessalonica. Then because of persecution, he was told to leave the city premises. Not only did he tell them about salvation, *the apostle's theology*, but also about the *apostle's eschatology*, the wrath prophecies to come. He wrote to them:

We give thanks to God always for all of you, continually mentioning you in our prayers. [...] Brothers and sisters beloved by God, we know that He has chosen you; for our good news [regarding salvation] came to you not only in word, but also in [its inherent] power and in the Holy Spirit and with great conviction. [...] And we also thank God continually for this, that when you received the word of God [concerning salvation] which you heard from us, you welcomed it not as the word of [mere] men, but as it truly is, the word of God, which is effectually at work in you who believe [exercising its inherent, supernatural power in those of faith] [*This was the apostle's theology to prepares the believer for their coming eschatological events*]. For the Lord Himself will come down from heaven with a shout of command, with the voice of the archangel and with the [blast of the] trumpet of God, and the dead in Christ will rise first. Then we who are alive and remain [on the earth] will simultaneously be caught up (raptured) together with them [the resurrected ones] in the clouds to meet the Lord in the air, and so we will always be with the Lord! Therefore, comfort and encourage one another with these words [concerning our reunion with believers who have died].

The Thessalonians learned really fast the message that Paul was conveying unto them, and they grew, matured spiritually by the word of God spoken to them by Paul about eschatology (1 Thess. 1:2–5, 2:13, 4:16–18). Paul assures them in this same letter: "For God did not appoint us to suffer wrath but to receive salvation through our Lord Jesus Christ." And from John, "Because you have kept the word of My endurance [My command to persevere], I will keep you [safe] from the hour of trial, that *hour* which is about to come on the whole [inhabited] world, to test those who live on the earth." The apostle's theology prepares us for the apostle's eschatology, and that is to escape it (1 Thess. 5:9; Rev. 3:10). They advised, "So we have the prophetic word made more certain. You do well to pay [close] attention to it as to a lamp shining in a dark place, until the day dawns and light breaks through the gloom and the morning star arises in your hearts," and this is into acquiring maturity. It is what their eschatology does (2 Pet. 1:19). It is by these reasons that we know that the word of God becomes an addiction in those who are lit up from darkness into the kingdom of light in Christ and must depend on the continued nourishing of God's words. At one time, God Jesus said in a prayer to the LORD: "Sanctify them in the truth [set them apart for Your purposes, make them holy]; Your word is truth." This gives the disciple the understanding that sanctity comes by the realization of the words content; therefore, we grow a dependence by ingesting, and we do it each day and as much as possible, because the word of God is spirit and is alive, as God Jesus taught: "It is written *and* forever remains written, 'Man shall not live by bread alone, but by every word that comes out of the mouth of God.'" The Bible student cannot miss this (John 17:17; Matt. 4:4).

These four characteristics, as we submerge deeper into the word, make us understand inevitably, with no doubts, that Scripture comes from the Father as testimony of His Son, *and it is growing in us* exclusively through the power of God the Holy Spirit. It is through Him we can get to understand and realize what she is producing in us, for our living state (*as persons*) is a product of God's word. We are God's word in living action. The natural men and women do not understand because they haven't been chosen, called, nor have been born again by the power of God since they haven't even asked. The apostle Paul said, "None of the rulers of this age knew; for had they known, they would not have crucified the Lord of glory" (1 Cor. 2:7–8). Isaiah (8:20) taught, "To the law and to the testimony! If they do not speak according to this word, it is because there is no light in them." John the apostle also wrote, "Whoever does not believe God has made him out to be a liar, because they have not believed the testimony God has given about his Son" (1 John 5:10). Paul the apostle, knowing the word, also wrote, "But all things that are exposed are made manifest by the light, for whatever makes manifest is light. Therefore, He says, 'Awake, you who sleep, Arise from the dead, And Christ will give you light.'" By God's testimony of His Son, we are awakened into true reality (Eph. 5:13–14). Therefore, it is important (*once born again*)to study, knowing the word in all the aspects. She demands, "*So now through the church the multifaceted wisdom of God [in all its countless aspects] might now be made known*," by us (Eph. 3:10). We must learn and understand all Scripture's characteristics, as Paul writes, saying the "*multifaceted wisdom of God.*" And so our hopes and prayers are that this literary work will guide you, pointing out this path.

The Word of God Carries His Attributes

Systematic theology supplies to the biblical structure a breakdown into the wisdom in the Bible's content and translates it into legible understanding. It gives the Christian disciples the ability to grasp the thoughts and path of God, as Isaiah the prophet was given to write: "For as the heavens are higher than the earth, So are My ways higher than your ways And My thoughts higher than your thoughts" (Isa. 55:9). This is what the word of God supplies to the disciple (*to learn from His word*), God's ways and thoughts, which He desires for us to know, which is the culture of the City of Light. His paths and thoughts are higher than ours, for they are to be discerned spiritually by our spirit/soul. This is by the realization of God's omniscient knowledge through His written word. The disciple must recognize, discerning these two aspects of the word of God: its path/ways (*literal*) and thoughts/ideas (*spiritual form*). These two complement each other and cannot be unperceived one away from the other. It would be like walking with one leg, not using the other as reference and balance. Let us take for instance what we know through the word's *literal aspect* (*reading*) and *our born-again experience* (*the sealed by God*). It is Him who holds all things together; therefore, *there is no Mother Nature*. Rid your mind from such delusional deceits. We now openly know that

> **The God who created the world and everything in it, since He is Lord of heaven and earth, does not dwell in temples made with hands; nor is He served by human hands, as though He needed anything** (*the God* BEING *does not needs the creation for Him to be the God* BEING, *but He made us to be His temple*) **because it is He who gives to all [people] life and breath and all things. And He made from one man every nation of mankind to live on the face of the earth, having determined their appointed times and the boundaries of their lands and territories. This was so that they would seek God, if perhaps they might grasp [seek] for Him and find Him** [*God is a personal God*] **though He is not far from each one of us. For in Him we *live* and *move* and *exist* [that is, in Him we actually have our being].**

Here you have the literary and spiritual aspects of knowing the word of God in action. He is causing all this to happen (Acts 17:24–28). If you accept its truth, He holds the physical and spiritual aspects of our life in His hands. Then you begin to see reality through the eyes of God, in accord with His holy written word, and this by living in the light of the gospel. As the disciple realizes that the word of God has His attribute of unchangeableness and it was spoken to us as omniscient knowledge (*which is also omnipresent*), the effect of the word in each one of us is yesterday, today, and tomorrow the same as when He said it. He is also omnipotent and changes us into the outcome of all the things He has spoken(*prophecies and promises*) for He prepared beforehand the works we were to walk in (*His written word*)so that we begin to stand in the rock, positioning our spirit/soul as living stones by His word's power. The disciple must also remember Paul's word of God's position: **"If we are faithless, He remains faithful [true to His word and His righteous character], for He cannot deny Himself"** (2 Tim. 2:13). God's word will do what He sent it to do in the disciples by them accepting it (*she is immutable*). Then they will stop swimming against the current and activate God's word in their spirit/soul to conquer. We were created by the spoken word of God, and that which has been given to us (*the word's content*) only works in us for God's purpose. It is like a radio that only picks up radio frequencies and/or television that only picks up television waves, for that is what they were created for. And the word of God was given for the elect, the chosen, before the foundation of the world. Paul, instructing the end goal of the word, said, **"So that the man of God may be complete and proficient, outfitted and thoroughly equipped for every good work,"** and those works were created by God beforehand (*at their first heavenly, divine summit*). He makes us fit in it as He changes our future outcome by His word, which is backed by His attributes: omniscience, omnipresence, and

omnipotence. And His word represents Him, and we are God's word active in action (2 Tim. 2:13, 3:17).

Building from the Biblical Foundation

Systematic theology exposes the central teachings (*doctrines*) of the Bible in their context and arguments. By this approach, the disciple advances, identifying the ways and thoughts of God for their individual growth. God the Father wants Christ's disciple to walk in the path/works that He has prepared beforehand for them, as they meditate in His ways and thoughts through the testimony He has given of the Son. It is written:

> For we are His workmanship [His own master work, a work of art], created in Christ Jesus [reborn from above—spiritually transformed, renewed, ready to be used] for good works, which God prepared [for us] beforehand [taking paths which He set [*in Their first divine, heavenly summit (Eph. 1:3)*], so that we would walk in them [living the good life which He prearranged and made ready for us].

As you can see, this is a work from God; and therefore, in theology, it is called *sanctification by position*, mainly because it has nothing to do with our doing and everything to do with what He has said and is doing in us (Eph. 2:10). Therefore, the word produces sanctification in practice, for the faith from the word transforms our behavior by our prayers (*she is omnipotent*). In this, we can understand James's words: "**Show me your faith** without deeds, and I will show you my faith by my deeds." The faith (*induced by the word of God*)in the believer creates good deeds that God prepared beforehand. Then you will show the works produced by your faith, the deeds/practice she produces through us (James 2:18). By the study of systematic theology, which is based on the shoulders of giants, we must abide and grow in the thoughts of God, which they fought in their eras for us to clearly see the path we must abide in. The apostle John goes on to say, "This is the revelation of Jesus Christ [His unveiling of the divine mysteries], which God [the Father] gave." Then it was the Father who gave Christ the revelation of His Word/Son to manifest it to us His disciples (Rev. 1:1 AMP). God Jesus said, "For I did not speak on my own, but the Father who sent me commanded me to say all that I have spoken" (John 12:49). The revelation the Father has given of His Son is for us to decipher who is the God BEING and understand what He wants of us. It was also said to John the apostle that "the testimony of Jesus is the spirit of prophecy [His life and teaching are the heart of prophecy]." Then it is in the words written by the prophets, psalmist, and the eyewitness apostles. We are to understand as the testimony the Father gives of His Son (Rev. 19:10 AMP). This is why John adds,

> The one who believes in the Son of God [who adheres to, trusts in, and relies confidently on Him as Savior] has the testimony within himself. [...] The one who does not believe God [in this way] has made Him [out to be] a liar, because he has not believed in the evidence that God has given regarding His Son.

This is not a good thing for those who reject the testimony given of Christ Jesus by God the Father (1 John 5:10–12). The book of Revelation chapter 5 is about the predestined reality the Father has changed and approved for our future directions because of what His Son has done in our present reality (*it is predestined and rearranged*), and the changes are in God Jesus's merits. The apostle Peter wrote: "**Through these [God Jesus's merits] he has given us his very great and precious promises, so that through them you may participate in the divine nature, having escaped the corruption in the world caused by evil desires**" (2 Pet. 1:4). In this same power, we change our tomorrow today by our prayers in His promises and prophecy. These were written in His Word for us. It is by the teachings extracted from the testimony of Jesus that we can strip a clear and vivid image of the plan of God the Father for us. This is as we get to know Him through His attributes and character, by His written word. Then we can understand His personal plan of redemption for all those who listen. This is also why He calls us friend (John 15:15; Jer. 9:23–24).

The following are the general teachings of systematic theology without their subdivisions. The complete knowledge we will not touch as it is an extensive work. This book's goal is to get the reader interested and have them search on their own the depth of this biblical knowledge:

- The teaching of what Scripture says is the Word of God.

- The teaching of who is (the) God (BEING) through the Word.

- The teaching of man in their fallen nature, how God sees us.

- The teaching of God Jesus and God the Holy Spirit (*as they are One*).

- The teaching of men's redemption by the merits of Christ.

- The teaching of the church by the apostle's theology.

- The teaching of future events by the apostle's eschatology.

In this Bible study, we are going to touch the surface of these topics to bring the disciple (*student of scripture*) into reaching the lifeline of the divine thoughts, which God wants us to learn. Remember when God says, **"For as the heavens are higher than the earth, So are My ways higher than your ways And My thoughts higher than your thoughts."** The LORD is challenging the disciple into reaching out and grasping His ways and thoughts (Isa. 55:9; Acts 17:28). Each of these doctrines and their subdivisions supplements each other, and you must begin by understanding the Word of God. She has been given/attributed by God, His attribute of unchangeableness. She is immutable. Then endowed with this truth, we must know that *she does not change.* We can rely on its content, its meaning, and assertion as God the Father intended for us to accept and move forward with its teaching(*once we are touched ignited by Him*), and that's the key to His revelation. The written word of God is the door to heavenly reality because she is spirit and alive connecting us to the Spirit of God, the Spirit of truth. The apostle Paul was led to write about this: **"For the gifts and the calling of God are irrevocable [for He does not withdraw what He has given, nor does He change His mind about those to whom He gives His grace or to whom He sends His call],"** and this is said about the gifts of salvation by His Holy Spirit, which is a gift given by God (Acts 2:32–33). Remember God is omnipresent and omniscient. He saves in the knowledge of His ability to see your future. We must ask ourselves: why would He spend His Son's precious blood on someone whom He knows will not accept His salvation terms and design? There is no wonder why God Jesus says, **"Do not give that which is holy to dogs, and do not throw your pearls before pigs."** Then He will not use a drop of His Son's precious blood for them either. It is for His chosen (Matt. 7:6). This is also why **"He chose us in Him before the foundation of the world"** (NIV), and that, at Their first divine, heavenly summit, **"He chose us in Christ [actually selected us for Himself as His own] before the foundation of the world, so that we would be holy [that is, consecrated, set apart for Him, purpose-driven] and blameless in His sight, in love"** (Eph.1:4 AMP). Paul also wrote:

"For it is by grace [God's remarkable compassion and favor drawing you to Christ] that you have been saved [actually delivered from judgment and given eternal life] through faith [*this was determined before the foundation of the world (Eph. 2:8 AMP)*]. And this [salvation] is not of yourselves [not through your own effort], but it is the [undeserved, gracious] gift of God." In other words, it is unappealable and inexorable. And it cannot be abolished, revoked, annulled, or invalidated once it's given to you; for it is a legal document signed by blood. And so the gift and calling of God through His word are irrevocable once He saves/touches you (Rom. 11:29). The disciple understands Paul's advice: "Do not be deceived, God is not mocked [He will not allow Himself to be ridiculed, nor treated with contempt nor allow His precepts to be scornfully set aside]; for whatever a man sows, this *and* this only is what he will reap [*which He knows been an Omni-God*]." God honors His Word for she contains His attributes of omniscience, letting the believer know and understand His omnipresent stand (*observation*). He said it is all in the past, touching the present, by His arranged (*prophecies/promises*) future events, expressed by God; and she is, for the believer, the omnipotent source guiding them to victory, as endowed by the hand of the LORD, Adonai, (Gal. 6:7). The Word of God is the foundation that He has established as an unchangeable testimony about the Son. And in that testimony, it is said of Christ's intervention for His body, the church: "Therefore He is able also to save forever (completely, perfectly, for eternity) those who come to God through Him, since He always lives to intercede [as High Priest] and intervene on their behalf [with God]." Our faith is provoked by His statements (Heb. 7:25 AMP). Paul taught this very thing to all disciples:

> According to the [remarkable] grace of God which
> was given to me [to prepare me for my task], like a
> skillful master builder I laid a foundation, and now

> another is building on it. But each one must be
> careful how he builds on it, for no one can lay a
> foundation other than the one which is [already]
> laid, which is Jesus Christ.

In other words, this foundation is God Jesus's testimony given by the Father (1 Cor. 3:10–11). Many people, intoxicated by their own sayings, have proposed opinions and interpretations that only bring viruses, as into a computer platform, which at end destroys/deter the spiritual growth of a believer. This is why Paul said about this foundation:

> But if anyone builds on the foundation (*erroneous doctrines*) with gold, silver, precious stones, wood, hay, straw, each one's work will be clearly shown [for what it is (*works of mere men, their super faith*)]; for the day [of judgment] will disclose it, because it is to be revealed with fire (*Holy Spirit*) and the fire will test the quality and character and worth of each person's work. If any person's work which he has built (*by faith*) [on this foundation, that is, any outcome of his effort] remains [and survives this test (*their faith/hope*)], he will receive a reward. But if any person's work is burned up [by the test (*because of the spirit of the word*)], he will suffer the loss [of his reward]; yet he himself will be saved, but only as [one who has barely escaped] through fire.

And so, again, many well-intentioned people who have not studied the Word through systematic theology have brought erroneous teachings that deterred the work of Christ instead of helping it (1 Cor. 3:12–15). Therefore, the author proposes that each disciple read and study well the structure of this book, for as a writer, I am building upon the foundation already established. Then you must investigate every cell of the idea spoken behind each word (*teaching*). God's Word is wisdom and omniscient knowledge from a living Omni-God. Everything is fresh at His sight, and because of this, we must look at reality through the eyes of God, according to His written word, to understand His proposition to our life. As we contemplate this, we can begin to see God's path and thoughts as Jeremiah (29:11) wrote: "**'For I know the plans and thoughts that I have for you,' says the Lord, 'plans for peace and well-being and not for disaster, to give you a future and a hope.'**" This is how we begin to understand God's plan once we know who God is by His living touch (*power*) and according to His written word. This is how we touch the thoughts of God and walk His path, and this is what He wants, for God is light (*He is not hiding anything*), and His word is life and spirit.

The Word Provokes Us to Believe

God's work in us is through ideas, thoughts of reasoning, and declarations, as if it has already happened (*for to Him, it has*). He has spoken it, and His word will not come back empty-handed but will do what it was sent/said to. She moves with His omnipotent power and sovereignty. He elevates us to His ways and thoughts by His word's ideas and reasonings. God Jesus prayed, "**Sanctify them in the truth [set them apart for Your purposes, make them holy]; Your word is truth.**" The word is truth as we read it, and the only way a disciple sanctifies him/herself from the ignorance of darkness is receiving it by the authority she ushers, "*Truth*" (John 17:17). The reader must understand that an idea is like a virus in the human spirit/soul, and until we don't accomplish what that idea is producing, we are not complete. God's Word is filled with His ideas of redemption and salvation for each one of us to accept. Therefore, we must understand the depth and foundation upon which we are constructing our spiritual edifice, that we may stand firm upon the rock, which is the word of God, and walk in the freedom, holiness, and purity that He has proposed for us. Sanctification by position is what God proposes as we read, for it will produce sanctification in practice. Scripture says, **"And you, who once were alienated and enemies in your mind by wicked works, yet now He has reconciled in the body of His flesh through death, to present you holy, and blameless, and above reproach in His sight."** This is our position, and if someone asks, tell them that "*God said so,*" because now you are heirs, sons/daughters, to get all the blessings He offers (Col. 1:21–21; John 1:12–12). God Jesus said, **"If you abide in My word [continually obeying My teachings and living in accordance with them, then] you are truly My disciples. And you will know the truth [regarding salvation], and the truth will set you free [from the penalty of sin]."** It is by the knowledge of the Word's truth that its authority sanctifies the believer on the merits of Jesus Christ, as scriptures say, and not on our physical works of the flesh (John 8:31–32). Sanctification by position leads us into sanctification in practice. It just does by His truth's authority. We build our reality upon the rock (*scripture*) by faith in Christ's priestly works and the hope of His return for us, which produces love, for the one we are believing through His holy words. It is in the spirit of His words that we obtain our victory. Christ taught, **"It is the Spirit who gives life; the flesh conveys no benefit [it is of no account]. The words I have spoken to you are spirit and life [providing eternal life]."** This leads into sanctification in practice, and therefore, the Word provokes us to believe in its content through its spiritual ideas and reasoning. You can't miss it (John 6:63).

The apostle John (1:1–3 AMP) said,

> **In the beginning [before all-time] was the Word (Christ), and the Word was with God, and the Word was God Himself. He was [continually existing] in the beginning [co-eternally] with God. All things were made and came into existence through Him; and without Him not even one thing was made that has come into being,**

This idea must rebound in the disciple's spirit/soul, for it is what sets us up into looking at reality through the eyes of God, according to His written word. Everything has been done by God, and it is God's ideas. It is God Himself wanting us to focus on His truth. The *Word was God*. Even before creation, He existed, for He is existence. "I AM THAT I AM," He states. This Word became flesh and walked among us but never stopped being God as the gospels give us to understand. The Word of the God BEING comes from the abundance of His heart. Now who can tell God that He cannot do what He wants to do? **"Will the thing formed say to him who formed *it*, 'Why have you made me like this?' Does not the potter have power over the clay."** God made our bodies to be a temple, His temple (Rom. 9:20–21). As we study scripture, we can see this was going to be an act of God, and it was a secret (*the church*) in the written word, a mystery (Isa. 53; Eph. 3:1–9). Scriptures goes on to say, **"He (Christ) was in the world, and though the world was made through Him, the world did not recognize Him."** And He said, **"All things that the Father has are Mine,"** because the Word comes from the abundance of God's heart (John 1:10, 16:15). In the same divine miraculous form, He referred to the written word, **"The words I have spoken to you are spirit and life."** It has the same power and essence for you to understand the activity of the Word in you. It is said of her: **"By His word the present heavens and earth are being reserved."** This includes all that is you and me in it by the same word (2 Pet. 3:7).

She touches us in its literal/spiritual way, and we cannot detach the one from the other—that is, be born of the Spirit and the water (*word*) as God Jesus said (John 3:5). Therefore, this is looking at reality through the eyes of God, according to His living word. This is how we enter the reality we were created to live in by God, to know Him clearly, not as through a darkened glass. In 1 Corinthians 13:12 (AMP), it says,

> **For now [in this time of imperfection] we see in a mirror dimly [a blurred reflection, a riddle, an enigma], but then [when the time of perfection comes, we will see reality] face to face. Now I know in part [just in fragments], but then I will know fully, just as I have been fully known [by God].**

Everything we have learned about this life we have to reexamine and renounce our thoughts from it in order to accept His ways in our front view and rear-view mirror. The apostle John reassure us that **"God is light and in Him there is no darkness at all."** Then we must accept His word as light, truth, and life. This is imperative for a disciple of Christ (1 John 1:5). We are as a writing page; and the God BEING, since He is omnipotent, omnipresent, and omniscient, He inscribed us into His consciousness (*reality*) by His written word, and all the codification written of our existence is programmed by Him. Our living is by His essence in becoming the center of His creation on earth, for in Him and through Him, we live. Our past is only a diminutive particle of His eternity as is our present stance, and our future projection is His proclamation. It is He that makes it happen, for *in Him, we live and move and have our stand* in Him. He defines who we are.

The Word Is Active and Full of Power in the Believer

God is light, and He is not hiding or covering up from us His truth, for it is written:

> **But when He, the Spirit of Truth, comes [*understand the four things He will assure*], He will guide you into all the truth [full and complete truth]. For He will not speak on His own initiative, but He will speak whatever He hears [from the Father—the message regarding the Son], and He will disclose to you what is to come [in the future].**

These four mandates were given by God the Father to His Spirit (Rom. 8:11; John 16:13). In these last words, He will disclose the present and future events (*prophecies and promises*) that have already been written in the past (*apocalypses*) but are being revealed by God to His chosen born-again believers each day. God Jesus declared that "*He* (**the Word**) *is the way, the truth, and the life and no one comes to the Father except through Him*" (John 14:6). He does the work to bring us to all truth and has given it to God the Holy Spirit (Himself, 2 Cor. 3:17). In Romans (8:11), Paul writes: "**And if the Spirit of Him [God the Father] who raised Jesus from the dead lives in you, He who raised Christ Jesus from the dead [the Father] will also give life to your mortal bodies through His Spirit, who lives in you.**"

The word of God is reinforced by the power of God the Holy Spirit. He is who makes the word work for us. The Holy Spirit as God the Father and the Son, they are One. God Jesus said, "**I and the Father are One [in essence and nature],**" and this is an ability of the God BEING. King David also wrote about the Holy Spirit being omnipresent: "**Where can I go from Your Spirit? Or where can I flee from Your presence?**" And Paul said about the Holy Spirit: "**The Lord is the Spirit, and where the Spirit of the Lord is, *there is* liberty**" (John 10:30; 2 Cor. 3:1; Ps. 139:7). They are a BEING, unlike us who are created creatures by Him. The LORD our God is the only BEING in existence ("*There is no God besides Me*" [Isa. 44:6]). He has attributes and abilities that we cannot understand (*they are called communicable and noncommunicable aspects of God*), but He created us with a certain ability to understand some of His godliness. That is what He has revealed to us through His Word, a special revelation. Moses wrote: "**The secret things belong to the Lord our God**" (Deut. 29:29). God is One and the only God BEING ever, and He looked and found no other. In His own words: "**Is there any God besides Me, or is there any other Rock? I know of none.**"

Therefore, He also has an ability to "see and be" Himself in these other selves of His BEING and acts on them as one with the same nature. Being the Father, the greatest by His choosing, God Jesus said, "**The Father is greater than I**" but also "**Anyone who has seen Me has seen the Father**" and "**All things that the Father has are Mine.**" This is His godly perspective, and "**if the Spirit of Him who raised Jesus from the dead [God the Father] lives in you, He who raised Christ Jesus from the dead [the Father] will also give life to your mortal bodies through 'His' Spirit, who lives in you.**" The Bible student can't miss out on this for it is written in His word (Isa. 44:8; John 14:28, 9, 16:15). In other words, God the Holy Spirit, in attributes, is also omniscient, omnipresent, and omnipotent, as are the Father who is the greater of His BEING in existence (John 10:29, God Jesus said, "*My Father [...] is greater than all.*") and it has been written that the Son is the image and substance of the invisible God; therefore, we must accept the God BEING as He says that He is (Col. 1:15; Heb. 1:2–3). It can be argued that God Jesus became second next to the Father when He took a body to the likeness of the first Adam, but He never lost His deity while in His human form (*He is part of the God* BEING. *He was not created*). Paul wrote:

> He existed in the form *and* unchanging essence of God [as One with Him, possessing the fullness of all the divine attributes—the entire nature of deity], did not regard equality with God a thing to be grasped or asserted [as if He did not already possess it, or was afraid of losing it]; but emptied Himself [without renouncing *or* diminishing His deity [*there is no other* BEING *but Them*] but only temporarily giving up the outward expression of divine equality and His rightful dignity] by assuming the form of a bond-servant, and being made in the likeness of men [He became completely human but was without sin, being fully God and fully man].

Then afterward, Paul writes: "He alone possesses immortality [absolute exemption from death] and lives in unapproachable light [*in flesh and bones*] whom no man has ever seen or can see. To Him be honor and eternal power and dominion! Amen" (Phil. 2:6–7; 1 Tim. 6:16).

In another look, Paul writes about the systematic agenda prepared by the God BEING, saying,

> After that comes the end (completion) when He hands over the kingdom to God the Father, after He has made inoperative and abolished every ruler and every authority and power. For Christ must reign [as King] until He has put all His enemies under His feet. The last enemy to be abolished *and* put to an end is death. For He (the Father) has put all things in

subjection under His (Christ's) feet. But when He says, "All things have been put in subjection [under Christ]," it is clear that He (the Father) who put all things in subjection to Him (Christ) is accepted [since the Father is not in subjection to His own Son]. However, when all things are subjected to Him (Christ), then the Son Himself will also be subjected to the One (the Father) who put all things under Him, so that the God BEING may be all in all [manifesting His glory without any opposition, the supreme indwelling and controlling factor of life].

The written word of God brings us to its conclusion that we may understand the Creator's cause and effect, and He has invited us to be with Him in His reality of invisibility for all eternity (1 Cor. 15:24–28; John 14:1–3).

In the beginning, the Spirit of God was the channel moving (*hovering, brooding, with a high degree of care*) upon the face of the waters and is the same through which all things are sustained. The Spirit of God and/or Holy Spirit God is by whom the personal body of Christ (*in flesh and bones*) was created, then resurrected, and is sustained through all eternity in a *glorified* state. He is also giving life to our mortal bodies:

For we are His workmanship [His own master work, a work of art], created in Christ Jesus [reborn from above—spiritually transformed, renewed, ready to be used] for good works, which God prepared [for us] beforehand [taking paths which He set] so that we would walk in them [living the good life which He prearranged and made ready for us] [...also stating] And if the Spirit of Him who raised Jesus from the dead [*God the Father*] lives in you, He who

raised Christ Jesus from the dead [the Father] will also give life to your mortal bodies through His Spirit, who lives in you.

This is not a mystery it has been revealed in Scripture, redemption is a work of the BEING called God (Rom. 8:11). As the author of this work, I am not manipulating the word of God to mean something she's not implying but bringing its objective ideas to life by His action worked in each one of us, to reason their content (Eph. 2:10). God's written word is the door to His reality of invisibility, His known universe: **"In My Father's house are many dwelling places."** And we know He lives above the heavens of the heavens (John 14:1–3). This is also why it is clarified for us by His anointing and we (*accept*) understand our body is the temple of the Holy Spirit, not only as we come together to worship but individually, and that anointing is God's special revelation. We must comprehend the act of God in us and grasp the importance the word is claiming about our being: **"Do you not know that your body is a temple of the Holy Spirit who is within you, whom you have [received as a gift] from God, and that you are not your own [property]?"** This is a powerful declaration that penetrates our entrails (*innermost*), realizing what we are now in Christ.

As a member of His body, we are not our own. Scripture states, **"You were bought with a price [you were actually purchased with the precious blood of Jesus and made His own]. So then, honor and glorify God with your body"** and **"He raised us up together with Him [when we believed] and seated us with Him in the heavenly *places* [because we are] in Christ Jesus."** We are actual members of His body and property by ownership of Christ (1 Cor. 6:19–20; Eph. 2:6). We are told to understand that **"His incomparably great power for us who believe. That is the same power as the mighty strength He exerted when he raised Christ** from the dead," the same and one power we are experiencing by his anointing (Eph. 1:19–20).

The price by which we have been bought is personal by God Jesus, not with gold or silver, nor credit cards of heaven but with something that makes it intimate from Him to us, His own blood and (soul)that is very personal to God the Father, God the Son, and God the Holy Spirit. This is why His word is a powerful living fountain in us, and she says, "**Do not be deceived, God is not mocked [He will not allow Himself to be ridiculed, nor treated with contempt nor allow His precepts to be scornfully set aside].**" Take this verse as part of the character of God for you to know Him closely and see how personal He is with you: "**For in Him we live and move and exist [that is, in Him we actually have our being]**" (Gal. 6:7; Acts 17:28). The disciple can sense the authority, clarity, realization, and addiction that the word makes us sense; for it is a living water stream of life within our spirit/soul. The psalmist (42:1) wrote: "**As the deer pants [longingly] for the water brooks, so, my soul pants [longingly] for You, O God.**" The addiction is real.

Therefore, God Jesus also said, "**He who believes in Me [who adheres to, trusts in, and relies on Me] as the Scripture has said** (*this produces faith/hope*) **from his innermost being will continually flow rivers of living water.**" The faith/hope is real. He makes it real. The word of God is alive in the believer, causing him/her to be sanctified through its truth. Christ said, "**Sanctify them in the truth; Your word is truth.**" And this goes even deeper as the disciple acquires the in-depth knowledge of God's word, sanctification (John 17:17). The knowledge of theology is the fuel that ignites your worship, and this is so because the word of God provokes us to believe in Him: "'*Test me in this,' says the Lord Almighty.*" Not taking these words out of context but hearing the Spirit words through Scriptures and of Scriptures, His word will not come back empty. Therefore, always expect the Spirit hand of

God searching your entrails (Mal. 3:10; Isa. 55:11). You have been washed by His blood, sealed by His Spirit, given the mind of Christ and, as a double portion (*to some*), the baptism of God the Holy Spirit with the evidence He gives, as in speaking in tongues (*for personal edification*). The apostle Paul was very specific about this and wrote it down (1 Cor. 12).

To understand the life, spirit, and light the Word expresses, the person must have had the experience of being born again by the Word's power. It is then when the Word takes real meaning in the spirit/soul of the believer and he/she understands that "**all Scripture is God-breathed [given by divine inspiration]**" (1 Tim. 3:16). The born-again theist believer receives, accepting with no restraints that Scriptures derive from the Almighty Creator, and He is who reveals Himself through her. As a writer of what the Lord has spoken and revealed to me, I must reverently respect what God has spoken and must provide to all readers through this work the total understanding received. He has given to my spirit/soul the knowledge to share with you sisters, brothers, and lectors. The high priest Eli asked Samuel not to cover anything that God revealed to him, saying, "**What is it that He said to you? Please do not hide it from me. May God do the same to you, and more also, if you hide from me anything of all that He said to you.**" The word of God has this stamp in her, and we must speak it and share it as she asks of us to, with no hiding any of its aspects, concepts, and precepts, which is the God BEING's multifaceted wisdom (1 Sam. 3:17; Eph. 3:10). In the same way the LORD asked the people of Israel to listen to Him, the LORD asks all believers of the testimony He gives of His only begotten (*unique*)Son to believe Him and said,

> **Say to them, "Thus says the Lord, the God of Israel, 'Cursed is the man who does not heed the words of this covenant which I commanded your fathers at the time that I brought them out of the land of Egypt [*the world*] from the iron furnace.' Saying, 'Listen to**

My voice and do according to all that I command you [*the New Testament is a continuation of the Old*] **So, you shall be My people, and I will be your God.'"**

In His omniscient knowledge, He knows who you are and challenges you to believe, for *everything is fresh at the eyes of whom we must give account* (Jer.11:3–4; 1 John 5:10; Heb. 4:12–13). God Jesus, as He taught the word, He said how a person must receive and how that which is received would make a change in them. This is not mere speculation; the word of God is alive: "**Jesus answered, 'I assure you and most solemnly say to you, unless one is born of water and the Spirit he cannot [ever] enter the kingdom of God.'**" This is another level for those who are Spirit born, "***born of water***" (John 3:5). To be born of the Spirit is to be sealed by God the Holy Spirit, but to be born of the water is to be born of the word of God. She is the living force in this universe. Paul was given to write "**so that He sanctifies the church, having cleansed her by the washing of water with the word [of God].**" This was explained in the author's first book published, *The Apostles Methodology to Interpret Scriptures*. And this book is a Bible study, a follow-up of that book (Eph. 5:26). We are repeating what we wrote that now we see, hear, talk, walk, handle with the senses/motion of the word of God. She is alive in us as we are temples of the Holy Spirit (*it's another level*). This is also in the understanding that the only thing that runs through a living physical body is its blood through the veins, which takes all impurities to the liver, for it to be expelled by the body. The blood/word of Jesus runs through His body of believer to cleanse them from all sins and create new living cells in them as they encounter bad decisions. This water (*word/blood*) as the testimony of God about His Son is in the understanding God speaks to us through ideas, thoughts, and reasoning by His word, and it affects all our spirit/soul, especially one that has just been brought to life by His living touch. We all have come with no discipline whatsoever into the ways of the LORD. This is intimate: **"The blood of Jesus, his Son, purifies us from all sin."** And this blood is in His water/word that cleanses His body of believers (1 John 1:7). We have become *prophecy* of God *manifested* and *witness* of His Son's testimony.

This Bible study, through systematic theology, drives the disciple to depth never experienced as its realization of the revelation lights up their spirit/soul. This first chapter has been modified to the understanding of systematic theology *first doctrine* to accept that the word of God has God's attribute of unchangeableness. She is immutable. Like Him, she does not change. Observe this spiritual transition:

> **For the word of God is living and active and full of power. It is sharper than any two-edged sword, penetrating as far as the division of the soul and spirit, and of both joints and marrow [the deepest parts of our nature], exposing and judging the very thoughts and intentions of the heart.** (*Observe the verse with no separation.*) **And not a creature [person] exists that is concealed from His sight, but all things are open and exposed, and revealed to the eyes of Him with whom we have to give account.**

God and His written word becomes *one*, and that was speaking about the Old Testament when this was written (Heb. 4:12–13). Two things are exposed here: our life is naked in front of God and we must give account to Him. In our physical reality, light and energy cannot be separated, only by name wording. They are one and the same. Light is energy, and energy is light. Whether we say lightning or electricity, their common source is energy. This same idea and reasoning can be said of God and His word:

In the beginning was the Word, and the Word was with God, and the Word was God. [...*remember He is a* BEING, *the only* BEING *and we (angels and man) are created creatures.*] Without him nothing was made that has been made. In him was life, and that life was the light of all mankind. [...*This is also meaning as Word about the Son.*] The true light that gives light to everyone was coming into the world. He was in the world, and though the world was made through him, the world did not recognize him. [...] The Word became flesh and made his dwelling among us. We have seen his glory, the glory of the one and only Son, who came from the Father, full of grace and truth.

This must be grasped spiritually as physically by the faith the Word gives as energy, for the Word is spirit and is life (John 1:1–14, 6:63). Our finite minds cannot comprehend the depth or in depth of these words of God, but we can sense His BEING behind it, and He gives it life.

We are placing three questions about this chapter for those of you who have acquired this book to be studied in a book club. Answer each question from the chapter's content:

1. Which personal attribute has the God BEING given to his word?

2. How is God BEING a personal God to us, and how can you prove it?

3. What manifestation are we of God, and how does His word affect each one of us?

SECOND LESSON

Knowing and Understanding God the Father through Scripture

L et us start this chapter with this powerful question: *Is it true that human creatures can know and understand God?* And *How much of God can she/he be able to know?* The only way that a weak and fragile human creature can know and understand God is if He wants to reveal Himself to them. God Jesus said,

> All things have been handed over to Me by My Father; and no one fully knows and accurately understands the Son except the Father; and no one fully knows and accurately understands the Father except the Son, and anyone to whom the Son [deliberately] wills to reveal Him. (Matt. 11:27 AMP)

No human creature can know God the Father, for He lives in an *attribute (reality) of invisibility*, but Christ came to reveal the Father to the church, and this is through the promise of His Holy Spirit's anointing and by His word, which comes alive by the anointing. Therefore, the apostle John was able to declare, "**I am writing to you [...the born again] because you have come to know the Father.**" And this was to the believers in the first century (*mainly Gentiles*), but this has been open for all born-again believers through the centuries: "*To come to know the Father*" (1 John 2:13). God wants you to know and understand Him in His terms and design, not in yours. This was one of the inquiries the disciples made to God Jesus while being trained by Him, and He taught them, openly answering as

> **Philip said to Him, "Lord, show us the Father and then we will be satisfied." Jesus said to him, "Have I been with you for so long a time, and you do not know Me yet, Philip, nor recognize clearly who I am?** [*part of the God* BEING]. **Anyone who has seen Me has seen the Father. How can you say, 'Show us the Father?'"**

This was not an answer like if God Jesus was in a spiritism trance but that the Father, the Son, and the Holy Spirit are one and the same God BEING; and that is Their spiritual reality and ability as a BEING (John 14:8–9, 4:24). The Old Testament ancient rabbis featured two powers in heaven as they read the scriptures, which was changed by the other rabbis in the first century to differentiate the belief of the Jews from the Christians in those days, but that change is an abomination of scripture. The New Testament writers capture what Christ came to reveal: the truth and that there are three powers in heaven—the *I* AM, the *Word*, and the *Spirit* (as in Gen.1:1–4).Christ revealed it to the apostles, and they to us, as Father, Son, and Holy Spirit; and they are *One*. Let's start with the apostle John, a Jewish writer of the first century who wrote God Jesus's spoken words: **"No one has seen God at any time; God the only Son, who is in the arms of the Father, He has explained Him."** This verse speaks of two Gods (John 1:18 NASB). Moses in his first encounter with the LORD wrote:

> **And came to Horeb, the mountain of God. Then the <u>angel of the LORD</u> appeared to him [Moses] in a blazing fire from the midst of a bush; and he looked, and behold, the bush was burning with fire, yet the bush was not being consumed. So, Moses said, "I must turn aside and see this marvelous sight, why the bush is not burning up!" When the LORD saw that he turned aside to look, <u>God</u> called to him from the midst of the bush and said, "Moses, Moses!" And he said, "Here I am."**

The lector can see the emphasized words, which are of different characters, and *the angel of the LORD is not any regular angel* (Exod. 3:2–4 NASB). In Judges 6, Gideon had an experience with these different characters, and it was written:

> **Then the <u>angel of the Lord</u> came and sat under the oak that was in Ophrah, which belonged to Joash the Abiezrite, as his son Gideon was beating out wheat in the wine press in order to save it from the Midianites. And the <u>angel of the Lord</u> appeared to him and said to him, "<u>The Lord is with you</u> [*spoken in third person*] valiant warrior."**

In this chapter, Gideon ask for a sign to the LORD, and these three characters declared a truth that makes us understand the God BEING and Their revelation, and

Yet <u>the LORD said to him</u>, "I will certainly be with you."
[...] Then Gideon went in and prepared a young goat
and unleavened bread from an ephah of flour; he put the
meat in a basket and the broth in a pot and
brought them out to him under the oak and
presented *them*. And the <u>angel of God</u> said to him,
"Take the meat and the unleavened bread and
lay them on this rock and pour out the broth." And he
did so. Then the <u>angel of the Lord</u> put out the end of the
staff that was in his hand and touched the meat and the
unleavened bread; and fire came up from the rock and
consumed the meat and the unleavened bread. Then the
<u>angel of the Lord</u> vanished from his sight. When Gideon
perceived that he was the angel of the Lord, he said,
"Oh, Lord God! For I have seen the angel of
the Lord face to face!" But the <u>Lord said to him</u>, "Peace
to you, do not be afraid; you shall not die."

We can notice these three characters speaking and reacting
with Gideon (Judg. 6:13–23 NASB). The prophet Daniel also
expresses his God experience and taught us about these characters:

I kept looking Until <u>thrones</u> were set up, and the <u>Ancient
of Days</u> took His seat [...and] I kept looking in the night
visions, and behold, with the clouds of heaven One like
a son of man was coming, and He came up to the
Ancient of Days and was presented before Him. And to
Him was given dominion, honor, and a kingdom, so,
that all the peoples, nations, and populations of all
languages Might serve Him. His dominion is an
everlasting dominion which will not pass away; and His
kingdom is one which will not be destroyed.

The lector can understand that *thrones* were set up (*more than one*) and that One (*a man*) was given power in the heaven of the earth (Dan. 7:9, 13–14 NASB). We also read how David, the psalmist, wrote: "**The** LORD **says to my Lord: 'Sit at my right hand until I make your enemies a footstool for your feet.'**" A word quoted by God Jesus and the apostles to clear up the understanding that God is a BEING with attributes, characteristics, and abilities like none other (Ps. 110:1 NIV). This questioning of knowing God Jesus still exists today among believers. The LORD has left and maintains His word through the centuries to reveal Himself to us. As we have already mentioned, by His creation, His special revelation, and His written word, the God BEING has revealed Himself to humanity. God is light, and He has nothing to hide, and it is all revealed on our sinful blindness.

The apostle Paul describes this first revelation of God by our senses, saying,

> **Because that which is known about God is evident within them [in their inner consciousness], for God made it evident to them. For ever since the creation of the world His invisible attributes, His eternal power and divine nature, have been clearly seen, being understood through His workmanship [all His creation, the wonderful things that He has made], so that they [who fail to believe and trust in Him] are without excuse and without defense. (Rom. 1:19–20)**

Then as a special revelation, He seals each born-again believer in their heart, as it is written:

> **In Him, you also, when you heard the word of truth, the good news of your salvation, and [as a result] believed in Him, were stamped with the seal of the promised**

Holy Spirit [the One promised by Christ] as owned and protected [by God].

This power has opened, lighting up our spirit/soul (Eph. 1:13, 4:30). When Paul wrote to the Thessalonians, he reminded them of how they received the word of God and said,

> You welcomed it not as the word of [mere] men, but as it truly is, the word of God, which is effectually at work in you who believe [exercising its inherent, supernatural power in those of faith].

The word of God is spirit and is alive in those who believe. How have you received it? (1 Thess. 2:13). This special knowledge about God cannot be encountered by natural human wisdom, for it is written:

> For since the world through all its [earthly] wisdom failed to recognize God, God in His wisdom was well-pleased through the foolishness of the message preached [regarding salvation] to save those who believe [in Christ and welcome Him as Savior].

And this message is not foolishness, but sinful men see it as foolish, because the point-blank truth is shown to them right in their faces but are too proud to accept (1 Cor. 1:21 AMP). Their ignorance occurs because of sin venom, as it's written:

> For even though they knew God [as the Creator], they did not honor Him as God or give thanks [for His wondrous creation]. On the contrary, they became worthless in their thinking [godless, with pointless reasonings, and silly speculations], and their foolish heart was darkened.

Sin's darkness does not let them see the truth. Some even declare that there is no God (Rom. 1:21; Ps.14). Scripture also says of them:

> **But even if our gospel is [in some sense] hidden [behind a veil], it is hidden [only] to those who are perishing; among them the god of this world [Satan] has blinded the minds of the unbelieving to prevent them from seeing the illuminating light of the gospel of the glory of Christ, who is the image of God.**

They are enslaved in their mental prisons of darkness (*worldviews*), as we already established in our first published book, *The Apostles Methodology*. Therefore, God is whom He reveals Himself to us (2 Cor. 4:3–4 AMP). It is because of this reason that we need Scripture in order to know the God of Abraham who called us to serve Him. They are God the Father, God the Son, and God the Holy Spirit through their word. Creation tells us there is a God, but His word teaches us about sin and how to know and understand Him. Without the word of the gospel in its revelation, man cannot approach, reach, acquire what is revealed in nature, and therein by God Almighty, for them. Scripture tells us about men understanding the things of God that are impossible to them: **"Great is the Lord, and highly to be praised, And His greatness is [so vast and profound as to be] unsearchable [incomprehensible to man]"** and **"Great is our [majestic and mighty] Lord and abundant in strength; His understanding is inexhaustible [infinite, boundless],"** where finite man cannot know God by his/her own physical knowledge, except through the faith produce by His word. That is how He reveals Himself to them (Ps. 145:3, 147:5 AMP). Scripture also teaches:

> **He has also planted eternity [a sense of divine purpose] in the human heart [a mysterious longing**

which nothing under the sun can satisfy, except God]—yet man cannot find out (comprehend, grasp) what God has done (His overall plan) from the beginning to the end.

Therefore, God is the one to reveal Himself to us. He created us with this (*code*) capacity, planting eternity in our hearts so that we can now understand Him for who He is, God Almighty (Eccles. 3:11). He is a personal God for each human person descendant of Adam (*not Nephilim who are just human/animal and do not have a spirit/soul but a demon/abomination (Cain Descendants)* [Matt. 13:18–30; Gen. 6:2, 4]), and He is not too far from each one of us. It is written: "**God did this so that they would seek him and perhaps reach out for him and find him, though he is not far from any one of us. 'For in him we live and move and have our being.'**" How can anyone miss that? We are God's spoken word manifested (Acts 17:27–28 NIV). Now though God has given us this ability to know Him, it is because of sin, death, evil, and darkness that the reasoning in man has become conceited, darkened, and totally egocentric (*like a human animal*), not wanting to accept the plain truth of God's reality. Scripture teaches:

> For by Him all things were created in heaven and on earth [things] visible and invisible, whether thrones or dominions or rulers or authorities; all things were created and exist through Him [that is, by His activity] and for Him. And He Himself existed and is before all things, and in Him all things hold together. [His is the controlling, cohesive force of the universe].

In other words, there is no *Mother Nature.* That is just the rebellious statement of sinful women and men (Col. 1:16–17).

God Has Spoken to Man

We need Scripture to interpret the natural revelation of God properly. In the beginning, God spoke the word and created the cosmos. Then He spoke to Adam, Abram, Moses, and the prophets. To the prophet Ezekiel (3:4) God said, "**Then He said to me, 'Son of man, go to the house of Israel and speak My words to them.'**" God personally spoke to man (Ezek.3:4). He told them to write a copy as a recount of His word: "**Then the Lord said to Moses, 'Write this in the book as a memorial,'**" and this is how we have the Word of God (Exod. 17:14). He told Jeremiah, the prophet, "**Write in a book all the words which I have spoken to you.**" And He also told the apostle John, "**Write the things which you have seen [in the vision], and the things which are [now happening], and the things which will take place after these things.**" And this is how the Word of God has reached us (Jer. 30:2; Rev. 1:19). In the last word that God spoke to us, His Son became flesh and walked among us:

> **The true Light [the genuine, perfect, steadfast Light] which, coming into the world, enlightens everyone. He (Christ) was in the world, and though the world was made through Him, the world did not recognize Him [...] And the Word (Christ) became flesh and lived among us; and we [actually] saw His glory, glory as belongs to the [One and] only begotten [*unique*] Son of the Father [the Son who is truly**

unique, the only One of His kind, who is] full of grace and truth (absolutely free of deception).

The promise given in Genesis (3:15), to the Adams, was fulfilled (John 1:9–10, 14 AMP). Now in this verse, He tells man of His ultimate words, like into telling us, "I will speak to you no more":

> **God, having spoken to the fathers long ago in [the voices and writings of] the prophets [about His Son] in many separate revelations [each of which set forth a portion of the truth], and in many ways, has in these last days spoken [with finality] to us in [the person of One who is by His character and nature] His Son [namely Jesus], whom He appointed heir and lawful owner of all things, through whom also He created the universe [that is, the universe as a space-time-matter continuum].**

The God BEING revealed Himself. God reveals Himself to a spiritually dead people, dead in their spirit/soul: **"And you [He made alive when you] were [spiritually] dead and separated from Him because of your transgressions and sins"** (Eph. 2:1). It has been written: **"But God [the Father] demonstrates his own love for us in this: While we were still sinners, Christ died for us"** (Heb. 1:1–2; Rom. 5:7–8). This is how God has spoken to us until His last resolution made in love to finish all things, as the Hebrew writer (*also the apostles Paul and John* [1 Thess. 4:13–18; 1 John 3:2]) explains. His last event is to transform our bodies to match our living spirit/soul in Christ and walk into the City of Light.

Today there are hundreds of false religions in the world. They are the evidence of how people without the proper education distort the truth of the gospel. It is only the words of scripture that makes us understand the testimony of the Father about Jesus and the divine nature of God. In the same form, it is only scripture that makes us understand the revelation of Christ in us as members of His body through His Holy Spirit. The writer of the book of Hebrews, writing about Christ, said,

> **The Son is the radiance and only expression of the glory of [our awesome] God [reflecting God's Shekinah glory, the Light-being, the brilliant light of the divine], and the exact representation [*substance*] and perfect imprint of His [Father's] essence and upholding and maintaining and propelling all things [the entire physical and spiritual universe] by His powerful word [carrying the universe along to its predetermined goal]. When He [Himself and no other] had [by offering Himself on the cross as a sacrifice for sin] accomplished purification from sins and established our freedom from guilt, He sat down [revealing His completed work] at the right hand of the Majesty on high [revealing His Divine authority].**

The Son is more than what humans can come to understand, and what he/she is able to understand is given to them through scripture. Believing that scriptures have God's attribute of immutability creates our understanding of the divine BEING (Heb. 1:3). There have been a lot of arguments about the Son as a deity, but scripture is the one that elaborates on the position God the Father has given the Son, and it is plain to read: "So that **all will give honor (reverence, homage) to the Son just as they give honor to the Father. [In fact] the one who does not honor the Son does not honor the Father who has sent Him.**" And this is a clear statement on how we must understand our God, who is *"One"*

(John 5:23). God Jesus said, "I am going [back] to the Father, for the Father is greater than I" […and] "I am the [only] Way [to God] and the [real] Truth and the [real] Life; no one comes to the Father but through Me." By these words, God Jesus canceled all other worldviews and religious teachings expressing that there is only one way to come to God the Father; and that it is the Father, through His spoken word, that reveals the greatness of the Son He loves (John 14:28, 6). Scripture teaches of the unity of the deity and how they have ownership of all things: "He will glorify and honor Me, because He (the Holy Spirit) will take from what is Mine and will disclose it to you. All things that the Father has are Mine." Now who can argue that, for He got up from the dead declaring victory! "The Lord our God, the Lord is one!" His written word declares it (John 16:15–16; Deut. 6:4). God the Holy Spirit is also a permanent person of the God BEING and substance of the godly divinity. It is said of them: "Now the Lord [Christ] is the Spirit." And this is as substance consisting of one and the same (Father, Son, and Holy Spirit), for it is also said of God the Father: "And if the Spirit of Him who raised Jesus from the dead [God the Father] lives in you, He who raised Christ Jesus from the dead [the Father] will also give life to your mortal bodies through His Spirit, who lives in you." They are "*one*" and the same (*It's a God thing* [2 Cor. 3:17; Rom. 8:11 AMP]). There is no wonder why God Jesus said on the cross, "Eli, Eli, lama sabachthani?" That is, "My God, My God, why have You forsaken Me?" or "My God (Father) and My God (Spirit), why have you abandoned me." Again, scripture shows the unity of the God BEING (Matt. 27:46; Ps. 22:1). This unity is of most importance to both the *Father* and the *Son*. They are very *protective* of their *Holy Spirit* and said,

> Therefore, I say to you, every sin and blasphemy will be forgiven men, but the blasphemy against the Spirit will not be forgiven men. Anyone who speaks a word *against* the Son of Man, it will have forgiven him;

but whoever speaks against the Holy Spirit, it will not be forgiven him, either in this *age* or in the age to come.

From a divine standpoint, the God BEING is love and merciful, and we must understand this unity and ability between them and honor it reverently. The God BEING is one (the only BEING), and in His intimate persona, His abilities to be who He is are multiple (Matt. 12:31–32). There is no wonder that scripture teaches that "In Him we live and move and exist [that is, in Him we actually have our being]." "*In Him*" it is written, and it's a God thing (Acts 17:28).

It is through God's Spirit that the world's mysteries are revealed to us, as scripture teaches:

> For God has unveiled them and revealed them to us through the [Holy] Spirit; for the Spirit searches all things [diligently], even [sounding and measuring] the [profound] depths of God [the divine counsels and things far beyond human understanding]. For what person knows the thoughts and motives of a man except the man's spirit within him? So also no one knows the thoughts of God except the Spirit of God (*and this is where things become different for the born-again believer, for scripture compares our existence to God's existence; we are created to His image and likeness, in other words with a spirit/soul alive*). *Now we have received, not the spirit of the world, but the [Holy] Spirit who is from God, so that we may know and understand* [God (*Jer.* 9:24)] *the [wonderful] things freely given to us by God* [*and it was paid by His oath (Heb. 6:13–20)*]. We also speak of these things, not in words taught or supplied by

human wisdom, but in those taught by the Spirit, combining, and interpreting spiritual thoughts with spiritual words (*verses to verses, chapters to chapters*) [for those being guided by the Holy Spirit]. But the natural [unbelieving] man does not accept the things [the teachings and revelations] of the Spirit of God, for they are foolishness [absurd and illogical] to him; and he is incapable of understanding them, because they are spiritually discerned and appreciated, [and he is unqualified to judge (*know*) spiritual matters]. But the spiritual man [the spiritually mature Christian] judges all things [questions, examines and applies what the Holy Spirit reveals], yet is himself judged by no one [the unbeliever cannot judge and understand the believer's spiritual nature]. For who has known the mind and purposes of the Lord, so as to instruct Him? But we have the mind of Christ [to be guided by His thoughts and purposes].

This passage teaches how God reveals Himself to man through His Holy Spirit's special revelation, by the seal of His Spirit and provoked by His written word to believe the purpose He declares: redemption from these present evil ages (1 Cor. 2:10–16; Isa. 55:11; Eph. 4:30 AMP).

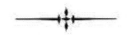

Humanities Glory Is to Know and Understand the LORD Our God

In the first chapter, we touched on realizing how Scripture is the immutable word of God. She is tagged with God's attribute of unchangeableness. Scripture gives the believer prophecies and promises encrusted to empower them by its authority of truth into the reality of God's unity with His Word/Son and Holy Spirit to bless our life and living. This is so because God loved His creation since before He created it and decided to empower them with the authority of truth to overcome their misfortune. Many people somehow think that God found Himself alone; and therefore, He created us, meaning that He had a necessity. But that would take away His attribute of freedom, independence, and unchangeableness; and God does not change. In 2 Chronicles (6:18), King Solomon said, **"But will God really dwell on earth with humans? The heavens, even the highest heavens, cannot contain you. How much less this temple I have built!"** Also, scripture explains,

> **The God who made the world and everything in it is the Lord of heaven and earth and does not live-in temples built by human hands. And he is not served by human hands, as if he "Needed" anything. Rather, he himself gives everyone life and breath and "Everything" else [*their needs, God is the Potter*]. From one man he made all the nations, that they should inhabit the whole earth; and he marked out their appointed times in history [*destiny*] and the boundaries of their lands.**

We must add: **"A man's mind plans his way [as he journeys through life], But the Lord directs his steps and establishes them."** We are living in and as part of the God BEING's reality (Prov. 16:9). *God did this so that they would seek him* (this is how God seeks us, His not begging but calling through His word) and perhaps reach out for him and find him, though he is not far from any one of us. **"For in him we live and move and have our being."** (*Christ, the God* BEING*'s Word, sustains our life [Col. 3:3–4]*). As some of your own poets have said, **"We are his offspring"** (*Paul was talking to nonbelievers. How much more does this apply to us, for now we are sons/daughters of God [John 1:12–13]*). **"Therefore, since we are God's offspring,** (*now He made us kindred*) **we should not think that the divine being is like gold or silver or stone—an image made by human design and skill** (*once again God wants us to see His revelation/realization in scripture, not our human imagination*). **In the past, God overlooked such ignorance, but now he commands all people everywhere to repent"**—that is, to turn from their worldviews (Acts 17:24–30). This, hence, reminds us of that God the Father does not live in our physical reality but in His (*reality*) attribute of invisibility, even away from the heavens (*as Solomon said*) and its City of Light. He also, through His Spirit, makes His dwelling in men and women, which He created to His image and likeness and are washed by Christ Jesus's blood and God's Spirit seal. Consequently, who can tell God that He cannot do so? The Israelites seem not to have wanted God's revelation, (*a majority*), and the *Gentiles* grabbed hold of it, receiving the blessings they rejected. It is written:

> **He came to that which was His own [that which belonged to Him—His world, His creation, His possession], and those who were His own [people— the Jewish nation] did not receive** *and* **welcome Him. But to as many as did receive** *and* **welcome Him, He gave the right [the authority, the privilege] to become children of God** [*sanctification by position/from offspring of Adam through Seth, now we are kindred*]**, that is, to those who believe in (adhere to, trust in, and rely on) His** <u>Name</u> [*Christ/Word*]**.**

No one can tell God how to apply His will in creation. He is the Potter. **"Who has known the mind of the Lord so as to instruct him?"** It is His sovereign right (John 1:11–12; 1 Cor. 2:16; Isa. 40:13).

Christ spoke of the glory He had next to the Father and the Holy Spirit before creation, and John the Apostle wrote His words, saying,

> **After Jesus said this, he looked toward heaven and prayed: "Father, the hour has come. Glorify your Son, that your Son may glorify you** [*the Word/Messiah always knew His position as the Son of God*]. **And now, Father, glorify me in your presence with the glory I had with you before the world began** [*and He also knew He took a body like ours but was still the Son/Word of God*]. **Father, I want those you have given me to be with me where I am, and to see my glory, the glory you have given me because you loved me before the creation of the world."**

Christ Jesus came to save us by bringing us back to the Father, to be with Him from everlasting to everlasting, (John 17:1, 5, 24). In the church's past, there were disputes about God Jesus being complete man and complete God, but it seems that those disputing this to create a Christendom doctrine missed out, in that God said, **" *You are gods, and all of you are children of the Most High. But you shall die like [fallen] men.*"** Our spirit/soul is in essence like God's spirit/soul. He said it. This is where God's image and likeness can be applied to us. God is spirit and has a soul (Isa. 42:1; John 4:24).

In the author's book *The Apostles Methodology to Interpret Scriptures*, we said the following about God being one in the Old

Testament. He has the ability to be the I AM, the *Word*, and the *Holy Spirit* in creating all things; and He revealed in the New Testament His BEING as "the Father, the Son, and the Holy Spirit." These three *self-expressions* are one being. As a BEING, and to that the only BEING that exists (*not created like we are*), He has abilities in and on His godly BEING that no one can compare (*uncommunicable*). Therefore, He establishes that He does not share His glory with no one. We can sense His persona, but we do not have His godly attributes. The Word establishes that God made us to His image and likeness (*man and women*) and He called us gods (*adopting us*). In our first published book called *The Apostles Methodology to Interpret Scriptures* (41–42), we explained the following:

The Apostles Methodology to Interpret Scriptures

> Some would say the Apostles never spoke about a Triune God, but God Jesus was the one to teach them this concept by saying: "*No one has ever seen God, but the one and only Son, who is himself God and is in closest relationship with the Father, has made him known,*" (John 1:18 NIV). He told them: "*Anyone who has seen me has seen the Father,*" (John 14:9). The Apostle also said Christ taught them: "*I am going to the Father, for the Father is greater than I,*" (John 14:28 NIV). These teachings about a Father/Son God relation is of course from the many Hebrew texts as some would point out to a '*Lord who said to my Lord*' (Ps. 110/Isa. 61:1) in other words more than one person (two Powers in heaven). Even in the beginning God speaking to someone said: "*Let Us make man in Our image, according to Our likeness,*" now this is not a person speaking to Himself, but this is God Almighty and His

Son, the Word of God, (Gen. 1:26). God Jesus taught His disciples: "*I and the Father are one,*" (John 10:30).

As the Bible student can perceive this view is a covenantal interpretation made by Peter from the forefathers' a divine legal writing about God's Persona. Stephen Martyr used this same method with boldness telling the Jews about the third person of the Trinity, '*God the Holy Spirit.*' In Acts 7:47–51, (NIV) he began to explain Scriptures to them about who is really the temple of the Holy Spirit by his speech and how through Scripture this was meant to be part of Israel covenant, he said: "*However, the Most High does not live, in houses made by men. As the prophet says: "Heaven is my throne, and the earth is my footstool,*" (Isa. 66:1/2 Ch. 6:18, a rider). *What kind of house will you build for me? says the Lord. Or where will my resting place be? Has not my hand, made all these things?*" (The Church is the temple of God's Holy Spirit, His chosen people, created by God Himself, and this is why nothing can fill the soul of men but Almighty God Himself, [1 Cor. 3:16, 6:19-20/Act 17:24–31/Rom. 8:11]), "*You stiff-necked people, with uncircumcised hearts and ears! You are just like your fathers: You always resist the Holy Spirit!*" (Gen. 6:3). In his interpretation, there was a sense of a new revelation given to him by God the Holy Spirit, that of being a temple. Paul extended this teaching saying: "*Don't you know that you yourselves are God's temple and that God's Spirit dwells in your midst? If anyone destroys God's temple, God will destroy that person,*" see how there's a condition here to a person who after being safe continues to seek darkness, (1 Cor. 3:16–17). This verse declares the church is a temple saying: "*God's Spirit dwells in your midst,*" but Paul also writes: "*Or do you not know that your body is the temple of the Holy Spirit who is in you, whom you have from God, and you are not your own? For you were bought at a price; therefore, glorify God in your body and in your spirit, which are God's,"* then not only when we gather as a church, we are God's temple, but our body individually is also temple of God, (1 Cor. 6:19–20). We must walk in the light of God's Spirit, through His sound doctrine in communion with God shining in us, (1 John 1:3–5). Stephen also gave a mystery in his words, *'they and their fathers'* as of a different breed of people walking among us. God Jesus called them, *'Tare and Goats,'* two different natures in contrast to the *Wheat* and *Sheep,* (Matt. 13:24–30, 36–43, 25:32–41). Jesus went as far as to tell them: *"You are not of my sheep,"* and, *"You are of your father the devil,"* a mystery to reveal ahead, (John 10: 27, 8:44).

In another example in their method of interpretation let's look at a passage in Psalm 82, which some scholar says this was referring to the kings and prince' of the Israelites courts but in true God Jesus, when interpreting these verses spoke of the common people to whom the word of God came and of Himself. In John 10:34–36, (NKJV) God Jesus is quoted saying: *"Is it not written in your law, 'I said, "You are gods"'? If He called them gods, to whom the word of God came (and the scripture cannot be broken)? Do you say of Him whom the Father sanctified and sent into the world, 'You are blaspheming,' because I said, 'I am the Son of God'?"* In this view's explanation we see an obvious meaning to these verses' interpretation and how God Jesus taught them that, *"scripture cannot be broken."* The apostle's method of interpretation was like the Lord's bold and simple not looking for *"Five feet on a Cat,"* (a Puerto Rican proverb) meaning : "Looking at reality without adding to it," but with the simplest of understanding in the authority of truth, Jesus is the '*Suffering Servant,*' and the '*Prophet*' they had been waiting for all along. Prophesied by Moses and the prophets as our *sin offering,* (Deut. 18:15/Isa. 53:10). It is by the blood of Jesus you have been washed and sealed by God the Holy Spirit, changing your sinful heart.

Then this body is like a spacesuit, to keep us in this physical reality created by God for humans and for Jesus of Nazareth, who now has a body like ours (*in flesh and bones*). He is in a state of glorification as our bodies will be in the next covenant of the transformation at the trumpet sound (Ps. 82:6–7; 1 Thess. 4:16–17). As we recognize the immutability of the Word and the reason behind it (the God BEING), we make this truthful declaration: Jesus Christ is God, and the Triune God is a family and has communicated in eternal love to their creation. God the Father has never been alone and will never be without and/or away from His creation because of His attributes. God does not need to hide His truth from no one, for God is Light, and He declares, "Come near me and listen to this: 'From the first announcement I have not spoken in secret; at the time it happens (*creation*) I am there[omniscient/omnipresent].' And now the Sovereign Lord [*The Father*] has sent me [the Son] endowed with his Spirit." In other words, this is Christ speaking to man (*in the Old Testament*) by the knowledge He has since before They created all (Isa. 48:16).

There is no other god or being as the God BEING of the Bible. It does not exist, and this is a declaration by the God of Abraham, saying, "Do not tremble, do not be afraid. Did I not proclaim this and foretell it long ago? You are my witnesses. Is there any God besides me? [*remember He is a* BEING, *not creation like us*] **No, there is no other Rock; I know not one.**" He proved it to Israel in Egypt and how He liberated them from the stronghold of the pharaoh (Isa. 44:8). God the Father exists in His spirit/soul existence. He was never created, nor began to exist. He always was, is, and will be, even before this dimension called time (*was, is, and be*) was spoken into creation by Him. The prophet wrote of God: "**Do you not know? Have you not heard? The Lord is the everlasting God, the Creator of the ends of the earth. He will not grow tired or weary, and his understanding no one can fathom**" (Isa. 40:28). Let me declare something about God's attributes that explains Him, His BEING's abilities. He is omniscient, meaning He cannot learn anything new, for He knows it all; and if there is anything new happening, it is because He is creating it to happen (*like grace into redemption, something new*). He is omnipresent, meaning He always existed above time as He is omniscient of it all. He sees and knows everything and is new and fresh to Him always. God Jesus said, "**My Father has been working until now [He has never ceased working], and I too am working.**" We will see greater things than these as He calls us home (John 5:17 AMP). We must always remember He is a BEING (*omnipotent, Almighty Being*) unlike us created creatures (*angels and man*). We are His creation.

The Triune God (*this word is a man-made term, as the anthropomorphic language, for as a* BEING *and into His awareness, God is* "*one*") worked together in their creation and Their redemptive work. Scripture uses anthropomorphic language to describe God's persona and Their actions, where *anthropo* means "man" and *morphic,* "form." Scripture says, the Father is the *Gardner,* Christ is the *Vine* of the branches (*which are His believers*), and the Holy Spirit is the *Counselor* in their work of redemption. Christ came as the last and final Adam for this reason (*innocent, immaculate, new blood in the likeness of sinful man, with the first Adam stamina, and kingship [Rom. 8:3]*). He is the

Seed of the woman with a purpose from before time (Gen. 3:15). Scripture explains, "For He was foreordained (foreknown) before the foundation of the world" (*in their first heavenly, divine summit*) for our redemption (1 Pet. 1:20). Paul reveals this mystery to us, saying,

> Therefore, just as sin came into the world through one man, and death through sin, so death spread to all people [no one being able to stop it or escape its power] because they all sinned [...*and ever since birth, we were imputed with the death of Adam*] So then as through one trespass [Adam's sin] there resulted condemnation for all men, even so through one act of righteousness [Christ] there resulted justification of life to all men (*one cancels out the other*). For just as through one man's disobedience[his failure to hear, his carelessness] the many were made sinners, so through the obedience of the one Man (*Jesus Christ*) the many will be made righteous and acceptable to God and brought into right standing with Him.

The God of Abraham since before the beginning of time united in a divine, heavenly summit to resolve the condition that man was going to encounter, and this work was through Himself as a responsible party, not that He was responsible for what happened (*God is not tempted by evil [James 1:13]*), but He took steps to resolve it since before the creation, for it is His creation (Rom. 5:12, 18–19). The writer of Hebrews says,

> But we do see Jesus, who was made lower than the angels for a little while [by taking on the limitations of humanity], crowned with glory and honor because of His suffering of death, so that by the grace of God [extended to sinners] He might experience

death for [the sins of] everyone. For it was fitting for God [that is, an act worthy of His divine nature] that He, for whose sake are all things, and through whom are all things, in bringing many sons to glory, should make the author and founder of their salvation perfect through suffering [bringing to maturity the human experience necessary for Him to be perfectly equipped for His office as High Priest].

God Jesus accepted the challenge placed in Their first divine, heavenly summit before creation (Heb. 2:9–10). The question was asked, and the response was given. And that is to admire, love, and worship our God the Word. The prophet Isaiah (*in an omniscient revelation*) heard and wrote the words spoken in that first divine, heavenly summit, but it seemed that as he did this, there was a lot of hiding of the words' meaning. But this is written, and with little words, it alerts a person to see through the verse: "**Then I heard the voice of the LORD, saying, 'Whom shall I send, and who will go for Us?' Then I said, 'Here am I** [*or I am, who is this but God*]. **Send me!'**" The question was an omniscient one: "**Who will go for Us?**" In a meeting of more than one person—the I AM, the Word, and the Spirit—the Word was the one to respond, "Here am I. Send me!" (*with an exclamation mark*); for *what could a mere man in a fallen nature (like Isaiah) could have done?* We can't even save ourselves (Isa. 6:8; John 1:14). The redemptive work of God is the main and central topic of the Scripture. God Jesus said, "**For the Son of Man has come to seek and to save that which was lost.**" This is the greatest topic to us in Scripture (Luke 19:10). It is by the will of God for us all, as it is written:

Because it is written, "You shall be holy (set apart), for I am holy." (*This is called sanctification by position. God declares, positioning us fallen creatures.*) If you address as Father, the One who impartially judges according to each one's work, conduct yourselves in [reverent] fear [of Him] and with profound respect for Him throughout the time of your stay on earth (*this is a must, follow the sound doctrine*). For you know that you were not redeemed from your useless [spiritually unproductive] way of life inherited [by tradition] from your forefathers with perishable things like silver and gold [*nor heaven's credit cards, this is personal*] but (*understand this well*) [you were actually purchased]with precious blood, like that of a [sacrificial] lamb unblemished and spotless, the priceless blood of Christ. For He was foreordained [note: *the Son of God always existed and it was always known (by the God BEING*) that He would be the Redeemer of mankind] [foreknown (*means to be aware of an event before it happens, only God can do that*)] before the foundation of the world (*this is where the first divine, heavenly summit of creation was conducted by the I AM, the God BEING*) but has appeared [publicly] in these last times for your sake and through Him you believe [confidently] in God [the heavenly Father], who raised Him from the dead and gave Him glory, so that your faith and hope are [centered and rest] in God.

In other words, "*Before the foundation of the world*" means that before the angels and Adam were created, God already knew the angels and man's failure and still loved us (1 Pet. 1:16–21; Job 4:18). As we analyze the following verse: "**For God so loved the world** [*man and woman*] **that He gave His only begotten Son,**" this happened at their first heavenly, divine summit before creation, where Christ was foreordained. This was when God so loved us (*angels and humans alike*) that He gave the closest thing to His heart before the creation of all (John 3:16). Scripture states,

> **For it was the Father's good pleasure for all the fullness to dwell in Him** [*our Man/God in flesh and bones*] **and through Him to reconcile all things to Himself, having made peace through the blood of His cross; through Him** [*Jesus of Nazareth, the Word became flesh*] ***I say*, whether things on earth or things in heaven** [*for*] ***it was fitting.*** (Col. 1:19–20; Heb. 2:10)

This is when God so loved the world (*human's spirit/soul*)—for it does not say He fell in love but "so loved"—and He gave us redemption before creation took place; therefore, the Son was foreordained before creation. We must understand God is the only BEING in all existence and has attributes like no one ever, and He does not share His glory (*attributes*) *with no one.* He is the storyteller, producer, and director of this reality that we are living. The story that He became a part of, or the *main part* of, through His Son. God is omniscient. He knows everything, always. He is omnipresent. There is nothing new for Him to learn, nor anything new existing that hasn't been done by Him and in Him. All is sustained. In that *divine, heavenly summit,* all the secrets of reality in heaven and earth started; but this is the topic for a *future book* if the LORD wills it.

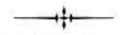

Redemption Is for the Adam's Descendants

Gentiles are grafted, implant to the real Vine (*Christ*), where now we give fruits to God the Father through God the Holy Spirit, who reveals to us our situation as sons/daughters of God. This is in a new covenant under better promises in the order of Melchizedek, where Christ Jesus is our high priest coming out of the tribe of Judah, not the Leviticus priesthood (Heb. 7:11–16, 8:13). The Lord Christ said, **"I am the true Vine, and My Father is the vinedresser,"** and **"But when the Helper (Comforter, Advocate, Intercessor—Counselor, Strengthener, Standby) comes, whom I will send to you from the Father, that is the [*promise*] Spirit of Truth who comes from the Father, He will testify and bear witness about Me."** This expresses the true work of redemption by our God and LORD through His Holy Spirit, which at blank sight is the work of Scripture for us all (John 15:1, 26; Rom. 8:11). The Father is the One involved in our redemption. God Jesus said, **"This is the will of Him who sent Me, that of all that He has given Me I lose nothing, but that I [give new life and] raise it up at the last day."** The Father is the greatest evangelist ever, and Christ is our Savior, producer of our redemption as He was preordained (John 6:39). This is where the story of predestination in God's terms begins, and we must accept it. Christ Jesus's life was predestined (Luke 15:3–7). This must make you think about the parable of the one hundred sheep (*predestination*). He started with one hundred sheep, and when He comes for them, He will take one hundred. Now God the Holy Spirit was given the greatest job of all: to guide, reveal, and restore as He would counsel us. Scripture says,

> But when He, the Spirit of Truth, comes, He will guide you into all the truth [full and complete truth]. For He will not speak on His own initiative, but He will speak whatever He hears [from the Father—the

message regarding the Son], and He will disclose to you what is to come [in the future]. He will glorify and honor Me, because He (the Holy Spirit) will take from what is Mine and will disclose it to you. All things that the Father has are Mine. Because of this I said that He [the Spirit] will take from what is Mine and will reveal it to you.

The Spirit of the Father is the one involved in all the affairs of the living God. He loves our spirit/soul image of Himself (John 16:13–15; Rom. 8:11). In this work of redemption, we can understand how our God is a personal God and He wants us to know this and understand in faith (*true confidence*) how all things are in His hands. This includes all of mankind, for we are all creations of the God BEING, and in Him *we live and move and have our being.* The apostle Paul wrote, "If some of the branches have been broken off, and you, though a wild olive shoot, have been grafted in among the others and now share in the nourishing sap from the olive root." This is speaking (*as anthropomorphic language about the church*) of Gentiles who are saved, bought/brought to the work God Jesus started for Israel (Rom. 11:17). This grafting is a miracle of God the Father, who chose us for the love of His Son, for He came to His own, but His own (*Israel*) did not receive Him (John 1:11). Paul is asking us to walk (*the sound doctrine*), being grateful for the choosing by God of our life. He considered us to be His sons and daughters before the foundation of the world. In looking into this redemption, we must understand that this is the greatest investment ever made in the universe. It was a personal investment given by offering His only begotten (*monos genes,* Greek word for "only" and "unique/kind"), not like Isaac who was a begotten but was also a second son. God the Father offered His Word/God and the Son of the God BEING (*see Hebrew 11:17 NKJV*). We must understand the following words of God Jesus when He said, "For out of the abundance of the heart the mouth speaks." Christ is said also to be the Word of the God BEING (Matt. 12:34; Luke 6:45). He has come from the deepest part of the heart of the God BEING. He declared it. Christ was a propitiatory sacrifice of blood (*from His own human body*) on a tormented agony of spirit/soul to the last drop of His human blood.

Let's dig deeper into the condition He was to come and do God's bidding: "**Yet it pleased the Lord to bruise Him; He [the Father] has put Him to grief,**" "**When You make His soul an offering for sin,**" and "**He shall see the labor of His soul and be satisfied.**" Christ's very *soul* was the expiation, the sacrifice offering; therefore, this is *so personal to Him* (Isa. 53:10–11 NKJV). This speaks to us so deeply about the persona, character of this divine BEING. There is no wonder that the apostle John called and said that God is love (1 John 4:8). The apostle Paul, making us act upon this bold attitude of God, show us how we can do this and said,

> **Have this same attitude in yourselves which was in Christ Jesus [look to Him as your example in selfless humility], who, although He existed in the form and unchanging essence of God [as One with Him, possessing the fullness of all the divine attributes— the entire nature of deity], did not regard equality with God a thing to be grasped or asserted [as if He did not already possess it, or was afraid of losing it]; but emptied Himself [without renouncing or diminishing His deity, but only temporarily giving up the outward expression of divine equality and His rightful dignity] by assuming the form of a bond-servant, and being made in the likeness of men [He became completely human but was without sin, being fully God and fully man]. After He was found**

> in [terms of His] outward appearance as a man [for
> a divinely appointed time], He humbled Himself
> [still further] by becoming obedient [to the Father]
> to the point of death, even death on a cross. (Phil.
> 2:5–8 AMP)

God Jesus put everything aside (*even His newly acquired human body*) to make this act personal, from Him to God the Father and their love for us all. God Jesus fulfilled: "**Honor your father and your mother, so that you may live long in the land the Lord your God is giving you.**" And in equal share, God the Father fulfilled this, saying, "**He who loves father or mother more than Me is not worthy of Me. And he who loves son or daughter more than Me is not worthy of Me.**" In giving His unique Son, the God BEING leads by example (Exod. 20:12). Many people complain of God, saying, "**Where was God when this and that happened to my son or daughter?**" And the answer is in the same place He was (*suffering*) when they killed His only Son. He was sitting at His throne watching His Son suffer for you and me (*it marked Him eternally*). The apostle Paul exposes what is being asked of us as a result of this, saying, "**For the love of Christ compels us, because we judge thus: that if One died for all, then all died; and He died for all, that those who live should live no longer for themselves, but for Him who died for them and rose again.**" Can you comply? (Matt. 10:37; 2 Cor. 5:14–15). This is why the LORD exalted His Son to the highest of all things because He humbled Himself to the lowest and became obedient to the redemptive work of God, honoring His Father. This is why it is written of Him:

> For this reason also [because He obeyed and so
> completely humbled Himself], God has highly
> exalted Him [*in flesh and bones*] and bestowed on

Him the name which is above [All] every name, so
that at the name of Jesus every knee shall bow [in
submission], of those who are in heaven and on earth
and under the earth, and that every tongue will
confess and openly acknowledge that Jesus Christ is
Lord (sovereign God), to the glory of God the Father.

A man in flesh and bones. Can you obey the Father as well?
This is a godly thing for us, and only we can understand this act of
love. The redemption work is one that involves us believers in it,
and as disciples, we must get involved in its action by also obeying
God Jesus (Phil. 2:9–11). Listen, you must fully understand the
implication of the death of His Son at the Cross on Calvary, for it
is eternally present at His Father's sight in an omnipresent stand,
for everything is fresh to Him who we must give account to (Heb.
4:13). The priestly works of Christ affects the Father's will as He
became indebted to Christ. Scripture says, "**Now to a laborer, his
wages are not credited as a favor or a gift, but as an obligation
[something owed to him].**" This is said of Christ's works of the
law: perfect, the Adam without sin (Rom. 4:4). Then He will
forgive those who repent, turn to Him, and/or punish those who
will not, as accomplices and guilty of the killing of His Son.
Question: *which one are you ready to accept?* This is in Scripture,
and it touches God's nature. In Him all absolutes are manifested.
Being Him, the absolutes [His nature] of all absolutes. That is
absolute power, absolute authority, absolute justice. (*Sovereignty
is an attribute by His deity.*) They all are manifested in and by Him,
and there is one aspect that Paul wrote about God's persona that
keeps Him together: "**He cannot deny Himself**" (2 Tim. 2:13). The
evil one sought to place a breaking fact in God's nature, for if you
break an absolute, then it is not what it is said to be. The evil one
contested that God is love and merciful (*like many people like to
do*). He stated with his evil act, "How dare He give an eternal

punishment?" In his evil plot, he sought to trap in his schemes the living God by His own words, but the answer to God's power is **"For it pleased the Father that in Him [Christ Jesus] all the fullness should dwell, and by Him to reconcile all things to Himself, by Him, whether things on earth or things in heaven, having made peace through the blood of His cross."** Again, *which one are you ready to accept?* Eternal life or death? You must choose today (Col. 1:19–20). The God BEING knew the evil one's schemes! And an absolute eternal act of Christ crushed all the evil one's aspiration (1 Cor. 15:24–28).

Paul continues to teach the sound doctrine, saying,

> **So then, my dear ones, just as you have always obeyed [my instructions with enthusiasm], not only in my presence, but now much more in my absence, continue to work out your salvation [that is, cultivate it, bring it to full effect, actively pursue spiritual maturity] with awe-inspired fear and trembling [using serious caution and critical self-evaluation to avoid anything that might offend God or discredit the name of Christ].**

This is our service in worship, the love produced by the words of faith and hope. In all truth, this is the result of sanctification by position. God said we are justified in Christ, and it produces sanctification in practice to our God by His Holy Spirit for **"God prepared beforehand the works [*at the first heavenly summit*] that we should walk in them."** The words *faith/hope* in our spirit/soul makes us powerful beings of light to produce godly works (Eph. 2:10). In Hebrews, it's written: **"Through Him, therefore, let us at all times offer up to God a sacrifice of praise, which is the fruit of lips that thankfully acknowledge and confess and glorify His** name" (Phil. 2:12; Heb. 13:15). When Paul makes his prayer to the Father in Jesus's name about us, he prayed:

> [I always pray] that the God of our Lord Jesus Christ, the Father of glory, may grant you a spirit of wisdom and of revelation [that gives you a deep and personal and intimate insight] into the true knowledge of Him [for we know the Father through the Son]. (*This is how the doctrine of God the Father in its systematic theology begins to be understood.*) And [I pray] that the eyes of your heart [the very center and core of your being] may be enlightened [flooded with light by the Holy Spirit], so that you will know and cherish the hope [the divine guarantee, the confident expectation] to which He has called you, the riches of His glorious inheritance in the saints (God's people), and [so that you will begin to know] what the immeasurable and unlimited and surpassing greatness of His [active, spiritual] power is in us who believe.

In this prayer of Paul, we can understand how God the Father is our Gardener. He is who plows, enlightening by His Holy Spirit's light, wisdom, revelation, and knowledge in our understanding so that we can know His redemptive work in us: "These are in accordance with the working of His mighty strength which He produced in Christ when He raised Him from the dead and seated Him at His own right hand in the heavenly places." God Jesus cut a deal with God the Father for us, His chosen, which cannot be denied (Eph. 1:17–20 AMP). We must understand that the (*surpassing greatness of His power is in us who believe*) the *"mighty strength"* manifested in Jesus when resurrected from the dead is the same and one power manifesting in us through God the

Holy Spirit always in our life and especially when we gather to worship the Father, the same and one power. The apostle Paul wrote about Christ in us: **"For in Him all the fullness of Deity (the Godhead) dwells in bodily form [completely expressing the divine essence of God]. And in Him you have been made complete [achieving spiritual stature through Christ]."** We must stop minimizing the work of God Jesus in us (Col. 2:9–10). This redemptive work is powerful as the God that provides it, and we must understand who is it that provides this power to Christ so that we may move in His light, for it is by this power of light, we are move into the culture of the City of Light, the power of the God BEING, the only BEING.

Scripture continues to say:

> **In Him you were also circumcised with a circumcision <u>not made with hands</u>** [*the anointing touch of God*] **but by the [spiritual] circumcision of Christ in the stripping off of the body of the flesh [the sinful carnal nature], having been buried with Him in baptism and raised with Him [to a new life] through [your] faith in the working of God, [as displayed] when He raised Christ from the dead** (*in theology, this faith is called sanctification by position for is produced by God*). **When you were dead in your sins and in the uncircumcision of your flesh (worldliness, manner of life), God made you alive together with Christ, having [freely] forgiven us all our sins** (*clearly, this state's all, again sanctification by position because we believe as it is written*) **having canceled out the certificate of debt consisting of legal demands** (*this term refers to a debtor's handwritten note acknowledging a debt*) **[which were in force] against us and which were**

hostile to us. And this certificate (*the requirements found in the Mosaic law, which were violated. This debt is the punishment due for violators through sin. Gentiles were never directly liable to the law, but as Paul explains in the letter to the Romans (2:12–16) God holds us also accountable, responsible for violating the principles of the law violated of our own will, choice*). He has set aside and completely removed by nailing it to the cross. (Col. 2:11–14)

Such is the redemptive work of God the Father in Christ for all who acknowledge His word. Therefore, the apostle John was given to write:

He came to that which was His own [that which belonged to Him—His world, His creation, His possession], and those who were His own [people—the Jewish nation] did not receive and welcome Him. But to as many as did receive and welcome Him, He gave the right [the authority, the privilege] to become children of God, that is, to those who believe in (adhere to, trust in, and rely on) His name—who were born, not of blood [natural conception], nor of the will of the flesh [physical impulse], nor of the will of man [that of a natural father], but of God [that is, a divine and supernatural birth—they are born of God—spiritually transformed, renewed, sanctified].

This is the narrative of the gospel: that God the Father in Christ Jesus has worked His redemption through God the Holy Spirit for us, His chosen believers, by His grace (John 1:11–13 AMP). It is written:

And if the Spirit of Him who raised Jesus from the dead [The Father] lives in you, He who raised Christ Jesus from the dead [The Father] will also give life to your mortal bodies through His Spirit, who lives in you. (Rom. 8:11)

In the same manner, James asked of the power of the faith we claim, for she produces the outcome: "**Show me your faith without your works, and I will show you my faith by my works.**" The word of God has the power to turn your life around into His kingdom of light, producing the works of faith that she declares (James 2:18).

God the Father's Attributes Are Also in God Jesus and God the Holy Spirit

When we contemplate all the *attributes, absolutes,* and *characteristics* of God the Father's persona, we can understand the Son/Spirit of God, for He is (*They are*) like Him (*the Father*), possessing it all. God Jesus said, "**All things that the Father has are Mine**" (John 16:15). God Jesus is the substance, the exact image and representation of the invisible God. It is declared of Christ Jesus that "**He is the exact living image [the essential manifestation] of the unseen God [the visible representation of the invisible]**" (Col. 1:15). Jesus Christ is the exact image of the Father. They are one BEING, and it is said of Him: "**He alone possesses immortality** (*He became a mortal, so that He could die for us and be resurrected*) **[absolute exemption from death] and lives in unapproachable light, whom no [***mortal***] man has ever seen or can see. To Him be honor and eternal power and dominion!**" Paul wrote this with an exclamation, for Christ is more than what man has said and thinks of Him (1 Tim. 6:16). Christ, the Word/Messiah, is interceding (*as part of the God BEING*) for all humanity that they may reach eternal salvation placed in front of us by His word. This interceding is as written:

> **But, on the other hand, Jesus holds His priesthood permanently and without change, because He lives on forever. Therefore, He is able also to save forever (completely, perfectly, for eternity) those who come to God through Him, since He always lives to intercede *and* intervene on their behalf [with God]. It was fitting for us to have such a High Priest [perfectly adapted to our needs], holy, blameless, unstained [by sin], separated from sinners and exalted higher than the heavens. (Heb. 7:24–26)**

We must think and know God in the terms of His written word. Therefore, Scripture reveals to us the direction we must follow when it comes to knowing God. Luke the Evangelist wrote of Paul, telling the Athenians who worshiped even an unknown god:

> **Therefore God overlooked and disregarded the former ages of ignorance (*and this because of Christ act for us*); but now He commands all people everywhere to repent [that is, to change their old way of thinking (worldviews)], to regret their past sins, and to seek God's purpose for their lives], because He has set a day when He will judge the inhabited world in righteousness by a Man whom He has appointed and destined for that task, and He has provided credible proof to everyone by raising Him from the dead. (Acts 17:30–31 AMP)**

We must understand who God Jesus is by His written revelation—and this after accepting His word as a steady rock/immutable—and, through prayer, ask that His revelation be realized in your spirit/soul. By the written revelation of Him and our special revelation (*born-again touch*), we can get to understand some of who He is, the God BEING; for as He touches our spirit/soul, the realization of His persona is exposed. He is the One revealing Himself, for God is light. He has nothing to hide (1 John 4:8).

Let us study God the Father's attributes, absolutes, and characteristics that He has revealed for us to know Him. Then as we see these aspects of His persona, we begin to understand Him, His Son, and Spirit. He has communicable/expressible attributes and absolute aspects and incommunicable aspects of His BEING. We can understand the first (*communicable*), for He has placed eternity in our heart so that we may know and understand Him as He also gave us His image and likeness (*a spirit/soul*) and can address, drawing these views to know Him. There are attributes nevertheless that are non-communicable or indescribable by our finite humanity, but it's what's revealed by God that we get to realize that we can know and understand Him as He asked, keeping this in mind: "**The secret things belong to the Lord our God, but the things which are revealed and disclosed belong to us and to our children forevermore.**" Then a disciple seeks to understand what God has revealed through His word, and once we know (*what He wants us to know*), then we can understand His redeeming purpose for His chosen, as He explained that "they may know and understand me," and that is His delight (Jer. 9:23–24).

Attributes That Describe God's Being According to His Word

- *Spirit*: The apostle John wrote what God Jesus said: "God [the Father] is spirit [the Source of life, yet invisible to mankind], and those who worship Him must worship in spirit and truth." And so we understand that God is Spirit (John 4:24).

- The LORD, God the Father, *has a soul*: The prophet Isaiah was given to write: "Behold, My Servant, whom I uphold; My Chosen One *in whom* My soul delights. I have put My Spirit upon Him; He will bring forth justice to the nations." This verse is found in seven Bible versions of the Old Testament, and it's something to deeply ponder (Isa. 42:1 AMP, KJV, NASB, ASV, NKJV, DRA, GNV). We must add that God has a heart: "The Lord regretted [...] and his heart was deeply troubled." A quality of His godly BEING this is shared with us, His creatures/creation, to know God's spirit/soul (Gen. 6:6).

- *Invisibility*: It was said to Moses by God Himself, with an exclamation mark: "He said, 'You cannot see My face, for no [*mortal*] man shall see Me and live!'" God lives in His own invisible reality (*above the heavens*), and it's an attribute of His persona (Exod. 33:20). Solomon said, "But will God actually dwell with mankind on the earth? Behold, heaven and the highest heaven cannot contain You; how much less this house which I have built!" In other words, His BEING and reality is over the heavens (*City of Light*) and earth (*the physical creation*), but He is alert to all that happens in both and made us to be His temple (2 Chron. 6:18; 1 Cor. 3:16, 6:19; Heb. 4:13). Scripture also states, "No one has seen God [His essence, His divine nature] at any time; the [One and] only begotten Son of God [*begotten means **unique/only** Son, not as a point of origin*] who is in the intimate presence of the

Father, He has explained Him [interpreted and revealed the awesome wonder of the Father]" (John 1:18 AMP).

- *Immutable or Unchangeableness*: The prophet Malachi was given by God to write: "For I am the LORD, I do not change [but remain faithful to My covenant with you]." And Moses wrote: "God *is* not a man, that He should lie, Nor a son of man, that He should repent. Has He said, and will He not do? Or has He spoken, and will He not make it good?" And scripture says of His Son, "Jesus Christ *is* the same yesterday, today, and forever" (Num. 23:19; Heb. 13:8). This is His central attribute, which He also gives to His word (*covenants*). Notice in all versions, capital letters are used for "LORD" to address God the Father (Mal. 3:6 AMP). Paul also saw this character of God and said, "If we are faithless, He remains faithful [true to His word and His righteous character], for He cannot deny Himself." God cannot deny Himself and does not share His glorious attributes with no one: "I am the Lord, that is My Name; My glory I will not give to another, Nor My praise to carved idols." He gives His written word equal honors, giving it His attribute of unchangeableness (2 Tim.2:1; Mark 13:31; Isa. 55:11).

- *Independence and Freedom*: The psalmist wrote: "For every beast of the forest is Mine, and the cattle on a thousand hills. I know every bird of the mountains, and everything that moves in the field is Mine. If I were hungry, I would not tell you, for the world and all it contains are Mine." This is another attribute. He has no need of His creation. He is not like the other god's people worship (Ps. 50:10–12). Scripture states, "Nor is He served by human hands, as though He needed anything, because it is He who gives to all [people] life and breath and all things" (Acts 17:25).

- *Almighty*: God told Abraham, "I am God **Almighty; Walk [habitually] before Me [with integrity, knowing that you are always in My presence], and be blameless and complete [in obedience to Me].**" This is a statement from God BEING Himself. *It applies to born-again believers* also, who are counted to have the faith of Abraham: "**For with God nothing [is or ever] shall be impossible.**" The God BEING is almighty (Gen. 17:1; Luke 1:37; Rom. 4:12).

- *Omniscient*: The apostle John said, "**God is greater than our heart, and knows all things.**" It can be said that because of this attribute, God can't learn anything new because He knows it all, and if there is anything new, it is because He created it (1 John 3:20). He told Jeremiah, "**Before I formed you in the womb, I knew you**" (Jer. 1:5). The psalmist wrote: "**Before a word is on my tongue you, Lord, know it completely.**" This is God's omniscient attribute, and "**nothing in all creation is hidden from God's sight. Everything is uncovered and laid bare before the eyes of him to whom we must give account.**" The God BEING knows everything about you (vs. 16). "**Your eyes saw my substance, being yet unformed. And in Your book they all were written, The days fashioned for me, When *as yet there were none* of them**" (Ps. 139:4, 16; Heb. 4:13).

- *Eternal and Omnipresent*: He has always been, and this is something incommunicable to our mind. The psalmist and prophet said, "**Before the mountains were born or before You had given birth to the earth and the world, even from everlasting to everlasting, You are [the eternal] God "** and "**Do you not know? Have you not heard? The Everlasting God, the Lord, the Creator of the ends of the earth does not become tired or grow weary; there is no searching of His understanding.**" King David wrote: "**O Lord, you have searched me [thoroughly] and have known me. You know** when I sit down and when I rise up [my entire life, everything I do]; You understand my thoughts from afar [...] Even before there is a word on my tongue [still unspoken], Behold, O Lord, You know it all" (Ps. 90:2, 139:1–2; Isa. 40:28).

Attributes that Describe God's Perceptiveness According to His Word

- *Knowledge*: The psalmist describes this as "Even before there is a word on my tongue [still unspoken], Behold, O Lord, You know it all." The writer of Hebrews said, "**Nothing in all creation** [*mainly each one of us*] **is hidden from God's sight. Everything is uncovered and laid bare** [*your life*] **before the eyes of him to whom we must give account**" (Ps.139:4; Heb. 4:13). The prophet Jeremiah was given to write: "**Now the word of the Lord came to me, saying, 'Before I formed you in the womb, I knew you'**" (Jer. 1:4–5). There is nothing new that God could learn, for He knows it all, and if there were to be something new, it is because He has made it to be (*like this grace He is giving us*). Peter told God Jesus, "**Lord, you know all things.**" Peter knew, and God told Job to recognize: "**Have you understood the expanse of the earth?** [*He calls it expanse, not a globe?*] **Tell Me if you know all this**" (John 21:17; Job 38:18). This is an incommunicable attribute of the God BEING to our human faculty.

- *Wisdom*: In Proverbs, it is written about wisdom as if it is God Himself: "**If you will turn and pay attention to my rebuke, Behold, I [Wisdom] will pour out my spirit on you; I will make** my words known to you." But in which other way do we know who God is if He doesn't tell us He is wisdom itself (Prov. 1:23). He advises, "My son, if you will receive my words and treasure my commandments within you." God told Moses about how He anoints and empowers people: "I have filled him with the Spirit of God in wisdom and skill, in understanding and intelligence, in knowledge, and in all kinds of craftsmanship." It is written: "the fear of the Lord is the beginning of knowledge." The disciple cannot ever miss this (Prov. 2:1, 1:7; Exod. 31:3). God Jesus said, *"But when He, the Spirit of Truth, comes, He will guide you into all the truth [full and complete truth]."* They are the one and the same, the God BEING (John 16:13).

- *Faithfulness*: The LORD God is faithful in all His way (*word*) with His covenant to us: "Know therefore that the Lord your God is God; he is the faithful God, keeping his covenant of love to a thousand generations of those who love him and keep his commandments." As we are reminded in scripture: "If we are faithless, he remains faithful, for He cannot deny Himself." He is *absolute* (Deut. 7:9; 2 Tim. 2:13). The New Testament is the fulfillment of the Old Covenant as the new will prepare us for the covenant of the permanent or the *transformation* (Heb. 12:26–28). Read *The Apostles Methodology to Interpret Scriptures*. This is discussed in the author's first published book.

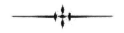

Moral Attributes of God According to His Word

- *Love, Merciful, Loving-kindness*: The prophet wrote of God's moral attributes: "It is because of the Lord's loving kindnesses (*other versions say mercy*) that we are not consumed, because His [tender] compassions never fail. They [God's mercy] are new every morning; great and beyond measure is Your faithfulness." God is love (Lam. 3:22–23; 1 John 4:8). He told the prophet Jeremiah, "I am the Lord who practices loving-kindness, justice and righteousness on the earth, for in these things I delight." *He practices.* How much more can we, the sound doctrine? (Jer. 9:24).

- *Holiness, God is Light*: The psalmist David sang, "But You are holy, O You who are enthroned in [the holy place where] the praises of Israel [are offered]." We must understand there is a river of worshipers throughout eternity at this very moment worshiping the God BEING (Ps. 22:3). The apostle John wrote of God Jesus, saying to them, "This is the message [of God's promised revelation] which we have heard from Him and now announce to you, that God is Light [He is holy, His message is truthful, He is perfect in righteousness], and in Him there is no darkness at all [no sin, no wickedness, no imperfection]." Darkness is confused at the splendor of light (1 John 1:5). God's wrath is known mostly because darkness cannot withstand its splendor. When God stands up from His throne and reality of invisibility to all, evil and darkness it will be as wrath and punishment, for they are not able to withstand God's glory. But that is not the wrath of God; it's His glory exposed. And for those living in darkness, it is a terrible consuming fire, and they will perish. His judgment is the epitome of His wrath in an eternal fire for what they did to His Word/Son.

- *Just and Peaceful*: The apostle Paul was given to write: "**We have been justified [that is, acquitted of sin, declared blameless before God] by faith, [let us grasp the fact that] we have peace with God [and the joy of reconciliation with Him] through our Lord Jesus Christ (the Messiah, the Anointed).**" In other words, we will stand in peace on God's judgment day by His will. The prophet Daniel wrote: "*For the Lord our God is [uncompromisingly] righteous and openly just in all His works which He does—He keeps His word.*" Also, King David said, "**The Lord God of Israel, has given peace and rest to His people.**" This is all written as God's testimony (Rom. 5:1; 1 Chron. 23:25).

- *Jealous*: The prophet Isaiah wrote of God, saying, "**I am the Lord, that is My name; And My glory I will not give to another,**" that is, in His attributes and absolutes. He shares with no creature, and so the evil one is not like our God at all but an abomination. The apostle Paul asked, "**Are we trying to arouse the Lord's jealousy? Are we stronger than Him?**" James also wrote, asking, "**Do you think Scripture says without reason that he jealously longs for the Spirit he has caused to dwell in us?**" God said He corrects those He loves: "**Those whom I [dearly and tenderly] love, I rebuke and discipline [showing them their faults and instructing them]; so be enthusiastic and repent [change your inner self—your old way of thinking, your sinful behavior—seek God's will].**" God's jealousy corrects our behavior (Isa. 42:8; James 4:5; Rev. 3:19).

- *Wrath and Angers against Evil*: As He is judge, He says, "**Therefore thus says the Lord God, 'Behold, My anger and My wrath will be poured out on this place [*it is not an uncontrolled anger but a measured control wrath*] on man and beast, on the trees of the field and the fruit of the ground; and** it will burn and [the fire will] not be quenched.'" Such is His power and glory: **"It is a fearful and terrifying thing to fall into the hands of the living God [incurring His judgment and wrath]"** (Jer. 7:20; Hab. 3:3–6; Heb. 10:31). This earthly reality is driven into the lake of fire that He created, but He has given us the power to escape it and asks, **"Do not love the world [of sin that opposes God and His precepts (behaviors)], nor the things that are in the world"** (1 John 2:15). It is also written: **"The wrath of God is revealed from heaven against all ungodliness and unrighteousness of men."** His light will wrap everything (Rom. 1:18).

Attributes of Excellence According to Scripture

- *God is Perfect*: The prophet wrote: **"As for God, His way is blameless and perfect"** and **"The Rock! His work is perfect, For all His ways are just; A God of faithfulness without iniquity (injustice), Just and upright is He"** (2 Sam. 22:3; Deut. 32:24).

- *Glorious*: Moses wrote: **"Reverence this glorious and awesome name, the Lord your God."** And Job said, **"God is awesome splendor *and* majesty [far too glorious for man's eyes]"** (Deut. 28:58; Job 37:22).

- *Majestic*: The psalmist wrote: **"On the glorious splendor of Your Majesty and on Your wonderful works, I will meditate"** (Ps. 145:5).

- *Indescribable*: Not only can He do indescribable things, but in truth, He is indescribable, for if He did not make Himself to be known by creating beings with such gifts (*angels and humans*), God could not be described at all. The apostle Paul wrote: "**Now thanks be to God for His indescribable gift [which is precious beyond words]!**" (2 Cor. 9:15). God has placed eternity in our heart that we may know and understand Him. Scripture says, "**He has made everything beautiful and appropriate in its time. He has also planted eternity [a sense of divine purpose] in the human heart [a mysterious longing which nothing under the sun can satisfy, except God]—yet man cannot find out (comprehend, grasp) what God has done (His overall plan) from the beginning to the end.**" God and His works are indescribable to His creation. We cannot explain any of them how are we alive, where are we going after (Eccles. 3:11 AMP).

- *The God BEING is Sovereign*: This attribute is based upon His creative power, which also sustains all things together. He created heaven and earth and has full authority to do whatever He desires. It is written: "**All things were created and exist through Him [that is, by His activity] and for Him. And He Himself existed *and* is before all things, and in Him all things hold together [His is the controlling, cohesive force of the universe]**" (Col. 1:16–17). The God BEING in all His nature is limitless.

We can understand two things about God the Father's attributes through Scripture; and that is, that they are communicable attributes, which we get to understand on their surface because He has placed eternity and understanding in our heart to know and understand Him. These are attributes of God's persona as the God BEING (*and there is no other Rock*). He is love, justice, grace, mercy, light. He has made us understand, in this fallen nature, His ideas, reason, and concepts through His word. Now those that are incommunicable or inexpressible to our understanding, they are those as follows: He is eternal (does not change); He is always present; and He knows everything (*always, yesterday, today, and tomorrow*). Everything is fresh in His sight, and there is nothing new to Him unless He creates it, and of course, nothing is impossible for Almighty God. He has created all things and maintains them as they are. Look around. It is God, not Mother Nature. He has given us abundance in us to perceive the abundance He created. God Jesus said, **"My Father has been working until now [He has never ceased working], and I too am working"** (John 5:17). Scripture teaches us these things of God, and it is He who describes Himself to us through scripture. Let's contemplate some of these descriptions: **"Worthy are You, our Lord and God, to receive the glory and the honor and the power; for You created all things, and because of Your will they exist, and were created and brought into being."** And by God's will, all things hold together as scriptures declare. The apostle Paul wrote: **"Yet for us there is but one God, the Father, who is the source of all things, and we exist for Him; and one Lord, Jesus Christ, by whom are all things [that have been created], and we [believers exist and have life and have been redeemed] through Him."** The apostle John wrote: **"All things were made and came into existence through Him; and without Him not even one thing was made that has come into being."** The apostle Paul continues to dialogue: **"Or who has first given to Him that it would be paid back to him? For from Him [all things originate] and through Him [all things live and exist] and to Him are all things [directed]. To Him be glory and honor forever! Amen."** The psalmist mentions as he sings, **"Before the mountains were born, Or before You had given birth to the earth and the world, Even from everlasting to everlasting, You are [the eternal] God."** Then we have Moses telling us what God told him: **"God said to Moses, 'I Am that I Am.'"** And I love to add: *"Like it whomsoever does not like it"* (Rev. 4:11; 1 Cor. 8:6; John 1:3; Rom. 11:35–36; Ps. 90:2; Exod. 3:14). Understand, God is a personal God to His creation (*you and me*). His BEING and His independence is defined by nothing or no one but by Himself: "*I AM that I AM.*"

We must understand that without the creation, God continues to be God Almighty, infinite, Omni-God, Trinitary (*this is a word made by theologians to describe: Father, Son and Spirit and/or the I AM, the Word, and the Spirit*). He is eternal, defined by all His absolute—power, justice, authority—which is His BEING. God does not need His creation because He does not need His creation for anything and/or to continue to be the God BEING. Paul said, **"The God who created the world and everything in it, since He is Lord of heaven and earth, does not dwell in temples made with hands; nor is He served by human hands, as though He needed anything, because it is He who gives to all [people] life and breath and all things."** He is who gives to all (Acts 17:24–25). There is no limitation, nor imperfection that can be projected by *us*, the creation, about the biblical God. He speaks about His creation in His liberty and independence, saying, **"For the sake of My Name I refrain from My wrath, And for My praise I restrain Myself from you, So that I do not cut you off."** [...*He lives in an attribute of invisibility for our benefit*] **"For My own sake, for My own sake, I will do it [I refrain and do not completely destroy you],"** [...*His reality in invisibility overlaps the heavens and earth*] **"And I will not give My glory to another."** The owner of the universe is a moral BEING (Isa. 48:9–11). Scripture tells us that it is possible for creation to bring joy and sorrow to God as these verses express: **"God saw everything that He had made, and behold, it was very good, and He validated it completely. And there was evening and there was morning, a sixth day"** [...and] **"The Lord regretted that He had made mankind on the earth, and He was [deeply] grieved in His heart."** Even though He knew what was going to happen, He so loved us that He made us (Gen. 1:31, 6:6). We must say that God's joy, His regret, and grief after, does not mean God recognized the creation of angels and man as a mistake on His part.

In His first divine, heavenly summit before the creation of everything, God, being omniscient (*that is, knowing everything*), saw the fall of angels and men. But He so loved the creation, the heavens and earth, that He made it to be a creation in all its *flavors* and all its *horror*. Scripture states (*looking through His attribute*) that "**God puts no trust or confidence, even in His [heavenly] servants, and He charges His angels with error.**" Then we must see that God saw the fall of one-third of the angels and the fall of man. Scriptures say of the dragon, the age-old serpent: "**His tail swept [across the sky] and dragged away a third of the stars of heaven.**" (*God deals in infinites, then this amount, "a third," is indescribable.*) This is a present sight in God's sight because to us, this is said of something to come in our future, but to God, it already happened; and all things are fresh at His sight (Ps. 139:16; Job 4:18; Rev. 12:4). God is the conductor, director, producer of our reality's storyline that took a wrong turn, and He is correcting what He wants to keep. There was a great plan by God once He decided to make creation, which we will elaborate ahead. God deals in absolutes and infinites.

Knowing that the creation would sin and become wicked, at God's first divine, heavenly summit in His invisible reality, the Word/God was preordained before the foundation of the world but not for the angels because they were created eternal, knowing good and evil, in contrast to man who did not know and were not eternal. It is said of Christ that "**He was foreordained (foreknown) before the foundation of the world.**" This knowledge is described in Scripture, that God knew all this at Their first divine, heavenly summit, before creation, for everything is fresh and present unto Him whom we call God (1 Pet. 1:20). Everything about the works of Christ/Messiah was predestined. The apostles were eyewitnesses to all of it: the prophecies of Messiah (Luke 24:44). It is written: "**And the Lord God said, 'Behold, the man has become like one of Us** (*Father, Son, and Holy Spirit, speaking with each other*), knowing [how to distinguish between] good and evil; and now he might stretch out his hand, and take from the tree of life as well, and eat [its fruit], and live [in this fallen, sinful condition] forever.'" Man was not eternal as the angels were when man sinned. *And* "for, as we all know, He (Christ) does not take hold of [the fallen] angels [to give them a helping hand], but He does take hold of [the fallen] descendants of Abraham [extending to them His hand of deliverance]." Remember God sees everything presently fresh in His attribute, foresight (*He is omnipresent in His here and now*) (Gen. 3:22; Heb. 2:16). This is why scriptures says,

> For it was fitting [*appropriate, proper, due, right, convenient*] for God [that is, an act worthy of His divine nature] that He, for whose sake are all things, and through whom are all things, in bringing many sons to glory, should make the author and founder of their salvation perfect through suffering [bringing to maturity the human experience necessary for Him to be perfectly equipped for His office as High Priest]. (Heb. 2:10)

God grieved over the sin of angels and man because it was appropriate for Him to, but He cannot deny Himself, for God is love personified. In His sovereignty, the God BEING does what is pleasing to Him, and all will work in His perfect path. Always remember it is His universe and His reality and existence.

God Does Not Needs Us for Anything

In scripture, there is this argument placed by Paul as he encounters this unsettling topic, and so he argues, "**What shall we say then? Is there injustice with God? Certainly not! For He says to Moses, 'I will have mercy on whomever I have mercy, and I will have compassion on whomever I have compassion.'**" So then God's choice is not dependent on human will, nor on human effort [the totality of human striving], but on God who shows mercy [to whomever He chooses—it is His sovereign gift] (*salvation is not on human efforts or terms*). *For the scripture says (to Pharaoh)* [symbolic to the evil one], "**I raised you up for this very purpose, to display My power in [dealing with] you, and so that My name would be proclaimed in all the earth.**" So then He has mercy on whom He wills (chooses), and He hardens (the heart of] whom He wills.) This was the apostle Paul's argument from scriptures, and he answered as well: "**You will say to me then, 'Why does He still blame me [for sinning]? For whom [including myself] has [ever] resisted His will and purpose?'**" Here you sense a carnal stand of justification (*condescension*) from it all, and Paul continues, "**On the contrary, who are you, O man, who answers [arrogantly] back to God and dares to defy Him? Will the thing which is formed say to him who formed it, 'Why have you made me like this?' Does the potter not have the right over the clay, to make from the same lump [of clay] one object for honorable use [something beautiful or distinctive] and another for common use [something ordinary or menial]?**" In other words, the God BEING has supremacy over all things. In Scripture, there are these two human natures: wheat and tare, and/or lamb and goats. As to "humans and Nephilims," the latter are offspring of fallen angels and the daughters of men, created from the same clay: one created by God; the other conceived through conception of fallen angels and the daughters of man (*tares and goats do not have a spirit/soul as they die but an abomination called demon*].

> **What if God, although willing to show His [terrible] wrath and to make His power known, has tolerated with great patience the objects of His wrath [which are] prepared for destruction? [*Goats and tares*] And what if He has done so to make known the riches of His glory to the objects of His mercy, which He has prepared beforehand [*predestined*] for glory, including us, whom He also called, not only from among the Jews, but also from among the Gentiles?**

And this is one of those secret things of God that scripture says must be left alone until the day when all truth is revealed (*what are tares and goats really?*). God Jesus explained it:

> **"Sir, did you not sow good seed in your field? How then does it have tares?" He said to them, "An enemy has done this. [...] Let both grow together until the harvest [...] gather together the tares and bind them in bundles to burn."**

This is the story of the tares and goats (Matt. 13:24–30, 25:41). Then we must say this: "**The secret things belong to the Lord our God, but the things which are revealed and disclosed belong to us and to our children forever, so that we may do all of the words of this law.**" We can think that these vessels of wrath are created with the desire to want the evil they created into the lake of fire and darkness (*God is merciful even in His wrath [Mark 5:11–13]*) (Rom. 9:14–24; Deut. 29:29). It's written: "***Nevertheless the solid foundation of God stands, having this seal: 'The Lord knows those who are His'*** [omniscient]." God knows and lift us up, giving us a mandate, for it is also written: "**He chose us in Christ [actually selected us for Himself as His own] before the foundation of the world, so that we would be holy [that is, consecrated, set apart for Him, purpose-driven] and blameless in His sight.**" To those who cannot accept God's predestination, the Father, or Ancient of Days, has given the Lamb a book with seven seals of a destiny pre-arranged by the God BEING (see Revelation chapter 5). You must remember, Messiah's life was pre-arranged by God, as the Seed of the woman and more (2 Tim. 2:19; Eph. 1:4; Luke 24:44).

God does not need us for anything, but it is glorious to know He chose us for His delight and glory. Being significant to God is the highest and greatest sense of purpose that can be imagined. Then not only did He create us, which gives us significance, but He came and died for us and doubled up on His purpose for the love of His Name. The apostle Peter was given to write: "**Receiving as the result [the outcome, the consummation] of your faith, the salvation of your souls. Regarding this salvation, the prophets who prophesied about the grace [of God] that was intended for you, searched carefully and inquired [about this future way of salvation].**" This romantic story (*movie script*) is by the God BEING. It's a God thing if you must know (1 Pet. 1:9–10). Only God can give significance to things, and if He sees us as significant, then for Him we are of importance. God Jesus said, "**I am the Vine; you are the branches. The one who remains in Me and I in him bears much fruit, for [otherwise] apart from Me [that is, cut off from vital union with Me] you can do nothing.**" Making us part of Himself is a love story (John 15:5). Let us elaborate a bit more. God Jesus asked of us, "**He who loves father or mother more than Me is not worthy of Me; and he who loves son or daughter more than Me is not worthy of Me.**" But the Lord would never ask us to do something that He would not do for us Himself (Matt. 10:37; John 3:16). We see this personal involvement of God, which gives us more significance: "For God so [greatly] loved and dearly prized the world [you and me] that He [even] gave His [one and] only begotten [unique] Son, so that whoever believes and trusts in Him [as Savior] shall not perish but have eternal life." This whole idea, concept comes from the God BEING (John 3:16). The purpose and counsel of God are permanent and immutable. What He says is by the power of His will: "The counsel of the Lord stands forever, the thoughts and plans of His heart [the Father is a BEING with an original heart/mind and spirit/soul] through all generations." God ensures His counsel, generation after generation, until the end of time (Ps. 33:11).

In the Lord's Nature, All Things Are Known and Exposed

As it comes to God's will for us, we can only understand it by knowing who God is. He gave Jeremiah a hint: "'But let the one who boasts boast in this, that he understands and knows Me. That I am the Lord, exercising lovingkindness, judgment, and righteousness in the earth [*He is a moral* BEING]. For in these I delight,' says the Lord" (Jer. 9:24). Clearly, we know that to understand a person you must first know that person and this through their character and traits. Then to know God, it must start by knowing His attributes, absolutes, and characteristics (*the God* BEING *is sovereign*) that we've mentioned, and it leads us to understanding His purposeful plan of redemption. We believe what He has described of Himself through His word. The prophet Jeremiah was given to write: "'[And acknowledges Me and honors Me as God and recognizes (His Sovereignty) without any doubt], that I am the Lord who practices loving-kindness, justice, and righteousness on the earth, for in these things I delight,' says the Lord." Then by knowing that God is light, we understand He is not trying to hide His truth from anyone, rather He is wanting for us to know it all and it is open for all to know (*He is good*). Scripture says, "**I will open My mouth in parables; I will utter things [unknown and unattainable] that have been hidden [from mankind] since the foundation of the world.**" The apostle was quoting the psalmist (*who also gave oracles*). God has revealed His divine power through nature by His Holy Spirit's touch and by His holy word for us to know and understand Him (Ps. 78:2; Matt. 13:35). This is what God has in store for us: "**Then the King will say to those on His right, 'Come, you blessed of My Father [you favored God, appointed to eternal salvation], inherit the kingdom prepared for you from the foundation of the world.**" This is called redemption, and it was prepared before the foundation of the world in His glorious counsel (Matt. 25:34 AMP). This was done in His omniscient knowledge, being legally established at His first divine, heavenly summit in His reality of invisibility, as the apostle Paul taught: "**Just as [in His love] He chose us in Christ [actually selected us for Himself as His own] before the foundation of the world, so that we would be holy [that is, consecrated, set apart for Him, purpose-driven] and blameless in His sight. In love,**" there is no missing it. God is (*acts out of*) love (Eph. 1:4). The apostle taught: "**In Him also we have received an inheritance [a destiny— we were claimed by God as His own], having been predestined (chosen, appointed beforehand) according to the purpose of Him who works everything in agreement with the counsel and design of His will**" (Eph. 1:11). There are lots of theologians and others who do not consider the word *predestination* properly, for they want to make God's redemption an act of (*man*) their own doing and choice, but how wrong are they (*even God Jesus's life was predestined*). Before this verse, Paul wrote: "**And to make plain [to** everyone] the plan of the mystery [regarding the uniting of believing Jews and Gentiles into one body] which [until now] was kept hidden through the ages in [the mind of] God who created all things." Everyone can see that this redemption and revelation (*touch of salvation*) is God's doing (Eph. 3:9). In other words, "He [the Father] chose us in Christ before the foundation of the world, so that we would be holy and blameless in His sight. In love," point blank and simple. This is an act and work of the God BEING, not us (Eph. 1:4). Let us say of God's way that by seeing all things, He designed a predestined act to save us. God created a narrow path from out of the wide, saying, "Enter through the narrow gate. For wide is the gate and broad and easy to travel is the path that leads the way to destruction *and* eternal loss, and there are many who enter through it." God rearranged the movie script to give us a special role (Matt. 7:13). We can see this with the parable of the one hundred sheep. He put aside the ninety-nine for that one (1 percent) that got lost in all our generations, and He went to find them. He brought them back, meaning that when He comes back to take His church to the place He prepared for them. He started with one hundred sheep, and He will take one hundred sheep, no questions asked. This is God's doing. It is His *redemptive work*, not us doing it. This is why it has also been written: "Nevertheless, the firm foundation of God [which He has laid] stands [sure and unshaken despite attacks], bearing this seal: 'The Lord knows those who are His.'" This was known to God in His heavenly, divine summit and provoked us by saying, "Let everyone who names the name of the Lord stand apart from wickedness and withdraw from wrongdoing," which we can accomplish through the anointing and the Word's determined sound doctrine by God the Holy Spirit, and 99 percent of us are doing so today as we name the name of the Lord before us (2 Tim. 2:19). Therefore, those who doubt the Word in this subject hate the predestination topic in biblical notes. They are not part of the faith in Christ without works (*the works which happen by faith is because of the power* in the word of God). God's predestination started at the God's BEING first divine, heavenly summit in His invisible reality. In Their godly agenda, they predestined "evil" to be burn in the lake of fire—that is, the beast, the false prophet—together with the dragon and his angels and all the tare and goats of human birth (Rev. 20:10; Matt .25:41). We must acknowledge God's awesome attributes as we read His word. He said,

> **The Lord has looked down from heaven upon the children of men** [*in His omniscient/omnipresent view*] **to see if there are any who understand (act wisely), who [truly] seek after God [longing for His wisdom and guidance]. They have all turned aside, together they have become corrupt** [*all of us in all time and epoch*]**; there is no one who does good, not even one.**

And Paul taught this to the Roman believers, saying, **"There is none righteous [none that meets God's standard], not even one. There is none who understands, there is none who seeks for God,"** meaning God knew of our fallen dead nature; and a dead person cannot hear, see, touch, walk because he/she is dead (Ps. 14:4–5; Rom. 3:10–11). Therefore, He looked yesterday, today, and tomorrow and found not one righteous, nor none looking for Him, so He decided to reveal Himself to us (**"*You did not choose Me, but I chose you and appointed you that you should go and bear fruit*"** [John 15:16]). He saw this before the creation of the world. Therefore, in the book of Revelation (*chapter 5*), the events are so important. About the book with the seven seals, they are the known (*arranged*) predestined future by the Father. This is His story line. Revelation 1:1 says, **"The Revelation of Jesus Christ, which God [the Father] gave Him to show His servants— things which must shortly take place."** It is a fix future by God

(NKJV). It is God giving us, by faith in His word, *sanctification by position*, where justification is an act of God and sanctification is a work of God. By these theological views, this verse explains, "**Yet Christ has now reconciled you [to God] in His physical body through death, in order to present you before the Father, 'holy and blameless and beyond reproach.'**" He positioned us, and these works are God's doing toward our salvation (Col. 1:22). But of course, there are those who will speak the opposite to those living by faith in Christ's priestly works, and this is their outcome, for God already knows who they are: "**All the inhabitants of the earth will fall down and worship him** (*the false prophet*), **everyone whose name <u>has not</u> been written since the foundation of the world in the Book of Life of the Lamb who has been slain [as a willing sacrifice].**" They are the tare and goats that God Jesus told the disciples to be aware of inside the flock (*the church*). They are the vessels of wrath God prepares for the last judgment, *tares, and goats* (Rev. 13:8; Jude 1:12–13; Rom. 9:21–24; Matt. 25:41). The apostles taught:

> **For such** *are* **false apostles, deceitful workers, transforming themselves into apostles of Christ. And no wonder! For Satan himself transforms himself into an angel of light. Therefore,** *it is* **no great thing if his ministers also transform themselves into ministers of righteousness, whose end will be according to their works.**

This was foreseen by God Jesus, who taught the apostles to tell us (2 Cor. 11:13–15).

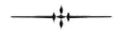

The God BEING Words of Affirmation

Scripture tells us how God had this redemption plan arranged and no one can't change what He has established. We are directing this point out to have you understand God's will. It is written:

> Remember [carefully] the former things [which I did] from ages past [*chosen historical events (see author's first publish book)*]; for I am God, and there is no one else; I am God, and there is no one like Me, Declaring the end and the result from the beginning and from ancient times the things which have not [yet] been done, saying, "My purpose will be established, and I will do all that pleases Me and fulfills My purpose." [*...as a sovereign God*] Truly I have spoken; truly I will bring it to pass. I have planned it, be assured I will do it.

The disciple must take this word and move in its power, for God is speaking about His godly attributes: "I, only I, am the Lord, and there is no savior besides Me" (Isa. 46:9–11, 43:11). Moses told the Israelites a word that it has been passed down to all believers in Christ, saying: "Look, I have taught you statutes and judgments just as the Lord my God has commanded me, so that you may do them in the land which you are entering to possess," and this land is called salvation by God the Holy Spirit's anointing (Deut. 4:5). The LORD God said, "You shall write on them all the words of this law, when you have crossed over, that you may enter the land which the Lord your God is giving you, 'a land flowing with milk and honey,' just as the Lord God of your fathers promised you." Then even from past times, it has been the LORD giving us salvation (Deut. 27:3; Josh. 5:6). The questions about this verse must be thought of: *when has the land (or earth) flowed with milk and honey?* This is clearly speaking about people (*humans*) who are created from the earth, and the "milk and honey" is the sweet salvation a born-again believer experiences when they are washed by the blood of Christ Jesus and sealed in their heart by God the Holy Spirit for the day of redemption (Eph. 4:30). The LORD our God has also declared it many times: "**Who declared it long ago? Was it not I, the Lord? And there is no other God besides Me, A [consistently and uncompromisingly] just and righteous God and a Savior; There is none except Me.**" God knows and declares all the things of this reality from His reality of invisibility and says, "***I am* God, and there is no one like Me, Declaring the end from the beginning, And from ancient times things which have not been done.**" He created the road beforehand in which we must walk, the narrow path (Isa. 45:21, 46:9–10). God said it in the past:

> **"You are My witnesses," declares the Lord. "And My servant whom I have chosen, that you may know and believe Me and understand that I am He. Before Me there was no God formed, and there will be none after Me. I, [only] I, am the Lord, and there is no Savior besides Me."**

No one saves beside God, and He repeated this truth to Isaiah the prophet, as we read his draft (Isa. 43:10–11). The apostle Peter affirms and confirms this truth by writing:

> **The God and Father of our Lord Jesus Christ, who according to His abundant and boundless mercy has caused us to be born again [that is, to be reborn from above—spiritually transformed, renewed, and set apart for His purpose] to an ever-living hope *and* confident assurance through the resurrection of Jesus Christ from the dead, [born anew] into an inheritance which is**

imperishable [beyond the reach of change] and undefiled and unfading, reserved in heaven for you, who are being protected and shielded by the power of God through your faith for salvation that is ready to be revealed [for you] in the last time.

Now more clear, a rooster can't crow (1 Pet. 1:3–5). God speaks as an *omniscient conscious* BEING to us His creation. In His omniscient knowledge (*His written word*), we must stand because this is who He is. The word of God is omniscient knowledge. It comes from a BEING who knows all things. Even the millions of millions of angels and man, He calls by name, for He also holds them together. It is written: "**Lift up your eyes on high and see: 'Who created these?** [*the stars/angels*] **He who brings out their host and numbers them** [*innumerable*] **calling them all by name; because he is great in strength, mighty in power, not one is missing'** [*in Him all things hold together*]." And of man, He said, "**But even the hairs of your head are all numbered.**" Then believe it. He got this (Isa. 40:26; Matt. 10:30 RSV). This idea of redemption by God is deeply rooted in scripture, and His counsel has been assured by Him: "**God is not a man, that He should lie, Nor a son of man, that He should repent. [He saves with knowledge.] Has He said, and will He not do it? Or has He spoken and will He not make it good and fulfill it?**" His word is immutable as He is unchangeable, and salvation is of the LORD (Num. 23:19; Isa. 43:11). He said, "**Believe in God. Believe also in Me**" (John 14:1).

Only God's Redemptive Work Makes Him to Move in Mercy

God has mercy and gives forgiveness when a person repents (*turns*) by a verbal petition, then He changes and is the only time in Scripture that shows that He will change in His decision of punishment. Let us look at some of these instances in Scripture: "**But Moses appeased and entreated the Lord his God, and said, 'Lord, why does Your anger burn against Your people whom You have brought out of the land of Egypt with great power and a mighty hand?'**" And this was the result: "**So the Lord changed His mind about the harm which He had said He would do to His people.**" God is merciful (Exod. 32:11, 14). The same thing happened in God's heart when He saw the Gentiles repent: "**When God saw their deeds, that they turned from their wicked way, then God [had compassion and] relented concerning the disaster which He had declared that He would bring upon them. And He did not do it.**" And we all know how Jonah was so upset about God's love and mercy to those (*Jonah's enemies*) who repented (John. 3:10). In this event, it is shown how different the God of light is from us hateful creatures. There is also this incident that shows how God will change the future of our life (*for He lives also in our [individual] future*) if we pray for guidance as David did in this passage. This incident was given (*chosen historic event*) to be written by the prophet Samuel as David spoke to God:

> "Will the men of Keilah hand me over to him? Will Saul come down just as Your servant has heard? O Lord, God of Israel, I pray, tell Your servant." And the Lord said, "He will come down." Then David asked, "Will the men of Keilah surrender me and my men to Saul?" The Lord said, "They will surrender you." Then David and his men, about six hundred,

arose and left Keilah, and they went wherever they could go. When Saul was told that David had escaped from Keilah, he gave up the pursuit.

See how God changes the outcome of our future by prayer, for He is omnipotent, God Almighty, merciful (1 Sam. 23:11–13). Also, we see the chosen historic event of King Hezekiah: "Go and tell Hezekiah, thus says the Lord, the God of David your father: 'I have heard your prayer, I have seen your tears; surely I will add to your days fifteen years.'" We must pray for tomorrow today (Isa. 38:5). To know and understand God, we must read His word; for it is scriptures that describe who He is and how He does things as He goes on with this, His reality. The false deities (*gods*) of the nations want you to give your life for them, the God of Abraham gave His Son's life (*Word/God*) for us. We were created by God to be His temples. Scripture states, "Heaven is My throne, and the earth is My footstool. Where, then, is a house that you could build for Me? And where will My resting place be?" But we were created by God (Isa. 66:1; 1 Cor. 6:19). Therefore, it is through the word that God gave to the prophets, psalmist, and His apostles that we can come to a concrete understanding of God's reality through His word. God is independent, sufficient in Himself. He does not need anything from us; for He is the One who gives all things, needed, to everyone. It is written:

> The God who created the world and everything in it, since He is Lord of heaven and earth, does not dwell in temples made with hands; nor is He served by human hands, as though He needed anything, because it is He who gives to all [people] life and breath and all things.

Then we must not think of the God BEING as if He is so far away from us. He created us to live in us (Acts 17:24–25). He is unchangeable, perfect in His promises/prophecies and purpose, and whoever does not believe the testimony He gives of His Son makes Him to be a liar, and no one wants to be on that position in front of Him on judgment day (1 John 5:10; Heb. 4:12–13). Let go and let God.

Scripture's Anthropomorphic Language

Theologians have described a language used in Scripture to describe the God BEING into our understanding, and in theology, it is called anthropomorphic. This is a Greek word compound of two meanings: *anthropo*, which means "man," and *morphic*, which means, "*form*." We have many examples in Scripture (*God's Word*) describing the persona of God through this anthropomorphic language, things pertaining to humans. It reflects God in human form with words such as *father, judge, king, commander of armies, architect, bridegroom, husband, shepherd/ pastor, gardener*. It also shows God with descriptions of things He created such as *lion, eagle, lamb, fire, fountain, rock, tower, shield, temple, castle*. We can see these throughout Scripture. Let us show one example: **"The Lord is my rock, my fortress, and the One who rescues me; My God, my rock and strength in whom I trust and take refuge; My shield, and the horn of my salvation, my high tower—my stronghold."** God's word uses this language in Scriptures for us men and women to understand His redeeming love. He acts on our lives as these words' meaning (Ps. 18:2). There are also traces in Scripture that reflect God having human senses, He can *see, hear, smell, taste, has hands, sits down, gets up, has* *feet for He walks and cleans up all tears.* We see these in verses as **"He who made the ear, does He not hear? He who formed the eye, does He not see?"** and **"For the Lamb who is in the center of the throne will be their Shepherd, and He will guide them to springs of the waters of life; and God will wipe every tear from their eyes [giving them eternal comfort]."** All these aspects about God in Scripture makes up the anthropomorphic language that lets us know that we are made to His image and likeness, as in having a spirit/soul and heart like He does (Ps. 94:9; Rev. 7:17). Scriptures also say of God the Father having *joy, wrath, love, pain*; and these are human emotions. God the Father also is spirit and has a soul, as Isaiah (42:1) wrote: **"Behold, My Servant, whom I uphold; My Chosen One in whom My Soul delights. I have put My Spirit upon Him; He will bring forth justice to the nations."** In this verse, we understand that God the Father or LORD is speaking about His Son, who was born taking a human form and now He lives in a human body in flesh and bones. Scripture speaks about the soul of God the Father, and we know scripture also states that God is spirit. God Jesus taught, saying, **"God is spirit [the Source of life, yet invisible to mankind], and those who worship Him must worship in spirit and truth."** Scriptures also states that God has a heart: **"And He was grieved in His heart."** God the Father also share His Spirit with His human sons and daughters (John 4:24; Gen. 6:6; Rom. 8:11; Joel 2:28). **"I will pour My Spirit in all mankind."**

We have observed that scripture describes (*also anthropomorphic language*) God the Father, the Son, and the Holy Spirit as He reveals Himself to us through His creation, His living touch, and His written word; and she demonstrates His glory and power. Scripture says,

> **For ever since the creation of the world His invisible attributes, His eternal power and divine nature, have been clearly seen, being understood through His**

workmanship [all His creation, the wonderful things that He has made], so that they [who fail to believe and trust in Him] are without excuse and without defense. (Rom. 1:20 AMP)

He also knows us from head to toe, from before and after, and this knowledge is through His personal attributes as we must apply them to scriptures in order to understand and know Him. He said of and to Jeremiah: "Before I formed you in the womb, I knew you." This applies to all of us (Jer. 1:5). Scripture speaks about this attribute of God and how we must understand them, saying,

O Lord, you have searched me [thoroughly] and have known me. You know when I sit down and when I rise up [my entire life, everything I do] (*this is God's omniscient/omnipresent attributes*); you understand my thoughts from afar. You scrutinize my path and my lying down, and You are intimately acquainted with all my ways (God is personal with His creation). Even before there is a word on my tongue [still unspoken], behold, O Lord, You know it all (*all things are fresh at His sight, always as He is omniscient/omnipresent*). You have enclosed me behind and before, and [You have] placed Your hand upon me. Such [infinite] knowledge is too wonderful for me; It is too high [above me], I cannot reach it [...and] You saw my body as it was formed. All the days planned for me were written in your book before I was one day old.

The point is, God lets us know these wonderful aspects of His BEING (Ps. 139:1–6, 16 NCV). God also said the knowledge of Him is our glory, and in this form, God is a personal God in Christ with His creation (Jer. 9:23–24). God Jesus taught His disciples so that we may also know this: "**All things have been handed over to Me by My Father; and no one fully knows and accurately understands the Son except the Father; and no one fully knows and accurately understands the Father except the Son, and anyone to whom the Son [deliberately] wills to reveal Him.**" And this is not *anthropomorphic language.* He (Christ) means this into reality, for He came to make God known (Matt. 11:27). We must understand the Son came to reveal God the Father to the church members. The apostle John, knowing this from God Jesus, said,

> I am writing to you, fathers [those believers who are spiritually mature], because <u>you know Him</u> who has existed from the beginning. I am writing to you, young men [those believers who are growing in spiritual maturity], because you have been victorious and have overcome the evil one. I have written to you, children [those who are new believers, those spiritually immature], because you have come to know the Father.

God reveals Himself (1 John 2:13). But you would ask, "But how do I know God the Father?" And His answer is, "**Have I been with you for so long a time, and you do not know Me yet, Philip, nor recognize clearly who I am? Anyone who has seen Me has seen the Father. How can you say, 'Show us the Father?'**" When you came to know Jesus (*His living touch*), literally you came to know the Father (John 14:9). The apostle John also wrote, stating this experience to believers those days, saying, "**I write to you, children, because you know the Father. I write to you, fathers, because you know the One who existed from the beginning.**" This is a profound statement, and the apostle was saying this of people like you and me in the first century (1 John 2:14).

God manifests Himself through all His absolutes to us, for "**all things are possible with [for] God**" (Matt. 10:27). If anything, He is all His absolutes—that is, absolute power, absolute justice, absolute authority—and there is no other one like Him. God the Father gives testimony of His Son, who has come to work the works of redemption for Them:

> **For it pleased the Father for all the fullness [of deity— the sum total of His essence, all His perfection, powers, and attributes] to dwell [permanently] in Him (the Son), and through [the intervention of] the Son to reconcile all things to Himself, making peace [with believers] through the blood of His cross; through Him [I say,] whether things on earth or things in heaven.** (Col. 1:19– 20)

This is the answer of God to the fall of His creation because God is love (1 John 4:8), God is light, (1 John 1:5), God is Spirit (John 4:24), He is the Just One and who justifies (Rom. 3:26), who does not change (Mal. 3:6). He is omniscient, omnipresent, omnipotent, God Almighty, the only God BEING. The "I AM" Jehovah; Existence; YHWH; and "I AM that I AM" God of Abraham, Isaac, and Jacob/Israel. He wants that our joy and sense of importance surges not from our own abilities, possessions, or wisdom but from the knowledge that He provides of Himself. The LORD states this: "**But let the one who boasts boast in this, that he understands and knows Me**" (Jer. 9:24). This was the agenda of Jesus of Nazareth when He walked the earth as He clearly said, "**Now this is eternal life: that they may know You, the only true [supreme and sovereign] God, and [in the same manner know] Jesus [as the] Christ whom You have sent**" (John 17:3). In God the Father's perspective/testimony, it is said,

> And the testimony is this: God has given us eternal life [we already possess it], and this life is in His Son [resulting in our spiritual completeness, and eternal companionship with Him]. He who has the Son [by accepting Him as Lord and Savior] has the life [that is eternal]; he who does not have the Son of God [by the word provoked personal faith] does not have the life.

They both interact with each other on our behalf, for they are "*one*" and the same (1 John 5:11–12). This is the covenant with God and man, as stated in scripture: "**Because they will all know me, from the least of them to the greatest.**" God has revealed Himself (*God is Light and has nothing to hide*), and He wants you to know Him face-to-face as it is appointed (Heb. 8:11, 4:13).

It is through Scripture that we can come to know the aspects and description of the persona of God and His plan of redemption in our spirit/soul. Scripture also teaches through the seven Hebrew names of God, a personal relationship with His believers. They demonstrated His divinity and blessings toward us: *Jehovah-Jireh*, "**the Lord will provide,**" was referred by Abraham (*Gentile*) at the land in Moriah after God provided the ram to sacrifice in replacement of Isaac (Gen. 22:14); *Jehovah-Rapha*, "**the Lord is my healer,**" for God cleanse the waters of Marah for Israel to drink once out the land of Egypt (*the world*) and told them, "**I am the Lord, who heals you**" (Exod. 15:25–27); *Jehovah-Nissi*, "**Moses built an altar and called it The Lord is my Banner**" (Exod. 17:15–16); *Jehovah-Shalom*, then Moses told them, "**The Lord turn his face toward you and give you peace**" (Num. 6:26); *Jehovah-Shamma*, "**The LORD is there**" (Ezra 48:35); *Jehovah-Tsidkenu*, "**The LORD is our Righteousness**" (Jer. 23:5–6); *Jehovah-Rohi*, "**The Lord is my shepherd**" (Ps. 23:1). These are also form in which the anthropomorphic language is used in Scripture and described how the LORD our God wants us to know Him in our daily living as a personal living God. This information was supposed to be given to the world by those whom He called, but **"He came to that which was his own, but his own did not receive him"** (John 1:11). This is mentioned for, in truth, this word was given to the people of another nation (Israel, but their God instead had to call a people that is not a people, *"from every nation, tribe, people and language, standing before the throne and before the Lamb,"* to heed His call (Rev. 7:9). It is written:

> **As he says in Hosea: "I will call them 'my people' who are not my people; and I will call her** [*the church of Christ*] **'my loved one' who is not my loved one"** **and "In the very place where it was said to them, 'You are not my people,' there they will be called 'children of the living God.**

Let the "New Jerusalenians" say Amen! (Rom. 9:25–26). No one goes to the Father except through Christ Jesus. All others are heretics without Him, stated in scripture (John 14:6).

In Christ, we have this great privilege of knowing the Father as we know the Son, and the apostle John said it was in a personal way. We speak to God in prayers, and God answers back by His Holy Spirit. We have communion with Him. We worship His presence. We sing to Him and are aware that He lives in us and among us. We are His living temple (*as a group and as individuals*). Scripture teaches us: **"Do you not know and understand that you [the church] are the temple of God, and that the Spirit of God dwells [permanently] in you [collectively and individually]?"** And again, **"Do you not know that your [individual] body is a temple of the Holy Spirit who is within you, whom you have [received as a gift] from God, and that you are not your own [property]? You were bought with a price [you were actually purchased with the** precious blood of Jesus and made His own]. So then, honor and glorify God with your body." This was said to Gentile believers in their sound doctrine training (1 Cor. 3:15–16, 6:19–20). The mature disciple seeks to know and understand the presence of God in Christ because God has revealed Himself to us in a personal and intimate relation. He touched us, making us to be born again, and that touch let us see Scripture in an intimate way. When we know God as Scripture teaches us through His attributes, then we can understand better what He is saying to us through His words. His word comes from an omniscient/omnipresent consciousness (*and its objective reality*). Then when we read God's word, we are reading omniscient knowledge from the mind of the God of Abraham from which both Gentiles and Jews were created into a new body. The apostle Paul writes to the Ephesians (2:15–16 AMP) that **"by abolishing in His [own crucified] flesh the hostility caused by the Law with its commandments contained in ordinances [which He satisfied** (*as it was established, predestined, preordained*)**] so that in Himself He might make the two into one new man, thereby establishing peace. And [that He] might reconcile them both [Jew and Gentile, united] in one body to God through the cross, thereby putting to death the hostility."** The gospel is the good news of God's salvation. This redemption is about a new priesthood in the order of Melchizedek, by a High Priest from another tribe, that alone abolishes the old Levi legalist priesthood (Heb. 7:11–22, 6:12–20). The apostle Paul repeated this good news of God positioning us, saying,

> There is [now no distinction in regard to salvation] neither Jew nor Greek [*race*] there is neither slave nor free [*status*] there is neither male nor female [*genders*]; for you [who believe] are all one in Christ Jesus [no one can claim a spiritual superiority]. And if you belong to Christ [if you are in Him], then you

are Abraham's descendants, and [spiritual] heirs according to [God's] promise. (Gal. 3:28–29)

In other words, the invisible church is not of gentiles nor of Jews, neither of man nor woman, but is a new body of people, members of the body of Christ. A new regeneration by God, as its written: "**But you are a chosen race, a royal priesthood, a holy nation, God's own people, that you may declare the wonderful deeds of him who called you out of darkness into his marvelous light**" (1 Pet. 2:9). He chose us:

> **God selected [(***people***) for His purpose] the foolish things of the world to shame the wise [...] the weak things to shame the things which are strong [...] the insignificant (base) things, that are despised and treated with contempt, the things that are nothing, so that He might reduce to nothing the things that are, so that no one may boast in the presence of God.** (1 Cor. 1:26–29 AMP)

The LORD Our God the LORD Is One

When the God BEING were in Their first divine, heavenly summit, they were called the "I AM," the WORD, and the SPIRIT (Gen. 1:1–4; Exod. 3:14; John 1:1–4); and after the creation, they decided to use commonly known names (*anthropomorphic*) to us. Today, we know the God BEING by God the Father, God the Son, and God the Holy Spirit. As a BEING, they possess the same attributes, absolutes, and characteristics; for they are One. We like to say that when God Jesus at the cross of Calvary cried out, "**Eli, Eli, lama sabachthani?**" that is, "**My God, My God, why have You forsaken Me?**" He meant, "My God [**Father**] My God [**Holy Spirit**]" (Matt. 27:46). We can see the One God BEING working together in the full aspects of the redemption of man as *the Gardener, the Vine, and the Counselor (anthropomorphic language used by God Jesus)*. But in the beginning, they were together making creation and then forming it (*a mystery in scripture [Isa. 45:18]*). Scriptures says:

> **In the beginning God (Elohim [*Hebrew word meaning "gods," plural*]) created [by forming from nothing] the heavens and the earth. The earth was formless and void or a waste and emptiness, and darkness was upon the face of the deep [primeval ocean that covered the unformed earth]. The Spirit of God was moving (hovering, brooding) over the face of the waters. And God said, "Let there be light"** (*the Word/Son spoke the light*) **and there was light. God [the Father] saw that the light was good.** (Gen. 1:1–4 AMP)

When the Word became flesh (John 1:14), He put aside His deity for the purpose of redemption, and it is written:

> **Who, although He existed in the form and unchanging essence of God [as One with Him, possessing the fullness of all the divine attributes— the entire nature of deity], did not regard equality with God a thing to be grasped or asserted [as if He did not already possess it, or was afraid of losing it]?** (Phil. 2:5)

In His doctrines to the disciple, God Jesus told them, "**For this reason the Father loves Me, because I lay down My [own] life so that I may take it back. No one takes it away from Me, but I lay it down voluntarily. I am authorized and have power to lay it down and to give it up, and I am authorized *and* have power to take it back. This command I have received from My Father,**" naturally showing how God the Father is head of the God BEING. This was determined in that first divine, heavenly summit between them. The God BEING for God so loved that He gave His unique Son for our redemption; and this was before the foundation of the world (John 10:17–18, 3:16 AMP). The God BEING gave a family member so that we can become part of Their family. (*This was explained in* The Apostles Methodology to Interpret Scripture). Therefore, God Jesus, in another teaching: "**You heard Me tell you, 'I am going away, and I am coming back to you. [...and] to the Father, for the Father is greater than I.**" And we must understand He said that because He was in a mortal body in the likeness to ours, but now He is the only immortal, for He was raised from the dead as He was found to have no sin. And if the wage of sin is death, who told the evil one he could end Jesus of Nazareth's life? (John 14:28; Rom. 8:11). Once He completed His redemptive work, it is said of Him: "**For in Him all the fullness of Deity (the Godhead) dwells in bodily form [completely expressing the divine essence of God],**" as it is also said that "**He is the exact living image [the essential manifestation] of the unseen God [the visible representation of the invisible], the firstborn [the preeminent one, the sovereign, and the originator] of all creation.**" Many want to call Him the second in deity, but that is not what Scripture states of God as a BEING. God Jesus now lives in a glorified body in "***flesh and bones,***" and He is the image of the invisible God BEING (Col. 2:9, 1:15). It is also said of God Jesus: "**Now to the King of the ages [the eternal Jesus Christ], immortal, invisible, the only God, be honor and glory forever and ever.**" The New Testament writers (also Israelites/Jews), like the Old

Testament writers, acknowledge the Name/Lord, Messiah/Christ as God and wrote: "He alone possesses immortality (*for He became a mortal, John1:14*) [absolute exemption from death] and lives in unapproachable light [*in the God* BEING *invisible reality*] whom no [*mortal*] man has ever seen or can see. To Him be honor and eternal power and dominion!" He now lives in a glorified, transformed body in *flesh and bones*, He said (1 Tim. 1:17, 6:16; Luke 24:39). On the other hand, God the Holy Spirit is called the third in the divine deity, but the apostle Peter said in an embarrassing situation: "Ananias, why has Satan filled your heart to lie to the Holy Spirit [...] You have not [simply] lied to people, but to God." The Spirit of the Father is God (Acts 5:3–4; Rom. 8:11). The Father, Son, and Holy Spirit are God with all the attributes, absolutes, and characteristics in their godly BEING. He also has the same power, and they are "One BEING." Scripture says, "The Lord is the Spirit" and also "And if the Spirit of Him who raised Jesus from the dead lives in you (*in other words, the Spirit of the Father*), He who raised Christ Jesus from the dead [God the Father] will also give life to your mortal bodies through His Spirit, who lives in you" (Rom. 8:11; 2 Cor. 3:17). We must understand and accept that God the Father, God the Son, and God the Holy Spirit, the God BEING, are One; and they have given their word, their attribute of immutability, so that we can take the descriptions of Himself in Scriptures as truth. This declaration is established by God, and He inspired John to write:

> The one who believes in the Son of God [who adheres to, trusts in, and relies confidently on Him as Savior] has the testimony within himself (*in other words all that you have read but in spirit form within*) [because he can speak authoritatively about Christ from his own personal experience]. The one who <u>does not</u> believe God [in this way] has made Him [out to be] a liar, because <u>he/she has not</u>

believed in the evidence that God [the Father] has given regarding His Son.

There is going to be a terrible day of judgment for all of them, and the accused is guilty as accomplices of the killing of His Son (1 John 5:10; Rom. 5:1).

The plan purpose of God is to bring back all things unto Himself. But this time around, He has placed all things under His Word's authority, who lives in a body of "*flesh and bones*" created to fit His BEING; for He is dealing with all His creatures(angels and humans)to be their God from everlasting to everlasting (1 Cor. 15:24–28). This plan was established in the Old Covenant and demonstrated in the new, saying, **"The Lord has sworn [an oath] and will not change His mind: "You are a priest forever According to the order of Melchizedek"** (Ps. 110:4; Heb. 7:17, 25, 6:13–20). Therefore, we can read in Scripture the order of things from beginning to end and on, as God is speaking through His attributes in Scripture, and it is said:

> **After that comes the end (completion), when He hands over the kingdom to God the Father, after He has made inoperative and abolished every ruler and every authority *and* power. For Christ must reign [as King] until He has put all His enemies under His feet. The last enemy to be abolished and put to an end is death. [The first Adam brought death into existence; the Second Adam canceled/destroyed it, with the evil one and his fallen angels who were eternal.] For He (the Father) has put all things in subjection under His (Christ's) feet.**

This revelation was given to us in scripture, and the apostle Paul explains it splendidly as we will show ahead.

> But when He says, "All things have been put in subjection [under Christ]," it is clear that He (the Father) who put all things in subjection to Him (Christ) is exempted [since the Father is not in subjection to His own Son]. However, when all things are subjected to Him (Christ), then the Son Himself will also be subjected to the One (the Father) who put all things under Him, so that[the]God [BEING]may be all in all [manifesting His glory without any opposition, the supreme indwelling and controlling factor of (the fabric)life]. (1 Cor. 15:24–28 AMP)

This is the will of God. It is also demonstrated in scripture, given to the apostle John to write of it, and he said,

> Then He [God the Father] who sat on the throne said, "Behold, I make all things new." And He said to me, "Write, for these words are true and faithful." And He said to me, "It is done! I am the Alpha and the Omega [*Aleph and Tav, God Jesus*] the Beginning and the End."

Here the deity becomes *one* and the same. This is a predestined future. It already happened in the God BEING's reality. Then He comes back to our timeline and says, "**I will give of the fountain of the water of life freely to him who thirsts. He who overcomes [uplifting this faith] shall inherit all things, and I will be his God and he shall be My son.**" It has always been known that the LORD our God is *One*, the eternal, a BEING not created; and it always has been known that He loves us dearly (Rev. 21:5–7). God Jesus is the image of the invisible God. In other words, He is everything the scriptures say about the Father in this chapter.

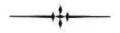

Answer the questions from this chapter to interact with others in a book club:

1. How can a human person know and understand who God is, and what gives us that affirmation?

2. How has the author arrived at the conclusion that Scripture points to a God BEING?

3. What are God's attributes, and how do they affect Scripture as we read it? Give an example.

THIRD LESSON

Understanding Christ's Victory and the Building of His Church

In this chapter, as we follow the systematic theology format, we are going to develop, according to scriptures, the doctrine of Christ. *Who was Christ? Who is He now, and how can men and women get to know Him?* Two thousand years have passed since Jesus Christ resurrected from the dead to live in inaccessible light. Scripture states of Jesus of Nazareth:

> Until the appearance of our Lord Jesus Christ that the blessed and only ruler will make manifest at the proper time, the King of kings and Lord of lords, who alone has immortality (*He became a mortal man and was like Adam before sinning but acquire immortality by God the Father after His death*

[*Heb.8:11*]) who dwells in unapproachable light (*God is Light*) and whom no [*mortal*] human being has seen or can see (*Christ now lives in an attribute of invisibility with the Father*). To him be honor and eternal power. Amen. (1 Tim. 6:14–16 NABRE)

If we were to resume the doctrine of Jesus of Nazareth as scripture explains, we would say that *Jesus was, and is, completely God and was, and is, completely man; He became and will always be* in a glorified body of *flesh and bones* as stated by Him. This discussion was one of the first heresy at the end of the first and beginning of the second to third centuries. It was created by Gnostics, a group of individuals with Greek philosophy and Judaism influence. They were stating Jesus was a common man, and the Spirit came into him in His water baptism by John the Baptist and left him at the cross of Calvary. The apostle John wrote about this condescending heresy establishing the statement of who was and is Jesus of Nazareth. His testimony is to be taken seriously, for he was an eyewitness. He said,

[I am writing about] what existed from the beginning, what we have heard, what we have seen with our eyes [*speaking of more than one person, "we have"*] what we have looked at and touched with our hands(a physical being, a man) concerning the Word of Life (*God*) [the One who existed even before the beginning of the world, Christ]—and the Life [an aspect of His being] was manifested, and we have seen [it as eyewitnesses] and testify and declare to you [the Life], the eternal Life who was [already existing] with the Father and was [actually] made visible to us [His followers]—what we have seen and heard we also proclaim to you, so that you too may have fellowship [as partners] with us. And indeed, our fellowship [which is a distinguishing mark of born-again believers] is with the Father, and with His Son Jesus Christ. We are writing these things to you so that our joy [in seeing you included] may be made complete [by having you share in the joy of salvation].

The apostle John shared the personal experience he had with God's Son, for he knew Him since he was a young man (*Apostles Methodology [50–51]*) (1 John 1:1–4). The apostle John, a Jew and ocular witness, declared this testimony against that heresy for future believers to be able to denounce and clarify this important doctrine. The declaration of John in the book of Revelation is more direct, stating God Jesus words as he was told to write:

When I saw him, I fell at his feet as though dead [*John was in spirit/soul, Rev.1:10*]. Then he placed his right hand on me and said: "Do not be afraid. I am the First and the Last. I am the Living One; I was dead, and now look, I am alive for ever and ever! And I hold the keys of death and Hades.

God Jesus spoke to him as in the maturity of being the substance and image of the living God, standing in *flesh and bones* in His new revelation (Rev. 1:17–18). Jesus of Nazareth is God, and He has the keys of death and hell, for He took them from the evil one who now lies **"destroyed, judged and condemned"** and next to be thrown into the lake of fire (John 16:11; Heb. 2:14; Rev. 20:10). Scripture describes who and what God Jesus is at this very moment in time. This was promise by God the Father to the Adams, and the result of the Seed of the woman was to have victory over their enemy, the serpent (Gen. 3:15). This virgin birth was a miracle of God into this reality in order to correct what the evil one destroyed. God's Word/Name would take a human body and enter our reality by God the Father's almighty power. Our reality became bound by God's word/promise of redemption. It was bound by chains of God's promise, oath, and laws in His word, which was given to Adam and legalized by Moses, the prophets' oracles, and the psalmist hints/riders about the birth and life of the Son of God once in this reality (*predestined life, see Isa. 53*).

In the illustrations below (*A and B*), we have the God BEING's reality of invisibility above heaven's reality, the city of angels, then bounding earth by chains of words, laws, promises, and prophecies of God. These were promised to the forefathers of the Israelites. God needed to create an environment to send His Son as the Seed of the woman and live among us. Moses wrote: **"The Lord did not set His love on you nor choose you because you were more in number than any other people, for you were the least of all peoples; but because the Lord loves you, and because He would keep the oath which He swore to your fathers** [*Abraham, Isaac, and Jacob/Israel*] **the Lord has brought you out with a mighty hand, and redeemed you from the house of bondage, from the hand of Pharaoh** [*the devil*] **king of Egypt,"** a promise made to the Israelites and further up to God Jesus's church (Deut. 7:7–8). He made them a nation and gave them laws to purify their carnal minds and animalistic living into a cleaner spiritual one. He told them what to eat; how to dress, how to worship and made them a people of law, promises, and prophecies. Paul writes the opposite of the Gentiles: **"At that time you were without Christ, being aliens from the commonwealth of Israel and strangers from the covenants of promise, having no hope and without God in the world"** (Eph. 2:12).

The law and the oracles were chains bounding earth's reality into the heavenly one because of Israel until the Seed of the woman would appear. At death, the faithful Israelite were sent to a waiting place (*Abraham's bosom*). The others were thrown into a burning hell (*Hades*) until the last judgment. Gentiles were thrown into a burning hell except for those who follow. As converts to Israel's promises (*since leaving Egypt*), they also waited in Abraham's bosom (*God had also dealt with Gentiles? like Balaam [Num. 22, 23]*). Scripture says, "**[Lazarus] the beggar died and was carried by the angels to Abraham's bosom. The rich man [*Jew*] also died and was buried. And being in torments in Hades, he lifted up his eyes and saw Abraham afar off, and Lazarus in his bosom.**" Those in Abraham's bosom were there in a "*faith on credit*" until the Lord would take the captivity captive once He paid the full price for their redemption (Luke 16:19–31). Scriptures teach about Messiah's priestly works that "**when He ascended on high, He led captivity captive, And gave gifts to men.**" (Now this, "He ascended"—what does it mean but that He also first descended into the lower parts of the earth? [Abraham's bosom] "**He who descended is also the One who ascended far above all the heavens, that He might fill all things.**") After Christ's expiation for sins, everything changed (Eph. 4:8–10). Jesus of Nazareth has made all things new, and now the new covenant is in effect as it was foretold in the writings of the prophets and psalmist.

God Jesus speaking to the Israelites of His days said,

> **I say to you that many will come from east and west [Gentiles] and sit down with Abraham, Isaac, and Jacob in the kingdom of heaven. But the sons of the kingdom [many Jews] will be cast out into outer darkness. There will be weeping and gnashing of teeth. (Matt. 8:11–12)**

Jews and Gentiles who do not accept God Jesus as the Father's Messiah are condemned, for there is only one way to the Father, and that is through Jesus Christ's sacrifice, His payment for our sins (John 14:6). Now the redeemed are called by God: "**But you** *are* **a chosen generation, a royal priesthood, a holy nation, His own special people, that you may proclaim the praises of Him who called you out of darkness into His marvelous light,**" chosen to enter the City of Light at death until the covenant of the transformation (1 Pet. 2:9).

The prophets wrote about this new covenant, saying, "**Therefore the Lord himself will give you a sign: The virgin will conceive and give birth to a son, and will call him Immanuel**" [...and] "**For to us a child is born, to us a son is given, and the government will be on his shoulders. And he will be called: Wonderful Counselor, Mighty God, Everlasting Father, Prince of Peace.**" The prophets were given to tell us a secret, which was to be revealed when it was to happen in the year AD "28, 30, or 33" (*no one knows which*); but it happened at the four thousand years in God's second week and two thousand years ago. We are living on the edge of the six days of God's second week after creation (Isa. 7:14, 9:6; Exod. 19:10–11; Hos. 6:2). The disciple can understand the child born is two thousand years old (*now*), but the Son given is Mighty God, Everlasting Father (*always has been*). There is no wonder why God Jesus told His disciples: "**Anyone who has seen me has seen the Father. How can you say, 'Show us the Father'?**" And now He is the image of the invisible "Living God" (John 14:9). This was written in the law about Messiah, and Moses wrote about what Jacob/Israel said, blessing his twelve sons on his bed of death: "**Judah, you are the one whom your brothers shall praise; your hand will be on the neck of your enemies; your father's sons shall bow down to you. Judah, a lion's cub; with the prey, my son, you have gone high up [the mountain].**" The reader can sense the break in thoughts here as Jacob begins to speak of someone greater:

> **He stooped down, he crouched like a lion** [*Lion of Judah, Rev.5:5*] **And like a lion—who dares rouse him? The scepter** [symbol of royalty, kingship] **shall not depart from Judah, nor the ruler's staff from between his feet, until Shiloh** [the Messiah, the Peaceful One (*Shiloh also means His gift*)] **comes, and to Him shall be the obedience of the peoples** (*understand this action caused by this Person's arrival*). **Tying his foal to the** [strong] **vine. And his donkey's colt to the choice vine** [*see Romans 11:16–20 and Ephesians1:4*]. **He washes his clothing in wine** [because the grapevine produces abundantly], **and his robes in the blood of grapes** [Zech. 3:3–4]. **His eyes are darker and sparkle more than wine, and his teeth whiter than milk** [speaking of redemption]. (Gen. 49:8–12)

The last prophet of the Old Covenant, John the Baptist, used what's called in theological terms to describe God's plan in an anthropomorphic *language* and explained the oath God the Father made about His only begotten Son (*"mono genes" means unique, not start of origin*). John the Baptist proclaimed, "**I have seen and testified that this is the Son of God**" and "**John saw Jesus coming toward him and said, 'Look, the Lamb of God, who takes away the sin of the world!'**" (John 1:29, 34). John B was declaring God the Father's testimony about His Chosen, the redemptive work as a sacrificial lamb, and remember, he got his head cut off for his testimony about Jesus of Nazareth (*the mark and sign of a real prophet of God*). We must ask ourselves though, What is impossible for God? Most of the people of Israel did not accept it then, nor they accept it today, that Jesus of Nazareth (*human born*) is the Son of God. But this is where this message has gone viral, for it is God the Father's testimony about His begotten (*only/unique*) Son (1 John 5:10). The prophet Isaiah started by asking, "**Who has believed our message?**" because it seemed he knew how the people of Israel would react against it (Isa. 53:1). God did what He had stopped Abraham from doing—that is, sacrificing His Son—for the redemption of humanity (*you must understand He already knew and created this event in Their first divine, heavenly summit*). We must ask: Who are we (*the clay*) to tell the Potter what to do with our form/body and existence created for this purpose in His reality? Who are we to tell God what to do? Once again, the word of God is immutable, and the testimony He has given about His Son is truthful and is important that our belief in this doctrine is well cemented and established: "*About the virgin birth of our Lord and God, Jesus [Christ] of Nazareth.*"

Our Lord Jesus took a physical body like ours to live in it permanently from everlasting to everlasting, and Scripture testifies:

> **Therefore, since [these His] children share in flesh and blood [the physical nature of mankind], He Himself in a similar manner also shared in the same [physical nature, but without sin], so that through [experiencing] death He might make powerless (ineffective, impotent) him who had the power of death—that is, the devil—and [that He] might free all those who through [the haunting] fear of death were held in slavery throughout their lives.**

Once redeemed, we don't have to live in fear of death the way we did (Heb. 2:14–15 AMP). The King James Version uses the words, "*destroy* **him that had the power of death, that is, the devil,**" to establish a truthful understanding that God's Chosen freed us from the power of darkness controlled by the evil one. Afterward, He resurrected in a body of *flesh and bones*, no blood included. As Bible students, let us research and compare the two events in Scripture that correlate to this event. In Genesis (2:23), it was written: **"This is now bone of my bones, and flesh of my flesh; She shall be called Woman, because she was taken out of Man."** As you can notice in the creation of the first Adam, no blood was included. After the fall into sin, their bodies went from the Holy Spirit empowered to flesh/blood strengthening. This is to see how Christ participated in flesh and blood (*but without sin*) to destroy him who had the power or empire of death: the evil one. (*We explained this in* The Apostles Methodology [116–128].) When Jesus of Nazareth resurrected from the dead, He told His disciples: **"See My hands and My feet, that it is I Myself; touch Me and see, for a spirit does not have flesh and bones as you see that I have."** Again, no blood was included, and this was declared by God Jesus as He stood in a glorified body (Luke 24:39). The words in Hebrew YHWH, the tetragrammaton, is said to mean *"**Behold the Hand, behold the Nail.**"* Jesus of Nazareth is God. The apostle John was told by Christ of this form in which now He lives and in which we will be one day: **"Do not be afraid; I am the first and the last, and the living One; and I was dead, and behold, I am alive forevermore** [*in flesh and bones*]**."** This is no wonder why John makes this exclamation in his first letter: **"Beloved, now we are children of God, and it has not appeared as yet what we will be. We know that when He appears, we will be like Him, because we will see Him just as He is"**—that is, in a glorified body of flesh and bones. (*This is also why we understand the apocalypses were written first* before *John's letters* [Rev. 1:17–18; 1 John 3:2].) Jesus Christ is completely man and completely God, even more after resurrected, for the Father gives testimony of Him in all the written scriptures, and **"the one who does not believe God [the Father] has made Him a liar"** (1 John 5:10). God resurrected Jesus, and now He is the first and only immortal who lives in inaccessible light (Rom. 8:11; 1 Tim. 6:16).

The Birth and Life of Jesus of Nazareth

Scripture establishes that Jesus of Nazareth is the prophetic Messiah, and it's well recorded in its documented genealogy. Matthew and Luke got these genealogies before the temple was destroyed in AD 70. They both took different route in recording them. Matthew wrote his in the line of Joseph coming from *Solomon*, and Luke wrote his from Mary coming from the line of *Nathan*. They were both sons of King David. Matthew writes: **"The record of the genealogy of** [*Yeshua/Joshua*] **Jesus the Messiah** [*Christos/Anointed*]**, the** son of David, the son of Abraham" (Matt. 1:1 NASB). We all know that Abraham was before David. The understanding that Matthew was giving to those who would research those days was that Jesus was the rightful (*and last*) heir of King David and an Israelite of the nation by legal birthright through the seed of Abraham, proven in the genealogical records. There's no wonder why the apostle Paul also researches and writes: **"Now the promises were spoken to Abraham and to his Seed. He does not say, 'And to seeds,' as** *one would in referring* **to many, but** *rather* **as** *in referring* **to one, 'And to your Seed,' that is, Christ,"** for scriptures were pointing to (Messiah) *the Seed* of Abraham (Gal. 3:16). This testimony stands against those who oppose the truth of God the Father. Joseph was not blood related to Jesus. He was married to Mary, giving Jesus the legal right of birth as heir: **"Jacob fathered Joseph the husband of Mary, by whom Jesus was born, who is called the Messiah"** (vs. 16). Then Matthew emphasizes, **"Mary had been betrothed to Joseph"** [unlike engagements today, a betrothed couple those days were considered married, but did not yet live together until the ceremony]. **"Before they came together, she was found to be pregnant by the Holy Spirit"** (vs. 18). Matthew also writes the testimony of Joseph, which he probably got from Jesus's family (brothers/sisters) or Mary herself (*or even God the Holy Spirit, the omnipresent storyteller*), saying,

> **An angel of the Lord appeared to him in a dream, saying, "Joseph, son of David, do not be afraid to take Mary as your wife; for the Child who has been conceived in her is of the Holy Spirit. She will give birth to a Son; and you shall name Him Jesus, for He will save His people from their sins."**

The facts are there to be accepted or not, but they are real facts (vs. 20–21). Understand God's word is immutable and carries His attribute of unchangeableness (*do not make Him a liar*).

Jesus grew from childhood to adulthood as all of us have. As a baby, He learned to eat, to talk, read, write and be obedient to His parents Joseph and Mary (*Joseph had the role of being Jesus's [step?] father. Wow, imagine how he felt*). This learning is part of every human existence, and Jesus honestly lived it as a human person, as one of us. The evangelist Luke wrote: **"The Child continued to grow and become strong, increasing in wisdom; and the grace of God was upon Him"** and also **"And Jesus kept increasing in wisdom and stature [age], and in favor with God and men"** (Luke 2:40, 52). Afterward, the writer of Hebrews wrote: **"Although He was a Son, He learned obedience from the things which He suffered."** Clearly, it can be noticed that the child was like every human person (*in our temporal time*), and the Son who learned obedience from the things He suffered was the Word/God. (*Remember His soul was the expiation/sacrifice, His soul, and He* is part of the God BEING. *The implication is deep* (Isa. 53:11; Heb. 2:9–10). Let's understand that He lived a natural life here on earth, but He is also the Word/God, and the apostles acknowledged it (Heb. 5:8; John 1:1–14). His reality was like every man and woman that will live and die in this plane of existence and beyond, but He clearly knew what had happened since the creation (*He created*) of the first man. Therefore, He has the right to claim ownership to our existence and reality. He conquered back what the first Adam lost. Jesus Christ was, and is, a man just like all of us (*in our earthly reality*); and He is also the Son of the God BEING (*in His godly reality*). We must remember the Potter/God created us to His image and likeness (*spirit/soul*). We are not descendants of a primate as the world's mad scientists have declared.

Jesus in His human body got tired as we do. He sweated in His human body. He had thirst, and we saw this as He sat down by a well and asked a Samaritan woman water from the well (John 4:6). Scripture also states that after fasting, He was hungry (Matt. 4:22). He had a spirit/soul like us and emotions. The apostle Peter wrote: "[The Prophets...] **which the Spirit of Christ in them.**" The Word of God was already working His mystery (*to become human*) through the prophets and psalmist (1 Pet. 1:10–12). The Father predestined, and it was written: "**Yet it pleased the LORD to bruise Him; He has put *Him* to grief. When You make His soul an offering for sin.**" His *soul* was the offering/expiation for our sins. It was not just the suffering of His human body (Isa. 53:10). This is so personal from Him to us (*the Son/Word of the God BEING*). In His earthly days, He declared at different times: "**Now My soul has become troubled; and what shall I say, 'Father, save Me from this hour'? But for this purpose, I came at this hour.**" He knew *it was predestined/prophecy, and* "**He became troubled in spirit**" (John 12:27, 13:21). Matthew writes of Him, saying, "**My soul is deeply grieved, to the point of death.**" God Jesus today is *spirit/soul* in a human glorified body of *flesh and bones,* and this is declared in the immutable scripture, true reality (Matt. 26:38).

Just like any of us in creation, Jesus marvels at things He experienced as a man. Matthew wrote of one of those moments: **"Now when Jesus heard this, He marveled and said to those who were following, 'Truly I say to you, I have not found such great faith with anyone in Israel.'"** And John wrote of an emotional moment in the life of Jesus of Nazareth, saying, **"Jesus wept,"** being this the shortest verse in scripture (Matt.8:10; John 11:35). Jesus marveled at the faith of a Gentile centurion, a Roman soldier, and wept at the despair of Lazarus's sisters, His beloved friends. He learned obedience as a man and was made High Priest forever according to the order of Melchizedek, qualifying His humanity for us, the redeemed. This is the whole point/theme of the book of Hebrews: **"For such a High Priest was fitting for us"** [...and] **"Now *this is* the main point of the things we are saying: We have such a High Priest, who is seated at the right hand of the throne of the Majesty in the heavens, a Minister of the sanctuary and of the true tabernacle which the Lord erected, and not man,"** fully human and fully God (Heb. 7:26, 8:1–2). The psalmist wrote of Him: **"The Lord has sworn and will not change His mind, "You are a priest forever According to the order of Melchizedek."** This is a prophecy that was to be fulfilled by the Messiah (Ps. 110:4). The writer of Hebrews took this promise to write about Jesus of Nazareth's nature and fulfilled prophecy, saying,

> **In the days of His flesh, He offered up both prayers and supplications with loud crying and tears to the One able to save Him from death, and He was heard because of His piety** [*reverence, devotion*]**. Although He was a Son, He learned obedience from the things which He suffered. And having been made perfect, He became to all those who obey Him the source of**

eternal salvation, being designated by God as a high priest according to the order of Melchizedek.

The writer made sure the readers understood he took this from a prophecy, which spoke of a man/Messiah, saying, **"For it is attested of Him, 'You are a priest forever, According to the order of Melchizedek,'"** and to that, in an order of a different priesthood, which canceled the other. He added what His work was going to be: **"Therefore He is able also to save forever (completely, perfectly, for eternity) those who come to God through Him, since He always lives [eternally] to intercede and intervene** (*as High* Priest) **on their behalf [with God]."** Understand this declaration: we do not serve God Jesus by the Leviticus priesthood (*it has been abolished for Christianity*) but by one who is High Priest from another tribe (*Judah*), and that alone disowns the Levi priesthood. Therefore, we walk in the order of Melchizedek by Christ's Spirit (Heb. 5:7–10, 7:17, 7:25; Rev. 1:6, 5:10 NASB, AMP). The people that lived near Jesus knew Him as an ordinary fellow before He took up His ministry. They spoke of Him with awe and wonder, even jealousy and envy, saying,

> He came to His hometown and began teaching them in their synagogue, so that they were astonished, and said, "Where did this man get this wisdom and these miraculous powers? Is this not the carpenter's son? Is not His mother called Mary, and His brothers, James and Joseph and Simon and Judas? And His sisters, are they not all with us? Where did this man get all these things?" And they took offense at Him. But Jesus said to them, "A prophet is not without honor except in his hometown and in his own household." And He did not do many miracles there because of their unbelief.

The people that grew up with Him didn't believe in Him and envied Him (Matt. 13:54–58 NASB). This also proved how He was also human.

Jesus of Nazareth and Adam are heads of humanity's creation, and this is also why Jesus Christ is called the second and last Adam by the apostles for there will not be another head of humanity ever (see Romans 5:12–21). He was also God in His humanity but with the powers of the first Adam over the earth (*which he lost when he sinned*). Jesus had Adam's dominion over the earth (Gen.1:26). It was said to Adam: **"When thou tillest the ground, it shall not henceforth yield unto thee her strength"** (Gen. 4:12 KJV). He also told Phillip how He was part of the God BEING, saying, **"Have I been with you so long, and yet you have not known Me, Philip? He who has seen Me has seen the Father [an argument this book is demonstrating], so how can you say, 'Show us the Father'"** (John 14:9). He walked upon waters: **"When they saw Him walking on the sea, they supposed it was a ghost, and cried out"** (Mark 6:49). This seemed like the powers of a God, but He performed this act following scriptures just as the first Adam and his ability to speak to animals and the elements and being able to walk on water. John said of Him: **"He was in the world, and the world was made through Him, and the world did not know Him"** (John 1:10). This is seen like what Paul said: **"Who, being in very nature God, did not consider equality with God something to be used to his own advantage."** The apostle Paul said Jesus left His deity for this reason and faced the devil blindfolded. Therefore, let's conclude that He came as the son of man and performed all the things as the first Adam would have, having the strength from the earth and the abilities/stamina Adam's body had before he sinned (Phil. 2:6 NIV). We must remind you that the evil one's nature is not of this reality but of the heavenly, and in this reality, he is out of character. He was bound into this world by God who said, **"The Lord God said to the serpent, 'Because you have done this, You are cursed** more than all the cattle, And more than any animal of the field; On your belly you shall go, And dust you shall eat All the days of your life,'" and all the ins and outs of this reality are to affect him as well, as we will demonstrate later (Gen. 3:14). But Jesus of Nazareth is not. He was born here, and God's covenant is about us and Him. The disciples knew Jesus was God after this happened to them, for no man ever did these acts: "But He said to them, 'Where is your faith?' And they were afraid, and marveled, saying to one another, 'Who can this be? For He commands even the winds and water, and they obey Him!'" (Luke 8:25). They began to understand the writing about the Messiah: "And so it is written: 'The first man Adam *became* a living being.' The last Adam became a life-giving spirit" [...and] "The first man *was* of the earth, *made* of dust; the second Man *is* the Lord from heaven. As *was* the man of dust, so also *are* those *who are made* of dust; and as *is* the heavenly *Man*, so also *are* those *who are* heavenly [born again]." They had no doubts about this, for not only were they eyewitnesses, but He declared unto them: "I and My Father are one." Let us not exclude Christ's humanity, for God made this body and it was good, and He took one like ours being born in it (1 Cor. 15:5, 47–48; Rom. 5:9–19; Gen. 2:7; Matt. 14:25; John 10:30). Our bodies are temples of God's Holy Spirit, scripture states; so let us accept, comply, and live.

Jesus had no sin in Him and was like the first Adam in his first state, who was created without sin, and so Jesus Christ walked the earth like the son of man. Leviticus (17:11) says, "For the life of the flesh is in the blood." Then it is known, when Adam sinned, his life/blood was stained by sin into death (*he went from Holy Spirit life to animalistic blood strengthening*)as were all his descendants who got imputed (*tagged*) with the stain of sin. Scripture states, "Therefore, just as through one man's sin entered the world, and death through sin, and thus death spread to all men, because all sinned." Then we must all die (Rom. 5:12). Jesus Christ was born of a virgin birth; and we know today, proved by science, the blood of the mother does not mix with the blood of the embryo. For if it did, the mother's body will reject it, abort it, and/or the child would be born abnormal (*research the Internet*). Jesus of Nazareth is born from a virgin birth as the promise/sign, says Isaiah (7:14) (*with new blood*). We are all walking in an abnormal situation (*fallen nature*), for the sin into death of Adam has been imputed to us. Therefore, scripture states, "**Blessed is the man to whom the Lord shall not impute sin**," and all who receive Jesus will receive this awesome blessing (Rom. 4:8). Jesus said, "**I am the light of the world.**" In other words, He had no sins. This is also why Pilate, after interrogating Him, said, "**I find no fault in Him at all**" (John 18:38). The apostle Peter wrote about Him: "**But with the precious blood of Christ, as of a lamb without blemish and without spot,**" comparing Him with Moses's sacrificial lamb (1 Pet. 1:19). Of Him, it is also written: "**But was in all *points* tempted as *we are, yet* without sin**" [...and] "**For in that He Himself has suffered, being tempted, He is able to aid those who are tempted**" [...and] "**For such a High Priest was fitting for us, *who is* holy, harmless, undefiled, separate from sinners, and has become higher than the heavens**" (Heb. 4:15, 2:18, 7:26). We hear how so many people talking about Jesus of Nazareth temptation as if it was like our fallen nature, and we must consider that His perfect body was not corrupted like ours. Let us give respect to the thought of what tempted Him. The evil one did try but was not able to move Him, even while in the weakness of fasting; and, not to take advantage, He did it in a human form, not a godly one, and He was not moved. Then for those carnal-minded sons of corruption, to say Jesus had a love affair like any sinful man is not only disgusting, but they will also pay eternally in the lake of fire for making such declarations—that is, if you do not repent and turn to Christ in forgiveness. This is said, for whoever confesses Jesus Christ was like all man and was not God. It is also a blasphemy to speak sacrilegiously against the God BEING's testimony of His Son (Himself). They who speak such, are, as the apostle John said, *Antichrist* (1 John 4:2–3; John 1:7). Jesus of Nazareth has a human body (*now glorified in flesh and bone*), and His original spirit/soul or image and likeness of the *Word God* as we are a copy of His spirit/soul from the God BEING. Scripture testifies of God, saying, **"You are 'gods.' You are all sons of the Most-High** [*knowing of our fallen condition, it is said*]**, but you will die like mere mortals."** God Jesus also pointed to this as a legal matter: **"Jesus answered them, 'Is it not written in your law? I said, "You are gods"** (**and the Scripture cannot be undone** *or* **annulled or broken)'"** (Ps. 82:6–7; John 10:34–35). These are the basis of our faith that Jesus Christ is completely God and completely man. His humanity is as important to us as His deity, for He made us part of the God BEING that He is, but without the attributes until He transforms our body into His glorified form. This doctrine is way most important for us, as people in this fallen condition. It is imperative to know God Jesus did not come to condemn us but to save us from eternal death (*this evil age*) and fallen nature. He took our nature in the purity that it should have been in each one of us, without death from sin, and then sacrificed it all for all to redeem us all.

His Redeeming Word and Victory over the Evil One

His ministry started when the prophet John baptized Him in the Jordan river. Immediately, God the Holy Spirit came upon Him. Matthew wrote the testimony John the Baptist spoke of Jesus of Nazareth and of what happened after coming out of the river's water. He wrote:

> When He had been baptized, Jesus came up immediately from the water; and behold, the heavens were opened to Him, and He saw the Spirit of God descending like a dove and alighting upon Him. And suddenly a voice came from heaven, saying, "This is My beloved Son, in whom I am well pleased." (Matt. 3:16–17)

If you notice this testimony, it seems to have been said to Matthew by God Jesus (*at this stage, Jesus hadn't yet called the disciples*). Then He was taken in the power of the Spirit to the desert and fasted for forty days and nights. Afterward, Christ told the disciples what had happened at the desert retreat. He bound/tied the devil and came healing the sick; resurrecting the dead; casting out demons, binding their power, and plundering the empire of death. Mark the Evangelist (*in testimony of the apostle Peter*) explains what Jesus told the disciples: "**No one can enter a strong man's house and plunder his goods, unless he first binds the strong man. And then he will plunder his house**" (Mark 3:27; Heb. 2:14). The serpent, full of terror and deep hate, screamed through his seed (*tare*), saying, "**You see that you are accomplishing nothing. Look, the world has gone after Him!**" because Jesus had tied him up and was destroying his empire of death (John 12:19; Gen. 3:15). Then the evil one went and did what an irrational animal would do: he had evildoers (*his seed*) put Him in a cross and killed His body. This was all designed, foreseen, and programmed into reality by God in His covenant with man in Genesis (3:15) and was executed in verse 21, which the evil one did not get: "**And the Lord God made garments of skin for Adam and his wife, and clothed them,**" a sacrifice, for the Adams and their descendants, until the promise came (Gen. 3:21 NASB).

The salvation of men was to commence, and the condemnation of the evil one was to be fulfilled. One must understand that the evil one was created for a celestial environment (*just like all the angels*) with likeness to God. But this earth was created for creatures with the image and likeness of God, meaning that the evil one was out of nature and could not understand nor see the beauty of this creation. Neither did he understand the covenant God made with man in Eden. The Seed of the woman was to come one day, Christ, taking a body like ours. The apostle Paul wrote about Jesus before and after His victory, saying,

> For it pleased the *Father* for all the fullness [of deity—the sum total of His essence, all His perfection, powers, and attributes] to dwell [permanently] in Him (the Son), and through [the intervention of] the Son to reconcile all things to Himself, making peace [with believers] through the blood of His cross; through Him [I say], whether things on earth or things in heaven.

See how He suffered, not only in His human body but also in His spirit/soul, sacrificed to acquire our redemption and moral authority over the heavens (Col. 1:19–20 AMP). Jesus of Nazareth came to earth and took a body like ours to fulfill the atonement. Said in Genesis 3:15 (*which was established at the first divine summit*), everything started with Christ's (*foreordained*) priestly work: "He indeed was foreordained before the foundation of the world" (1 Pet. 1:20). The writer of Hebrews wrote:

> For, as we all know, He (Christ) does not take hold of [the fallen] angels [to give them a helping hand], but He does take hold of [the fallen] descendants of Abraham [extending to them His hand of deliverance (*must add Romans 4:16–17, 23-25, those of the faith*

in Christ are also descendants of the faith of Abraham, scripture states)]. **Therefore, it was essential that He had to be made like His brothers (mankind) in every respect, so that He might [by experience] become a merciful and faithful High Priest in things related to God, to make atonement (propitiation, *sacrifice, appeasement*) for the people's sins [thereby wiping away the sin, satisfying divine justice, and providing a way of reconciliation between God and mankind]. Because He Himself [in His humanity] has suffered in being tempted, He is able to help *and* provide immediate assistance to those who are being tempted *and* exposed to suffering.** (Heb. 2:16–18)

Jesus of Nazareth's temptation (*as the child born [Isa.9:6]*) had to be without using His divine power (*as the Son given [Phil. 2:5–7]*), which He did not use. He used Adam's first state of powers over creation and physical stamina. This was the plan of God for you who reads and for all humanity, those that would respond to His call as He made this a personal act, written by the prophets and psalmists (*it was all predestined*) and witnessed by the apostles who wrote the outcome of His victory (1 Pet. 1:12). Moses clearly wrote: **"The Lord your God will raise up for you a prophet like me [Moses] from among you, from your countrymen (brothers, brethren). You shall listen to him."** In other words, Moses told them about Messiah, that when He came, forget about what he (*Moses*) had said and listen to Him. But as we all know most of the Israelites of Jesus's days (*and thereafter*) on earth did not listen to Him (Deut. 18:15).

In Leviticus 23, Moses wrote about the solemn festivities, which were events clearly revealing the works of the Seed of the woman to come, but they did not get it. Not only because of their state of sin (*fallen nature*), but they were blinded by the evil one's lies, false doctrines. (*This has been happening to the church since birth and until today.*) Scripture shows that in the same process of blinding the word from the Israelites and humanity, the written word dumb blinded the evil one, for she was written for creatures with the image and likeness of the living God (*those that are chosen, born again, and this is also why Peter wrote:* "**Things into which angels long to look**" [*Eph. 1:4; 1 Pet. 1:12*]).

The prophets wrote in scripture that a soul that sinned would die, and the apostle Paul intuitively wrote: "**For the wages of sin is death**" (Rom. 6:23). The evil one had the empire of death wide open to his snares/traps to enslave men and women, for they were born already in sin. The Lord said, "**For the intent (strong inclination, desire) of man's heart is wicked from his youth,**" and you must understand, youth (*in the body*) starts once the embryo is conceived (Gen. 8:21). The psalmist, King David, wrote: "**I was brought forth in [a state of] wickedness; In sin my mother conceived me [and from my beginning I, too, was sinful]**" (Ps. 51:5). He also wrote: "**There is no one who does good, not even one**" (Ps. 14:3). Humanity lives in a sinful fallen nature.

Scripture also reveals: "**Indeed, there is not a righteous man on earth who *always* does good and who never sins**" (Eccles. 7:20). The apostle Paul, intuitively by the Holy Spirit, wrote: "**Since all have sinned and *continually* fall short of the glory of God.**" This is where our fallen nature is so obvious (Rom. 3:23). The apostle John also wrote in that understanding: "**We know [for a fact] that we are of God, and the whole world [around us] lies in the power of the evil one [opposing God and His precepts].**" No human person that has existed is saved by his/her owns works, for we are trapped under sin (*strapped bound*) and all humanity needs a redeemer (1 John 5:19 AMP). To those who will say the contrary, it is written: "**For no person will be justified [freed of guilt and** declared righteous] in His sight by [trying to do] the works of the Law. [*Those rituals were performed as a credit, until Christ appeared to pay the debt*]. For through the Law we become conscious of sin [and the recognition of sin directs us toward repentance but provides no remedy for sin]" (Rom. 3:20).

The evil one, not understanding God's covenant with man, put the Second Adam, who had no sin in the cross of Calvary and left His body lifeless. But he overstepped his boundary of the power of death, for by this act, he sinned against God's Word who committed no sin. Then we must ask: *If the wage of sin is death, then why did the evil one take the life of the Messiah, who not only was born with no sin but never committed one?* Jesus of Nazareth was born with the first Adam's initial nature—with no sin, innocent, and pure—as He took a body of bones, flesh, and blood like ours but with the first Adam's stamina (*nature*) in pure blood. This is also why He was the woman's Seed and not the seed of man stained in its blood with death's sin naturally. The judgment, condemnation, and destruction of the devil are seen clearly, joined to the victory Christ obtained for our sins (Heb. 2:14).

We must ask: if Christ had no sin in His blood and the wage of sin is death, who told the evil one he could harm Jesus's innocent body? Then the evil one sinned against God's Chosen into death, bringing all his empire into the lake of fire. We must add, this is also the same act with any principalities and powers of darkness when they come against a born again (*Spirit-filled*) believer by the written word. We have the right to bind, tie, plunder, and send them into hell until the day of judgment by the word of our God— that is, when they overstep God's word against us, for they will lose all their rights (*if they even have one*). Therefore, rebuke them, pray them into the burning hell until the Day of Judgment (Matt. 16:19). Paul rebuked a demonic spirit from a girl who kept annoying their life. He personally rebuked the demon, but when you pray to the Father in Jesus's name, He will do the rebuking

(Acts 16:16–34). We can research this in Scripture (explained in the author's *Apostles Methodology* book) as the next biblical verses show how our High Priest Jesus was taken up to heaven.

Then to Him Was Given

Jesus was taken up to heaven in a cloud: **"While they watched, He was taken up, and a cloud received Him out of their sight"** (Acts 1:9). Years before, Daniel saw this vision, a look into infinite time (*predestined*), and wrote:

> **I was watching in the night visions, And behold, *One* like the Son of Man, Coming with the clouds of heaven! He came to the Ancient of Days, And they brought Him near before Him. Then to Him was given dominion and glory and a kingdom, that all peoples, nations, and languages should serve Him. His dominion is an everlasting dominion, which shall not pass away, And His kingdom *the one* which shall not be destroyed.**

This was already set up (*foreordained*) by our God in His first divine, heavenly summit (Dan. 7:13–14). The disciples saw Jesus taken on a cloud; and Daniel, many years before, saw Him coming in a cloud to the Ancients of Days (*God's omniscient foresight and ordained future*). And it is said that He was brought near Him, not to Him, for there was something about to happen, a judgment in the events that had just transpired on earth at the Passover feast, which had moved God the Father into justified mercy for humanity. The prophet Zachariah was given to write about this future vision, and he wrote:

> Then he showed me Joshua [*in Hebrew and Greek, Joshua means Jesus; this vision is a metaphor/ symbolism*] the high priest standing before the Angel of the Lord [God the Holy Spirit] and Satan standing at his right hand to oppose him [*clearly a judgment on someone greater than a mere man*]. And the Lord said to Satan [*understand, the God BEING who said, "Let there be light," is now rebuking a creature created by Him*], "The LORD rebuke you, Satan! The Lord who has chosen Jerusalem [*and the church, as the body of Christ*] rebukes you! Is this not a brand plucked from the fire [*from a burning hell to come*]?" Now Joshua was clothed with filthy garments [*stained by the sin carried for humanity*] and was standing before the Angel [*and spoke to Him as a representative of humanity, as their High Priest*]. Then He answered and spoke to those who stood before Him, saying, "Take away the filthy garments from him." And to him He said, "See, I have removed your iniquity from you [*mortality*], and I will clothe you with rich robes [*immortality*] [a glorified body]." (Zech. 3:1–7)

Then this is where we can contemplate Daniel's words:

> Then to Him was given dominion and glory and a kingdom, That all peoples, nations, and languages should serve Him. His dominion is an everlasting dominion, Which shall not pass away, And His kingdom *the one* Which shall not be destroyed.

This has already started at Jesus's resurrection (Dan. 7:14). Looking at reality through the eyes of the God BEING, let us see His predestined future, like Daniel saw it and John in Revelation chapter 5 about the *sealed book* of the future that is about to happen. We must understand that for God, temporal time does not exist (*or means what it means to us*). He turned around and made all things a new creation, for us to come back to life as a holy nation. Peter wrote from Moses: "**But you are a chosen generation, a royal priesthood, a holy nation, His own special people, that you may proclaim the praises of Him who called you out of darkness into His marvelous light**" (1 Pet. 2:9; Exod. 19:6). It is also written: "**For the creation was subjected to futility, not willingly, but because of Him who subjected it in hope.**" Again, predestination, so let's understand: this decision took place at God's first divine, heavenly summit, for this is where God fell in love with man (*starting point of, John 3:16*) and created a new time portal to save His elect and punish His foes (Rom. 8:20). At this vision, we can say John was in proximity to Daniel, watching the same vision (*the same event of the future to us mortals, so that we can compare and understand the God BEING's nature and power*]. John was given to write:

> And I looked, and behold, in the midst of the throne and of the four living creatures, and in the midst of the elders, stood a Lamb as though it had been slain [*...he saw God's omniscient foresight of things*] Then He came and took the scroll out of the right hand of Him who sat on the throne [*...with the seven seals of predestined future events*] Now when He had taken the scroll, the four living creatures and the twenty-four elders fell down before the Lamb, each having a harp, and golden bowls full of incense, which are the prayers of the saints. And they sang a new song, saying: "You are worthy to take the scroll,

And to open its seals; For You were slain, And have redeemed us to God by Your blood Out of every tribe and tongue and people and nation.

This already began (vs. 12–14). John wrote: "I saw thrones on which were seated those who had been given authority to judge [...] Then I saw a great white throne and him [*Ancient of Days*] who was seated on it." In other words, John was not so far from Daniel when he saw all these (Rev. 20:4, 11). Continuing, John wrote:

Saying with a loud voice: "Worthy is the Lamb who was slain, to receive power and riches and wisdom, And strength and honor and glory and blessing!" And every creature which is in heaven and on the earth and under the earth and such as are in the sea, and all that are in them, I heard saying: "Blessing and honor and glory and power Be to Him who sits on the throne, And to the Lamb, forever and ever!" [*John saw by God's foresight the future of the Lamb*] Then the four living creatures said, "Amen!" And the twenty-four elders fell-down and worshiped Him who lives forever and ever."

The victory of Christ for humans must be celebrated eternally in the greatest celebration and worship by all the redeemed (Rev. 5:6–9). The apostle Paul beautifully wrote:

After He was found in [terms of His] outward appearance as a man [for a divinely appointed time], He humbled Himself [still further] by becoming obedient [to the Father] to the point of death, even death on a cross. For this reason also [because He

obeyed and so completely humbled Himself], God has highly exalted Him and bestowed on Him the name, which is above every name, so that at the name of Jesus every knee shall bow [in submission], of those who are in heaven and on earth and under the earth, and that every tongue will confess and openly acknowledge that Jesus Christ is Lord (sovereign God), to the glory of God the Father.

The victory of Christ Jesus is plain and factual for all of His elect (Phil. 2:8–11). In the middle of all that omni-power, the God BEING is so glorious, being so self-effacing, modest, inconspicuous. This scenario is humbly written in the pages of the Bible for us to see, for God is not one to divulge victory in a vulgar way but with delight and divinity for the love to His Name (Son) and the glory of His creation. God is love, and He gives all for all.

Then after contemplating the salvation of man, we can see the Lord turning to destroy His enemies with impunity and excessive abuse. My brothers and sisters, these are events that already happened in God's eternal time, and we must worship Him and rejoice as we contemplate them by God the Holy Spirit's living light realization unto our spirit/soul. It is written:

And you, being dead in your trespasses and the uncircumcision of your flesh, He has made alive together with Him, having forgiven you <u>all</u> <u>trespasses</u> [*this all must be applied as He is omnipresent*] having wiped out the handwriting of requirements that was against us [*the power of the law (1 Cor. 15:5; Eph. 2:15)*] which was contrary to us. And He has taken it out of the way, having nailed it to the cross [*by His word omnipotent power, signed as a legal document by His Son's blood*].

> Having disarmed principalities and powers, He made a public spectacle of them [*destroying the evil one*] triumphing over them in it [at the cross of all places]." (Col. 2:13–15; Heb. 2:14)

Jesus Christ is now, stated in scripture and known in the heavens, as the *image* and *substance* of the invisible living God (*in a body of flesh and bones*). It is written: "**For in Him all the fullness of Deity (the Godhead) dwells in bodily form [completely expressing the divine essence of God]**" (Col. 2:9). He has *all power* up in heaven and down in earth and *the keys* to "***Hades [Hell] and Death***," and He has been made by God the Father the *head of all principalities, powers, authorities, and all hosts of darkness in the regions of death*. He has dethroned, destroyed, plundered the office of the evil one; for the church is to stand above all of them in the heavenly places in Christ so that when they overstep the word of God, against us, we can plunder their powers/position (Col. 1:15–17; 1 Cor. 15:55–57; Phil. 2:9–11). It is written: "**And raised *us* up together and made *us* sit together in the heavenly *places* in Christ Jesus, that in the ages to come He might show the exceeding riches of His grace in *His* kindness toward us in Christ Jesus**" and "**On this rock [Word] I will build My church; and the gates of Hades (death) will not overpower it.**" This word you are reading right now (Eph. 2:6–7; Matt. 16:18 AMP), do not let anyone fool you, for this has been written, intervened by the omnipotent power of God (*by His word*). And from the first century, this has been taking place for two thousand years now. Christ has been building His church. Therefore, it is said of her:

> [For God's] intent that now the manifold wisdom of God might be made known by the church to the principalities and powers in the heavenly *places* [*as they overstep God's word against us*] according to

the eternal purpose which He accomplished in Christ Jesus our Lord.

And this power is the power of His resurrection, do not let any demons overstep their boundaries in scripture against you (Eph. 3:10). Our fears must only be upon the fear of the LORD, our God.

A Foresight in Scripture of Christ's Victory

Unfolding some of the deep things of scriptures through systematic theology, we can notice that as we know and understand the God BEING (*by His attributes, absolutes, and character*), everything has been wrapped up by Them in Their [*DHS*] first divine heavenly summit since before the foundation of all creation (1 Pet. 1:20; John 3:16). It is written: "**The secret things belong to the Lord our God, but the things revealed belong to us and to our sons forever.**" Therefore, there are things we must know from Scriptures and others to leave them alone until (Deut. 29:29). We must understand, as we think and meditate in scripture, death did not exist until Adam's sin. God foresaw the rebellion of the angelic creation before they were created and that of man.

Scripture states, "**God does not trust his angels; he blames them for mistakes**" (Job 4:18 NCV). The angels were created knowing good and evil, and they are eternal. They could not die, and death did not exist. When a third of the millions of millions of angels rebelled, they were bound in chains of darkness until God dealt with their leader, scripture shows. It is written: "**And [the] angels who did not keep their own domain but abandoned their proper dwelling place, *these* He has kept in eternal restraints under darkness for the judgment of the great day**" (Jude 1:6).

God did not need to forgive man, for it is stated: "**For if God did not spare the angels who sinned,**" but He decided to use this heinous, abominable (*aberration*) situation for the glory of His Name (Word/Son) (2 Pet. 2:4). It might seem this (*death*) was predetermined, but it was not. For God paid dearly afterward on what He was about to do, and so death became a thing until the evil one, by death through sin, had humanity strapped in a *death time zone*, or this *evil age* as Paul calls it. And all things became bound and strapped in it, even the evil one, for he became the god of this world. But the God BEING saw and used this situation for His glory. Scripture states that after his defeat of Adam, "**the god of this world has blinded the minds of the unbelieving, so that they will not see the light of the gospel of the [victory] glory of Christ, who is the image of God.**" The wide path is where we were all walking until Christ made the narrow path for His born-again believers (2 Cor. 4:4).

Therefore, it is said of all humanity and God the Potter: "**He made from one man every nation of mankind to live on all the face of the earth** [*through conception*] **having determined their appointed times and the boundaries of their habitation** [*that is, vessels of honor and of wrath (Rom. 9:21–23)*]." And after the sin of Adam, every person (*vessel*) has been destined by God's omnipotent BEING and sovereign right to live by His predestined existence everyday of their life. It is also said: "**Your eyes have seen my formless substance; And in Your book were written All the days that were ordained *for* me, When as yet there was not one of them.**" The apostle Paul explains this argument to the Romans, chapter 9 (Acts 17:26; Ps. 139:16 NASB). It is also revealed:

For it was fitting for God [that is, an act worthy of His divine nature] that He, for whose sake are all things, and through whom are all things [*here we see His decision*] in bringing many sons to glory, should make the author and founder of their salvation [*Jesus of Nazareth*] perfect through suffering [bringing to maturity the human experience necessary for Him to be perfectly equipped for His office as High Priest].

The God BEING saw the outcome in Their first heavenly summit (Heb. 2:10 AMP). Now death was not a part of God's creation, but He had ordained it until Adams sinned (*disobeyed his pact with God*), then death came into existence. The evil one, taking advantage (*in a moment of weakness, the Adams were not a complete product*), stole from Adam his world as he (*the evil one*) set them up to sin, and (*as he stole*) he was charged with all the ins and outs of earth creation, including their new condition—death. He knew it but did not understand the ins and out of it because he is not a creature of this creation. It is written what he said for us to understand: "**The devil said to Jesus, 'I will give you all these kingdoms and all their power and glory. It has all been given to me [*lie, he swindled it*] and I can give it to anyone I wish.'**" Again, he was bound (Luke 4:6; Gen. 3:14).

When the evil one sinned against the Chosen One of God by killing the body of Christ who had no sin in this reality's earthly plain. He fell in the mire of sin he crafted for Adam. For on this earth, the wage of sin is death. The evil one is now charged, judged, condemned, and destroyed with all his (*followers as well*) fallen angels, tares, and goats into the death Adam brought into existence (Heb. 2:14; Rev. 12:7–9).

The God B<small>EING</small>, as it is written, "**made a public spectacle of them [...that is], the devil and his principalities, powers, rulers, and forces of darkness**" (Eph. 6:12). The devil was actually destroyed, as scripture states, "**Since these children are people with physical bodies, Jesus himself became like them. He did this so that, by dying, he could destroy the one who has the power of death—the devil.**" The devil has been destroyed, made powerless (*to* destroy *is to reduce something to nothingness or to take away its powers and functions, so that restoration is impossible*).

Scripture states "*destroy*" *the devil,* which blinds people from knowing the truth, but scripture is bold (Heb. 2:14 NCV). The evil one has been charged with all the sins of the fallen angels; and man (*and their aberration, tare/goats*), being him the cause of all rebellion, is now going to be executed (*he already was/has been predestined*) into the lake of fire created for him and his angels and all his human offspring, tares/goats established at the first divine, heavenly summit before creation (Matt. 25:41; Rev. 17:8).

This means that in him, all the fallen angels also lost their eternity as they became subjected to death by the act of the evil one (*whom they had followed*) as he dared execute a sinless man, *the Seed of the woman,* at the cross of Calvary. Scriptures explain of these last creatures (*tares and goats*) that they are of a different nature on earth. It is written: "**The Nephilim were on the earth in those days and, also later. That was when the sons of God [***fallen angels***] had sexual relations with the daughters of human beings. These women gave birth to children, who became famous and were the mighty warriors of long ago,**" still unto today, and if they are not offspring of the first Adam, then they don't have a soul/spirit but an abomination (*called demon*) coming out of them when they die (Gen. 6:4 NCV). God Jesus spoke of them, saying,

> **The kingdom of heaven is like a man who planted good seeds in his field. That night, when everyone**

was asleep, his enemy came and planted weeds [tare] among the wheat and then left [*to the God* BEING, *this is a true story and God Jesus is the truth*]. Later, the wheat sprouted, and the heads of grain grew, but the weeds also grew. Then the man's servants came to him [angels] and said, "You planted good seed in your field. Where did the weeds come from?" The man answered, "An enemy planted the weeds.' The servants asked, "Do you want us to pull up the weeds?" The man answered, "No, because when you pull up the weeds, you might also pull up the wheat. Let the weeds and the wheat grow together until the harvest time. At harvest time I will tell the workers, 'First gather the weeds and tie them together to be burned [*God knows where every one of them are (Ps. 147:4)*]. Then gather the wheat and bring it to my barn.'" (Matt. 13:24–30 NCV)

God Jesus, in another teaching, told His disciples:

The Son of Man will come again in his great glory, with all his angels. He will be King [sovereign] and sit on his great throne. All the nations of the world will be gathered before him, and he will separate them into two groups as a shepherd separates the sheep from the goats. The Son of Man will put the sheep on his right and the goats on his left. [...and] Then the King will say to those on his left, "Go away from me. You will be punished. Go into the fire that burns forever that was prepared for the devil and his angels."

The victory of Christ over His enemies is predetermined. They cannot escape it, and we must not fear any of them (Matt. 25:31–33, 41).

Therefore, it has been predestined in scripture that Michael the Archangel, whose angelic rank is lower than the evil one used to have (*a covering cherub*) now after being destroyed by Christ, he is thrown/kicked out of heaven into earth with all the fallen angels as the church has been taken up to heaven to the City of Light (Rev. 12). It is written: "**The stars in the sky fell to earth** [*which were bound in darkness (Rev. 18:1–2)*] **as figs drop from a fig tree when shaken by a strong wind**" (Rev. 6:13). Then seven years after this, another event, also predetermined, will happen.

A regular-ranking angel is going to knockout the dragon (*he will put up a fight but to no avail*) and tie him in chains, seal his mouth, and throw him into hell for one thousand years (Rev. 20:1–3). He has gone from bad to worse for his rebellious atrocity that he started and has been condemned, as he dared to say, "**You told yourself, 'I will go up to heaven. I will put my throne above God's stars. I will sit on the mountain of the gods, on the slopes of the sacred mountain. I will go up above the tops of the clouds. I will be like God Most High.' But you were brought down to the grave, to the deep places where the dead are**" (Isa. 14:13–15 NCV). He has been destroyed by Christ, kicked out of heaven by Michael, and will be (*silly slapped*) beaten up by an angel (*not the higher rank*) in heaven. It's like all God's angels lined up to take a lick at the one who destroyed their heavenly realm.

Answer the questions from this chapter to interact with others in a book club:

1. Who is Jesus of Nazareth today, and what were the reasons for Him to build a church?

2. As we observe reality through the eyes of God, according to His written word, what is the new condition for humanity on earth to enter heaven?

3. How did Christ destroy the empire of death and its leader? Explain what seems to have been the outer reason and the outcome of his destruction.

For we are members of His body, of His flesh and of His bones.

—Ephesians 5:30

FOURTH LESSON

Understanding the Church: Worship, Edification into Evangelism

The nature of the church is visible, invisible, local, and worldwide. The church is a spiritual community of believers born again by the faith produced on the merits of the blood shed by Christ. It is written, **"The solid foundation of God stands, having this seal: 'The Lord knows those who are His.'"** This community is founded by the God BEING, and They know (you) who their elect before the foundation of the world are—that is, since Their first heavenly, divine summit (2 Tim. 2:19; Eph. 1:4). The apostle Paul wrote about God Jesus work in the church, saying, **"Christ also loved the church and gave Himself for her."** He gave Himself into death to redeem us (Eph. 5:25). The apostle Paul said how, in scripture, it was foreseeing and wrote:

So understand that it is the people who live by faith [with confidence in the power and goodness of God] who are [the true] sons of Abraham. The Scripture, foreseeing [*forecast, anticipate beforehand*] that God would justify the Gentiles by faith, proclaimed the good news [of the Savior] to Abraham in advance [with this promise], *saying*, "In you shall all the nations be blessed." So then, those who are people of faith [whether Jew or Gentile] are blessed *and* favored by God [and declared free of the guilt of sin and its penalty and placed in right standing with Him] along with Abraham, the believer. (Gal. 3:7–9)

The plan of God the Father is so immense and personal that He exalted Jesus Christ to the highest position and has elevated the members of His body the church with Him, through the highest, over the top of creation, from the moment He saved us in Christ. And the reason is that "**He might show the exceeding riches** [*this is over the top; this is talking about the One who created and possess all riches*] **of His grace in** *His* **kindness toward us in Christ Jesus**." The redemptive plan is by God the Father. The God BEING has made it a personal endeavor to trim the life of each member of His body to encounter the highest riches of His abundance in Christ toward us, Himself, for He wants to meet with us personally. This is why it is written that "**[The Father] raised** *us* **up together and made us sit together in the heavenly** *places* **in Christ Jesus** [*...not with but in Christ, as a member of His body*] **And He put all** *things* **under His feet and gave Him** *to be* **head over all** *things* **to the church, which is His body, the fullness of Him who fills all in all**." This is an amazing plan from God, and though we might not understand all of it, to be part of it is an exciting proposition on His behalf for each one of us. We will meet Him as part of His Son's bride (Eph. 2:6–7, 1:22–23; Rev. 19:7–8). Fear not, it's going to happen in a transformed existence.

The word *ekklesia* derives from the Greek language and signifies the same as in Hebrew *qahal* (*assembly or congregation*) of people with one purpose: to worship the LORD. God told Moses, **"Gather the people to Me, and I will let them hear My words, that they may learn to fear Me all the days they live on the earth, and *that*they may teach their children."** This is the same as gather to worship and hear to edify their life and pass it on, evangelism (Deut. 4:10).

This purpose is the same as what the prophets and psalmists said about the work Jesus of Nazareth (Messiah) was to do with His chosen, and He gave a special touch to it by saying, **"[Upon] this rock [*His written word*] I will build My church, and the gates of Hades [or Death] shall not prevail against it."** Then we speak this word daily. Scripture teaches that this rock is God Himself, and this is who scripture speaks about: **"Is there a God besides Me? Indeed *there is*no other Rock; I know not one,"** the God/Word of the God BEING (Matt. 16:18; Isa. 44:8). The plan of Christ with His church is the same as that in the Old Covenant by God the Father with the people of Israel (*which He was not able to completely do with them, of reaching humanity for His Son's purpose*), that of "***Gather the people [...] to learn, to fear and to worship.***" But it is said to the church: **"[For God's] intent [is] that now the manifold wisdom of God might be made known by the church to the principalities and powers in the heavenly *places*."**

The members of the church are made born again/sealed and placed in a position of authority against God's enemies as a new man and woman, said through scriptures. We are the body of Christ (Eph. 3:10; John 1:11–12). The church member tells the enemy what to do, not the other way around, for once they overstep (*God's word, that is our rights written in scripture*) by attacking and hindering our godly purpose in Christ. They are out of character and into our hands to plunder their riches (*which are really ours in Christ; my advice, pray them into hell where they cannot hinder any of us or humanity any longer*). In other words, they belong to us, to do as scripture states, and in God Jesus's words: "**I will give you the keys of the kingdom of heaven; the things you don't allow on earth will be the things that God does not allow, and the things you allow on earth will be the things that God allows**" (Matt. 16:19, 18:18, 22; John 20:23).

Then the kingdom of God began as the kingdom of heaven "happened" by Christ's priestly works, as it is written: "**So that, by dying, he could destroy the one who has the power of death— the devil.**" The Spanish version (RV 1960) says, "**Para destruir** [*to destroy*] **por medio de la muerte** [*through death*] **al que tenía el imperio de la muerte** [*he who had the empire of death*] **esto es, al diablo.**" The second Adam (Christ) died as an innocent, no stain of sin, holy man, and destroyed by death the evil one, who now stands with no character of truth in his accusations against humanity because he sinned against the Anointed One of God. Therefore, everything started at Jesus's death on Calvary (Heb. 2:14).

After He resurrected, He started to create an assembly of Jews and Gentiles as a new people. Scripture states, "**There is neither Jew nor Greek […] there is neither male nor female; for you are all one in Christ Jesus.**" The members of God Jesus' body are a holy nation by God's will. Christ cut a deal with God the Father for us (Gal. 3:28; 1 Pet. 2:9–10). The apostle Paul explains it, saying, "**Now to a laborer, his wages are not credited as a favor *or* a gift, but as an obligation [something owed to him].**" The Second Adam placed God the Father in debt by His laborer on earth fulfilling the Leviticus law, all of it and more, for He was obedient unto death and death at a Cross, innocently. The God

BEING owed Him, and He cut a deal with God on our behalf (Rom. 4:4). This is the truth of the gospel; take it or leave it.

When Christ Jesus started to preach His good news, Matthew said, "**Jesus began to preach and to say, 'Repent, for the kingdom of heaven is at hand.'**" This is when the kingdom of heaven began (Matt. 4:17). The Second Adam (Jesus of Nazareth) was assuring that through His preaching, the defeat of the evil one had started, for in a sublime way, He had started the war against the enemy's forces. He would say, "**But if I cast out demons** [*the forces that tied people by their sin into guilt*] **by the Spirit of God, surely the kingdom of God has come upon you,**" a work of the church afterward. Christ also taught them about those forces, how He did the work of casting them: "**How can anyone go into a strong man's house and steal his property unless he first overpowers *and* ties up the strong man? Then he will ransack *and* rob his house,**" which He did at His forty-day fasting in the desert (Matt. 12:28–29; Luke 4).

The prophets had taught the Israelites, the kingdom of God was the destruction to be manifested on earth; and Jesus of Nazareth was teaching that first, He had to extinguish, shutdown, destroy His adversary's empire, as the prophets said, "**And you, son of man, thus says the Lord God to the land of Israel: 'An end! The end has come upon the four corners of the land.'**" And that end was to start with the destruction of the empire of death and its leader (Ezek. 7:2). It was taught to them: "'**Not by might nor by power, but by My Spirit,' says the Lord of hosts,**" a spiritual aspect that they (Israelites) did not seem to understand (Zech. 4:6). This mystery was later disclosed by the apostles for God was to include His salvation for the Gentiles. Paul wrote by God's inspiration:

> **At that time you were without Christ, being aliens from the commonwealth** [*an independent country or community joined into a kingdom, like Puerto Rico*

and the US of A today] of Israel and strangers from the covenants of promise, having no hope and without God in the world. But now in Christ Jesus you who once were far off have been brought near by the blood of Christ [*as New Jerusalenians*]. For He Himself is our peace, who has made both one, and has broken down the middle wall of separation, having abolished in His flesh the enmity, that is, the law of commandments [*ten*] contained in ordinances [*some 316, plus those added in the Jewish Talmud, which are cancel/abolished*] so as to create in Himself one new man from the two [*in the order of Melchizedek*] *thus* making peace, and that He might reconcile them both to God in one body through the cross, thereby putting to death the enmity [*none of them are worthy*]. And He came and preached peace to you who were far off and to those who were near. For through Him we both have access by one Spirit to the Father.

This is the plan of God Jesus for His church for two thousand years now (Eph. 2:12–19; Hos. 6:2). This started four days (*or four thousand years*) after creation (*second week in God's calendar*) and marked by the year of God Jesus's death and resurrection (*year 28, 30 or 33?*), and we are at the end of the two thousand years after. The seventh day after creation is God's rest (Shabbat), a millennium in scripture, and is about to happen again (*we are living in God's calendar*). Remember what the God BEING said, "*I am* God, and *there is* none like Me, Declaring the end from the beginning, And from ancient times *things* that are not *yet* done." This is what the written word of God reveals as she sanctifies us in its truth. His word is truth (Isa. 46:9–10).

The apostles taught what God Jesus told them, that He would move among us always, even until the end of the age; and they wrote: "**All that Jesus began both to do and teach.**" They wrote this after His resurrection, for this is Christ's ministry, and we are just collaborators. They said, "**The Lord added to the church daily those who were being saved.**" Even today, salvation is of the Lord as was then: "**I, [only] I, am the Lord, and there is no Savior besides Me**" (Acts1:1, 2:47; Isa. 43:11; Hab. 3:2). This was no different from what was taught by the prophet Hosea (*and his personal life*) about the people of Israel's infidelity. Apart from that, they did not all receive their Messiah Jesus of Nazareth when He showed up, and he wrote: "**After two days He will revive us** [same *as Paul (Rom.11:25–27 and Zech. 11:10 RSV)*]. **On the third day He will raise us up, that we may live in His sight**" (Hos. 6:2; John 14:1–4). It has been two thousand years now since God Jesus resurrected and has been healing, reviving people into His church (*generation after generation*). Daniel did not understand this and asked,

> Although I heard, I did not understand. Then I said, "My lord, what *shall be* the end of these things?" And he said, "Go *your* way, Daniel, for the words *are* closed up and sealed till the time of the end. Many shall be purified, made white, and refined [*the church mystery*] but the wicked shall do wickedly; and none of the wicked shall understand, but the wise shall understand. (Dan.12:8–10)

In His days on earth, Christ Jesus referred to this prophecy about Israel and said, "**And they will fall by the edge of the sword and be led away captive into all nations. And Jerusalem will be trampled by Gentiles until the times of the Gentiles are fulfilled**" (Luke 21:24). The prophet Zechariah (11:10 RSV) wrote: "**And I took my staff Grace, and I broke it, annulling the covenant which**

I had made with all the peoples." But God never made a covenant with the people or the nation, as other versions express, until John (1:11–12), who said: "He came to his own home, and his own people received him not. But to all who received him, who believed in his name, he gave power to become children of God." The apostle Paul taught this very thing. This is a great sign for those who are getting ready: "I do not want you, believers, to be unaware of this mystery [God's previously hidden plan]—so that you will not be wise in your own opinion—that a partial hardening has [temporarily] happened to Israel [to last] until the full number of the Gentiles has come in," into the invisible church of God (Rom. 11:25; Zech. 11:10; John 1:11–12).

The church of Jesus Christ has been constructed for the same purpose said by the prophets: to *fear, learn,* and *worship* God. This purpose was determined by the God BEING in their first divine, heavenly summit, and it was with a great sacrifice on His behalf but necessary, as the writer of Hebrews explains, "**Just as He chose us in Him before the foundation of the world** [*just remember, He chose us (John 15:16)*] **that we should be holy and without blame before Him in love, having predestined us** [*God's word is also omnipotent; God changes things by it*] **to adoption as sons by Jesus Christ to Himself, according to the good pleasure of His will**" [*...Paul said*] "**He did this** [**the Father**] **through Christ's death in the body** [**a payment**] **so that he might bring you into God's presence as people** [*sanctification by position*] **who are holy, with no wrong, and with nothing of which God can judge you guilty**" [*...and Peter adds*] "**But with the precious blood of Christ, as of a lamb without blemish and without spot. He indeed was foreordained before the foundation of the world** [*at Their first divine, heavenly summit*] **but was manifest in these last times for you**" [*...and John wrote*] "**For God so** [**greatly**] **loved and dearly prized the world** [**before He created us, at His first divine summit to this respect**]**that He** [**even**] **gave His** [**Only Son, the One who is** truly unique, the only one of His kind] only begotten Son, so that whoever believes *and* trusts in Him [as Savior] shall not perish, but have eternal life" (Eph. 1:4–5; Col. 1:22; 1 Pet 1:19–20; John 3:16). The Hebrew writer explains,

> Jesus, who was made a little lower than the angels, for the suffering of death crowned with glory and honor, that He, by the grace of God, might taste death for everyone [*the* God BEING *became the main actor of His reality's script and screenplay*]. For it was fitting for Him, for whom are all things and by whom are all things, in bringing many sons to glory, to make the captain of their salvation perfect through sufferings [*this gives us significance, for us to live eternally*]. For both He who sanctifies and those who are being sanctified are all of one, for which reason He is not ashamed to call them brethren, saying: "I will declare Your name to My brethren; In the midst of the assembly, I will sing praise to You."

How glorious that day will be when Jesus will sing His praises to the Father. The apostle Paul also referred to the redemptive work of Jesus and said,

> Let this mind be in you which was also in Christ Jesus, who, being in the form of God, did not consider it robbery [advantage] to be equal with God, but made Himself of no reputation, taking the form of a bondservant, *and* coming in the likeness of men. And being found in appearance as a man, He humbled Himself and became obedient to *the point of* death, even the death of the cross. Therefore, God

also has highly exalted Him and given Him the name which is above every name.

Therefore, the church must study, understanding God Jesus, for in Him we are also elevated to His glorious grace that we may be with Him wherever He will be. He said so (Phil. 2:5–9; John 14:1–3). And He lives in God's invisible reality above the heavens.

Jesus Christ is constructing His church in His merits, and the writers of scripture were shown to use an anthropomorphic language to describe her spiritual construct. We see this with the use of words in scripture to compare us (*in unity with Him*) such as *branches* (John 15:2) or *temple* (*not tabernacle, for a temple is in place, stable, constructed on a permanent surface*) (1 Cor. 6:19–20) or *as His human body* that has members (Eph. 1:22–23) or *sons and daughters* (2 Cor. 6:18) or a *spouse* (Rev. 19:1–9). These are words used to teach members of the invisible church that they are spiritually alive in God's invisible reality, based on God the Father's will (John 4:24). God is Spirit, and scripture says, **"Nevertheless the solid foundation of God stands, having this seal: 'The Lord knows those who are His.'"** This is sanctification by position, for it is God who separates us (*in His sovereign right [Rom.9:15]*) by His living light/anointing in us (2 Tim. 2:19).

As the wife of Christ, the church is a family of the divine family (*the I AM, the Word and the Spirit*). She is a daughter-in-law (Eph. 5:31–32). God Jesus prayed this prayer: **"That they also may be one in Us [...] And the glory which You gave Me** [*the Holy Spirit promise*] **I have given them, that they may be one just as We are one,"** the most intimate desire of Jesus Christ for the church (John 17:21–22). God knows us, for in His greatness, He says, **"Lift up your eyes on high, and see who has created these *things*, Who brings out their host by number; He calls them all by name, By the greatness of *His* might And the strength of His power; Not** one is missing." He knows all His creation and says of us: "**But the very hairs of your head are all numbered**" (Isa. 40:26; Matt. 10:30). The God BEING oversees all realities. He is omniscient, omnipresent, and an omnipotent BEING; but God Jesus gives it a touch of intimacy by saying of His body the church: "**That where I am, *there*you may be also**" (John 14:3). God Jesus elevates our relationship with God the Father over the top. This intimacy is very clear in the purpose He declares for us:

> **He who overcomes** [*this statement is on the continuity of scripture topic of redemption by faith, it is not a wonder who*] **I will make him a pillar in the temple of My God, and he shall go out no more** [*our permanent home is God's invisible reality*]. **I will write on him the name of My God and the name of the city of My God** [*the doors to God's invisible reality*], **the New Jerusalem, which comes down out of heaven <u>from</u> My God. And *I will write on him* My new name.**

Because of this, He gives us responsibilities, authority, and purpose (Rev. 3:12). He/she who overcomes it by the faith/hope in God Jesus's words. It's about Him. This is His prayer to the Father, and it will not be denied: "**That they all may be one; just as You, Father, are in Me and I in You, that they also may be one in Us.**" He is the one that saves, and again, this is sanctification by position, God Jesus said so (John 17:21). And His prayer will not be denied (Jn.17).

The apostle Paul explains how we must see the visible church and says, "**To the church of God which is at Corinth**" (1 Cor. 1:2), "**To all the saints in Christ Jesus who are in Philippi**" (Phil. 1:1), "**The churches of Asia**" (1 Cor. 16:19), "**The church that is in their house**" (Acts 9:31), "**The churches throughout all Judea, Galilee,** and Samaria." In other words, the churches in its beginning by houses, towns, regions, and nations. When the members of the body of God Jesus congregate, they become a church, not only in a temple but also in their houses and wherever in the world as they come together; for they are God's temple.

God Jesus said, "**For where two or three are gathered together in My name, <u>I am there</u>, in the midst of them.**" He meant in person (*not thinking of or looking to but there*), and He also said, "**Lo, I am with you always, *even* to the end of the age.**" The Lord does not leave His chosen, for those who He calls, He also seals and baptizes with His Holy Spirit (Matt. 18:20, 28:20; Rom. 8:29–30). Then the church of God Jesus is local and worldwide. There are also infidels among them (tares/goats), and He said, "**Let them grow together until the harvest**" and "**Satan himself masquerades as an angel of light. […] His servants also masquerade as servants of righteousness.**" And so this is even among ministers like the disciple Judas (Matt. 13:30; 2 Cor. 11:14–15). God knows who they are as they use the word of God mostly for condemnation, greed, and self-gloat (Jude 1:17–23).

God sees us as His temple. Let us increment the perception of how our Omni-God moves among our unity as a body. The apostle Paul points out how we must conduct ourselves, saying, "*I write* so **that you may know how you ought to conduct yourself in the house of God, which is the church of the living God, the pillar and ground of the truth**" (1 Tim. 3:15; Rom. 9:25). Paul told the Philippians: "**For we are the circumcision, who worship God in the Spirit, rejoice in Christ Jesus, and have no confidence in the flesh**" (Phil. 3:3). We are called to be collaborators in the ministry of Christ with all believers in the power of God's Holy Spirit, which are in this world, with the words of life from scripture. The apostles taught us that there are three pillars of truth we must uphold; and they are *worship, edification,* and *evangelism,* until we are called by God Jesus to the City of Light. There is no greater motive/calling.

The Apostles Theology Prepares Us for the Apostles Eschatology

The believer must understand how and why God Jesus built His church and for what purpose for it is Him preparing us. Peter wrote: **"Like living stones be yourselves <u>built</u> into a spiritual house, to be a holy priesthood, to offer spiritual sacrifices acceptable to God through Jesus Christ."** We are being built, and we must let ourselves be built here on earth. This is for now, for once transformed, it is a natural thing (1 Pet. 2:5). Peter asks *to offer spiritual sacrifice,* and the Hebrew writer explains how: **"Let us continually offer to God a sacrifice of praise—the fruit of lips [***this is worship***] that openly profess his name."** This is also why we built our spiritual house, for living in darkness has no fruits from your lips (Heb. 13:15; James 2:18). The psalmist proclaimed, **"Give unto the Lord the glory due to His name; worship the Lord in the beauty of holiness."** So it is in the beauty of holiness, we give unto the LORD. This also gives us the authority of truth to move forward (Ps. 29:2). Then let us never forget, it has been Christ, the builder of the church, who said, **"And the gates of Hades shall not prevail against it"** (Matt. 16:18). God Jesus is the one who sacrificed His life for all of us to have this position. This was the plan of God the Father, who has inspired us through His word by the testimony He spoke of His Son. Through it, He has shown us our present situation, fallen but in victory by faith, (*beforehand/predestined [Rev. 5])* God's future events about to happen. They are the times we are living right now (Rev. 1–3). We are being taken out, by the hope in His Son's promises, and unto the place God Jesus went to prepare for us. The apostle John wrote these words of Christ:

> **Let not your heart be troubled; you believe in God, believe also in Me** [*faith*]. **In My Father's house are many mansions; if it were not so, I would have told you. I go to prepare a place for you** [*hope*]. **And if I go and prepare a place for you, I will come again and receive you to Myself** [*love*]. See how these three are produce by His word—that is, faith, hope, into love [*The words in these verses speak about a snatching away (rapture), a relocation, for all believers, and a second coming, by mouth of God Jesus*], **that where I am, there you may be also. And where I go you know** [God's invisible reality (Heb. 6:20)] **and the way you know.**

He said, "I AM the Way" (John 14:1–4, 16:10). John also wrote of Jesus, saying, "**However, when He, the Spirit of truth, has come, He will guide you into all truth; for He will not speak on His own *authority*, but whatever He hears He will speak; and He will tell you things to come.**" By Him, we can understand the eschatological language in scripture (John 16:13). God Jesus wants for each of us to know the present and the future events individually, to have our hands on the plow (*to dig into, turning the bad soil out of our lives*). In other words, living according to the apostolic theology/tradition (Luke 9:26). The first thing the believer must do is to wear the armor of God. Therefore, we must understand Paul's metaphor of the armor. Let us contemplate those verses:

Stand therefore, having girded your waist with truth [*knowing God's word, John 17:17*]**, having put on the breastplate of righteousness** [*faith in the merits of Christ priestly works, Rom. 3:22*]**, and having shod your feet with the preparation of the gospel of peace** [*something clear to understand, share the good news, 2 Tim. 3:16*]**; above all, taking the shield of faith** [*in the merits of Christ*] **with which you will be able to quench all the fiery darts of the wicked one.** [*A dart doesn't kill a person; it's just meant to distract our purpose. We are not at war, for it has already been won and the battles have ceased. We are plundering the goods that belong to us in the first place (Gal. 5:22–24; Matt. 12:29).*] **And take the helmet of salvation** [*again, in Christ merits, Rom. 3:24*] **and the sword of the Spirit, which is the word of God** [*study and memorize her, Heb. 4:12–13*]**; praying always** [*the only physical act*] **with all prayer and supplication in the Spirit** [*the Spirit's gift evidence and citing the word*]**, being watchful to this end with all perseverance and supplication for all the saints.**

Pray for one another and watch for God's immediate answer (Eph. 6:14–18). These show the columns of the church stand: "*Worship, edification, and evangelism.*" We are ready to take the attack, instead of waiting for the struggle/wrestle from the enemy's forces: "*You plunder.*" And this is also why they will continue to frighten in their madness: "**The thief does not come except to steal, and to kill, and to destroy.**" Therefore, we use God's armor (*the Holy Spirit*) to attack back (John 10:10). It is done through wearing the armor of God—that is, God the Holy Spirit in our life, pleasing Him through the sound doctrine of the apostles and the intensive prayer in our life for each other and our future where God also resides. (We wrote about this in our book entitled *The Apostles Methodology to Interpret Scripture.*) Pastor James wrote about our personal struggles and said, "**Confess** *your* **trespasses to one another** [*as you can see, in the first century, strives among brethren existed*] **and pray for one another, that you may be healed** [*and they seemed to have been harsh*]**. The effective, fervent prayer of a righteous man avails much**" (James 5:16). The Lord knows about our interior personal struggles, and we must fix them, and it starts by the effective fervent prayer. The effective prayer changes even our future, for God lives in our future. Read how Peter wrote of it (1 Pet. 4:17).

Next to our daily prayers, the Holy Spirit intercedes with and for us: "**Likewise the Spirit also helps in our weaknesses. For we do not know what we should pray for as we ought, but the Spirit Himself makes intercession for us with groanings which cannot be uttered.**" This is speaking in tongues, and it is a gift (Rom. 8:26). Joined with prayers and the prayer in the Spirit, we also get prayers involved in our fasting but never as into buying anything from God. That would be tempting God as an extortion. We already get everything freely from Him. Scripture teaches: "**Do not be deceived, God is not mocked; for whatever a man sows, that he will also reap. For he who sows to his flesh will of the flesh reap corruption, but he who sows to the Spirit will of the Spirit reap everlasting life**" (Gal. 6:7–8). Paul said, "**If, in the manner of men, I have fought with beasts at Ephesus** [*false brethren...*] **besides the other things, what comes upon me daily: my deep concern for all the churches**" (1 Cor. 15:32; 2 Cor. 11:28).

As you can notice, Paul does not mention wars or physical battles because God Jesus already won the war, and the battles for our salvation have ceased. Paul mentions he fought in wrestles or struggles, which really means *to overcome, prevail, engage in deep thoughts, striving to trip or overthrow off balance an opponent, as to deal with a problem or difficulty, physical but mainly spiritual.* In the spiritual Christian realm, it is never about those forces killing their opponent. They don't have the authority, for even attacking us is overstepping the word of God. Therefore, even Job's life was spared. It's all in the hands of God. But in any circumstance, Paul wrote: **"For if we live, we live to the Lord; and if we die, we die to the Lord. Therefore, whether we live or die, we are of the Lord's."** Death has no power whatsoever over the Christian's spirit/soul (Rom. 14:8). Now understand that in this grace covenant, scripture says, **"Keep me as the apple of Your eye; Hide me under the shadow of Your wings [...and] For thus says the Lord of hosts [...] he who touches you touches the apple of His eye."** This is why we are also asked to learn about Him: **"Keep my commands and live, and my law as the apple of your eye [...and] What then shall we say to these things? If God is for us, who can be against us?"** Our victory is patented by the word of the God BEING, our Savior (Zech. 2:8; Ps. 17:8; Prov. 7:2; Rom. 8:31).

The apostle Paul points out: **"We do not wrestle against flesh and blood."** It is a spiritual struggle against invisible enemies (*not people*), which only, and only, God the Holy Spirit takes care of on our behalf. This is not a struggle against other human creatures (Eph. 6:12). Scripture says, **"'Not by might nor by power, but by my Spirit,' says the Lord Almighty"** (Zech. 4:6). The church is called to administer knowledge, letting the evil forces know God Jesus's powers: **"[For] now the manifold wisdom of God might be made known by the church** [*this would be quoting them the Word where we stand*] **to the principalities and powers in the heavenly places."** We already sit in Christ on top in heavenly places, (Eph. 3:10, 2:6). The apostles' theology prepares us for what's coming. *The apostle's eschatology,* foretold by God the Holy Spirit, is the end of all evil forces. This is the intention of God as we know the whole truth of what victory He has given us (*which victory was* *acquired by Christ*). We have the edge against the forces that have taken over (*hostage*) the whole human race and their society.

Sanctification by Position and Sanctification in Practice

The knowledge of the word of God, or theology, is the fuel that ignites our worship; for the word of God provokes us to believe in Him. And as we whole heartily do, we move the forces of evil by the power of God, the Holy Spirit, away from our life and living. The faith exercise as you hear the word of God (*which speaks about the priestly works of God Jesus*) elevates our worship, as we are touched by the divine knowledge realized in the spirit/soul. The word of God provokes us to believe in His love, forgiveness/justice, and mercy/sanctification, which gives us the power to stand in victory. It also induces physical and spiritual healings, miracles, and, of course, salvation from our eternal disorder in death; for now we can perceive, turn, and ordain according to His word our present and future existence. This happens because of God's prophecies and promises in His word for us. His word is the testament designed as a legal contract for humanity—those who receive, believing in the merits of Jesus Christ by the Father's proposition.

By the faith in His word, we are established into sanctification, and this is done by His will, His doing. He is the one saying we are justified, meaning good to go. Then justification is an act of God; and sanctification is a work of God, as He places us in the position of sons and daughters, complete, holy, and without stains. Scripture states, **"But as many as received Him, to**

them He gave the right to become children of God, to those who believe in His name" [...*this is a position proposed by God*] **"And you, who once were alienated and enemies in your mind by wicked works, yet now** [*here comes the act and work of God*] **He has reconciled in the body of His flesh through death, to present you holy, and blameless, and above reproach in His sight."**

This is sanctification by position (John 1:12; Col. 1:20–22; Eph. 2:10), as Paul was proclaiming this and all works out as you place your faith/hope in the works and merits of Jesus Christ, and he goes on to say, **"If indeed you continue in the faith, grounded and steadfast, and are not moved away from the hope of the gospel** [*grounded in the prophecies and promises, how can we not? It's by faith, not works*] **which you heard, which was preached to every creature under heaven, of which I, Paul, became a minister."** This condition is in the first faith when you accepted and (*was born again*) His gift, anointing (*which is perceptibly felt*), is irrevocable (*salvation also a gift, falls in that category [Rom. 11:29]*). There is no personal work or merits on that, but to continue to believe in the middle of this amnesty since works cannot save you (Col. 1:23; Eph. 2:8, 10). You must think, if no good works can save you, then bad works cannot get you lost, for it is only your faith/hope in Christ that cancels the wrath of God (*King David knew this truth and Paul wrote of them [Rom. 4:7 from Ps. 32:1]*), that is, for us to do the works prepared beforehand by Him (*which we also fail to do at times in this fallen nature*). God the Father's intent is to save you by the belief in the action taken for you by Christ. This is highly expressed to you in such a degree that rejecting God's testimony of His Son's priestly works is condemnable by eternal punishment. The apostle John assures, **"He who believes in the Son of God has the witness [anointing] in himself; he who does not believe God, has made Him a liar, because he has not believed the testimony that God [the Father] has given of His Son"** (1 John 5:10). Therefore, the believer is born again and sealed by God the

Holy Spirit and washed by the water (*which is the written word of God*), and that in the moment of your new conception, you are bought at the price of blood and you do not belong to yourself any longer. Jesus Christ, in His ministry on earth, said, "**Unless one is born of water** [word] **and the** [*Holy*] **Spirit, he cannot enter the kingdom of God.**" This is God's requisite to entering the kingdom, which act is done by God, not you. But by the faith/hope produced by His spoken word, for she provokes you to believe in Him, then immediately as He perceived it in your heart, He saves you eternally (John 3:5). The faith that the word produces has God's omnipotent power to save our spirit/soul from eternal condemnation: "**Therefore he** [Christ] **is able to save completely** [forever] **those who come to God through him, because he always lives to intercede** [**as High Priest in the order of Melchizedek**] **for them.**" It is written (Heb. 7:25). Our faith is now based on a High Priest from the tribe of Judah, that alone disowns the law and the Leviticus priesthood.

The apostle Paul established, by inspiration of God the Holy Spirit, about the church of Christ and the works done for her to be healed and ready to be snatched away. He wrote:

> [Jesus] **Christ also loved the church and gave Himself for her, that He might sanctify and cleanse her with the washing of water by the word** [*which cleansing are being obtained right now by the reading of His word, washing you, for she provokes you to believe*] **that He might present her to Himself a glorious church, not having spot or wrinkle or any such thing, but that she should be holy and without blemish.**

This, in theological term, is called *sanctification by position*, and this is an act and work of God through His Word/Spirit, (Eph. 5:25–27). Who can contradict that "**for God did not appoint us to** suffer wrath but to receive salvation through our Lord Jesus Christ?" This is the narrative of the apostle's theology (1 Thess. 5:9). It is God the Father who positions us by His grace powers (*obtained by Christ*) unto the gospel narrative, taking us out of the sinful world's storyline, which is being driven to a second death into a lake of fire. This is why John wrote from God to us: "[And] as many as received Him, to them He gave [*this is an act of God*] the right to become children of God [*a work of God*] to those who believe in His name [...*notice the next verse*] who were born, not of blood, nor of the will of the flesh, nor of the will of man, but of [the will of] God." By believing His word on His Son's testimony given through scripture, that makes us victorious (John 1:12–13). This simple fact is also given to a person by the writer of Hebrews, for scripture is provoking you to believe her spirit's truth: "**Faith is the assurance (title deed, confirmation) of things hoped for (divinely guaranteed), and the evidence of things not seen [the conviction of their reality—faith comprehends as fact what cannot be experienced by the physical senses] [...and] But without faith it is impossible to [*walk with the God* BEING *and*] please Him, for whoever comes [near] to God must [necessarily] believe that [*the*] God [*BEING*] exists and that He rewards those who [earnestly and diligently] seek Him**"—that is, following the faith in His words (Heb. 11:1, 6). This sanctification by position through your faith/hope in His written word advances you to walk into sanctification in practice. It just does, for the authority of truth (*wisdom*) becomes plain in your spirit/soul by His touch. Scripture states of sanctification in practice:

> **Wisdom will come into your heart, and knowledge will be pleasant to your soul; discretion will watch over you; understanding will guard you; delivering you from the way of evil, from men of perverted speech [*violent, bloodthirsty (also women)*] who forsake the paths of uprightness to walk in the ways**

of darkness, who rejoice in doing evil and delight in the perverseness of evil; men whose paths are crooked [*in vices*] and who are devious in their ways [*vessels prepare for wrath*]. You will be saved from the loose [*adulterous, married*] woman, from the adventuress [*strange woman*] with her smooth words [*as faith/hope in Christ's word calls you*]. (Prov. 2:10–16)

We all have heard: "*Tell me who you walk with, and I'll tell you who you are.*" Well, walking with God the Holy Spirit heals and transforms your inner self. This is no wonder why James said, "**Show me your faith without doing anything, and I will show you my faith by what I do,**" for faith produces the works prepared beforehand by God (James 2:18 NCV; Eph. 2:10). And this is where this has gone viral, for it is written: "**For we are His workmanship, created in Christ Jesus for good works, which God prepared beforehand** (*at His [DHS] divine heavenly summit*) **that we should walk in them.**" It is all in the anointing package received when we were saved again (Eph. 2:10). This has nothing to do with your works (*favor, good or bad*) or good pleasure but by the will and power of God encrusted in His word that produces/provokes us to believe.

It is said: "**For it is [not your strength, but it is] God who is effectively at work in you, both to will and to work [that is, strengthening, energizing, and creating in you the longing and the ability to fulfill your purpose] for His good pleasure.**" If you start by faith, let that faith produce the fruits of its vines, which is the gospel of Christ (the Vine) (Phil. 2:13 AMP). The apostle Paul was infuriated with the Galatians because of this and wrote to them: "**O foolish Galatians! Who has bewitched you, before whose eyes Jesus Christ was publicly portrayed as crucified? Let me ask you** only this: Did you receive the Spirit by works of the law, or by hearing with faith?" (Gal. 3:1–2).

The Word of God contains His attributes of omniscient, omnipresent, and omnipotent power to act through God the Holy Spirit in it as we walk by it. Scripture states: "**The things which are in agreement with sound doctrine [will produce men and women of good character whose lifestyle identifies them as true Christians** (*sanctification in practice*)]" (Titus 2:1). The fact to this truth is said to be: "**You were bought with a price [you were actually purchased with the precious blood of Jesus and made His own]. So then honor *and*glorify God with your body.**" This is something personal from our God to us and from us to our God (1 Cor. 6:20). It is because of erroneous doctrines you have doubts, then ask why. King David, in scriptures, wrote: "**Blessed *and*happy *and*favored are those whose lawless acts have been forgiven, and whose sins have been covered up *and*completely buried. Blessed and happy and favored is the man whose sin the Lord will not take into account *nor* charge against him.**"

This happens by continuing in the faith/hope honestly placed in Christ (Rom. 4:7–8; Ps. 32:1–2). King David had an adulterous affair, killed her husband (*abusing his power as king*), and spoke in denial to the prophet of God, until the word convicted him; and he understood he did not belong to himself but to the God BEING who called Him. Paul by the Spirit/Word wrote: "**For it is [not your strength, but it is] God who is effectively at work in you, both to will and to work [that is, strengthening, energizing, and creating in you the longing and the ability to fulfill your purpose] for His good pleasure.**" It is not that God let you do the evil we do; it's that He made an oath (Heb. 6:17, 7:25) to correct it after you accept His terms and designs (Phil. 2:13). It is God's anointing that programs us as we are sealed by God's Holy Spirit (Eph. 4:30), and we do what she asks of us once we move by the faith/hope in its settings. The Hebrew writer spoke of this option:

"This *is* the covenant that I will make with them after those days," says the Lord: "I will put My laws into their hearts, and in their mind, I will write them [*the anointing*]." Then He adds, "Their sins and their lawless deeds I will remember no more [*as we walk in His faith/hope, and these are omnipresent words*]." Now where there is remission of these, *there is* no longer an offering for sin.

Grace is an amnesty under better promises until the permanent comes. This is the priesthood order of Melchizedek (Heb. 10:16–17). The power of our faith/hope in the merits of Christ priestly works is forever, and there is no reason to doubt, for it is written: "**Therefore He is able also to save forever (completely, perfectly, for eternity) those who come to God through Him, since He always lives to intercede *and* intervene on their behalf [with God].**" It is in this new priesthood order, under better promises, that we walk by faith (Heb. 7:25 AMP). The theological precept of sanctification by position is understood from scriptures again, as it is written:

> For we are His workmanship [His own master work, a work of art], created in Christ Jesus [reborn from above—spiritually transformed, renewed, ready to be used] for good works, which God prepared [for us] beforehand [taking paths which He set], so that we would walk in them [living the good life which He prearranged and made ready for us].

And this was established *beforehand* at God's first divine, heavenly summit in the past to a future scale of knowledge for you, who He knows; and we will experience it one day (*we already have*), starting at the born-again conception (Eph. 2:10 AMP). Therefore, **"we proclaim Him, warning and instructing everyone in all wisdom [that is, with comprehensive insight into the word and purposes of God], so that we may present every person complete in Christ [mature, fully trained, and perfect in Him—the Anointed]."** We pray for tomorrow's *sanctification* today (Col. 1:28). This is the same faith experience as in our first encounter with God for salvation. Like that of a healing or a miracle, we use this same faith/hope to believe that our eternal disorder is being reshaped, prearranged until, by the power of God who lives in us, we know our future has completely been transformed. It is through studying Scripture that we come close to knowing and understanding God, for the study of theology is the fuel that ignites our worship into knowing more of Him, for the Word provokes us to believe in Him as she transforms us into the image of His Son. The Hebrew (*apostle*) writer wrote so fervently about this because it is a new priesthood succession according to the order of Melchizedek. This is also why even the Jews were against it; but if you believe in Christ Jesus, your faith is based in a new order, away from the Levitical law (*priesthood*) and into a new priestly position based on a *High Priest* of a different Israeli tribe and not of the Levi priesthood. This alone abolishes the Old Covenant making us walk in a new life order. The abolishing by Christ Jesus is explained like this:

> **For when the priesthood is changed, the law must be changed also. He of whom these things are said belonged to a different tribe** [*this is a legal matter*] **and no one from that tribe has ever served at the altar. For it is clear, that our Lord descended from Judah, and in regard, to that tribe Moses said nothing about priests. And what we have said is even more clear if another priest like Melchizedek appears, one who has become a priest not on the**

basis of a regulation as to his ancestry but on the basis of the power of an indestructible life. For it is declared: "You are a priest forever, in the order of Melchizedek." The former regulation is <u>set aside</u> because it was weak and useless (for the law made nothing perfect), and a better hope is introduced, by which we draw near to God. And it was not without an oath! Others became priests without any oath, but he became a priest with an oath when God said to him: "The Lord has sworn and will not change his mind: 'You are a priest forever.'" Because of this oath, Jesus has become the guarantor of a better covenant.

Faith *(in Christ merits)* replaces our self-inflated *(ego)* belief by our work. (Heb. 7:12–21 NIV) Paul wrote:

For the [remarkable, undeserved] grace of God that brings salvation has appeared to all men. It teaches us to reject ungodliness and worldly (immoral) desires [*sanctification in practice is a product (symbiotic) of sanctification by position*] and to live sensible, upright, and godly lives [lives with a purpose that reflect spiritual maturity] in this present age, awaiting *and* confidently expecting the [fulfillment of our] blessed hope [*this is by the word provoking the believer*] and the glorious appearing of our great God and Savior, Christ Jesus [*see we're provoked*] who [willingly] gave Himself [to be crucified] on our behalf to redeem us *and* purchase our freedom from all wickedness, and to purify for Himself a chosen and very special people to be His

own possession, *who are* enthusiastic for doing what is good.

This word provokes us to move ahead, walking in the glorious promises and prophecies given by God Jesus and the Father, who are the God BEING full power in action toward us, His Son's believers (Titus 2:11–14). Scripture states, "**Having abolished [crucified] in His flesh [the law with its commandment and legal claims].**" This is the testimony of God the Father toward His Son for us (Eph. 2:15). It is by the power of God Jesus that we move in this path designed by God the Father for us. It is written: "**And if the Spirit of Him [God the Father] who raised Jesus from the dead lives in you, He who raised Christ Jesus from the dead [the Father] will also give life to your mortal bodies through His Spirit, who lives in you.**" He promised this, and it has a personal (*connotation*) implication, implied in those who believe do not make Him out to be a liar (Rom. 8:11 AMP).

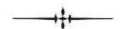

The Holy Spirit Work toward Evangelism

The anointing of God's Spirit does not stop in providing for us alone, for it provides us with extra power, (gifts and ministries) so that we (*collaborate*) multiply, sharing the anointing upon others, women and men, through *evangelism*. The worship and edification of our gatherings moves us to evangelize (*as collaborators*). We know the truth and what is happening right here and now in this plan of existence. The apostle Paul taught this with clear annotations that these gift and ministries are from God Jesus, saying, "**But to each one is given the manifestation of the**

Spirit [the spiritual illumination and the enabling of the Holy Spirit] for the common good" (1 Cor. 12:7). We must be reminded that worship and edification produce evangelism and are the three major columns of the Christian health as a body. Let us emphasize, God the Holy Spirit manifests His power through signs and wonders when the people of God walk according to the anointing of the sound doctrine (1 Tim. 1:9–11). The anointing separates us from the spirit of the world, its evil and sin (*whose desires are in the flesh pleasurable with its wicked acts*), and through sound doctrine practice until the day is perfect. This perfection does not happen immediately. Scripture says, **"But the path of the just (righteous) is like the light of dawn, that shines brighter and brighter until [it reaches its full strength and glory in] the perfect day."** The believer might fall, but he/she will get up, over and over (Prov. 4:18). The anointing elevates us above all principalities, powers, authorities, and host of evil in the celestial regions where God the Father has seated us in Christ. It is through sanctification by position that we must understand these words:

> **Giving thanks to the Father, who has <u>qualified us</u> to <u>share</u> in the inheritance of the saints (God's people) in the Light. For He <u>has rescued us</u> and <u>has drawn us</u> to Himself from the dominion of darkness and has <u>transferred us</u> to the kingdom of His beloved Son, in whom we have redemption [because of His sacrifice, resulting in] the forgiveness of our sins [and the cancellation of sins' penalty].**

There are five verbs underlined in these verses for you to see that this is God's doing and not us, and this surely makes our faith/hope morph/transform into love, to worship our God (Col 1:12–14 AMP). Under the kingdom of light, we have victory as members of the body of Christ, and therefore, we are "in Christ" not "with Christ" for we are part/members of His body (Eph. 2:6). In Christ, we stand over all principalities, powers, authorities, and host of darkness in the celestial regions (*and we don't stand alone*). They cannot touch us because we are like Christ's sheriffs here on earth, as God Jesus said that neither the powers of hell nor death will prevail against the church, so it is written. God Jesus has the keys to hell and death, and we seat in Christ over all the powers that had us enslaved. The grace of God is like an amnesty (absolution, remission) for the believer to build his/her lives brand new. Faith in Scripture creates our works as it explains, "**Show me your faith without works, I'll show you mine by my faith.**" The power of the word of God in the born-again believer comes from an omnipotent source. What she says, she also does in us.

Sanctification by position activates us into sanctification in practice but let us have precaution that we don't fall into the false self-belief that it is our own works that makes us holy and not recognize God Jesus's power/work in us each day, for by works, no one is save. And let us never fall into the lazy notion of not building with the Holy Spirit, our spiritual house. We are the priest of God's temple (*our body*), and we do find dirt in it every day. It is written: "**If we live by the Spirit, let us also walk by the Spirit**" (Gal. 5:25). Good works cannot save you, nor bad works can get you lost while you walk by faith in God's words, for it is God who prepared beforehand the works that those bought at a price of blood are to do. His word produces faith and gives us the power to do his good will. Scripture states, "**For no person will be justified [freed of guilt and declared righteous] in His sight by [trying to do] the works of the Law. For through the Law, we become conscious of sin [and the recognition of sin directs us toward repentance but provides no remedy for sin].**"

The belief in God's word/advice gives us the power and strength by its authority of truth (Rom. 3:20). It is starting with a new account. We do not owe God a thing by His forgiveness. Each day, by the following of His word, we maintain this truth. The sound doctrine (*sanctification in practice*) is the active action of the hand of the omnipotent God anointing in our life (*naturally through His word*) after cleaning us from sin by His blood. He is the one suggesting, by His word, that we are in peace with Him. It is written: **"Therefore, having been justified by faith, we have peace with God through our Lord Jesus Christ."** The faith in Christ justifies us by giving us peace with God (Rom. 5:1). This peace is not the peace when Jesus said, **"[My peace I] leave with you, My peace I give to you"** (John 14:27), neither is **"The peace of God, which surpasses all understanding"** (Phil. 4:7), but Paul was explaining that this is the peace that assures us that we will not be in God's last judgment, for we are at peace with God.

The new priesthood order of Christ assures us that salvation is a gift of God, as written: **"For by grace you have been saved through faith [...] not of yourselves;** *it is* **the gift of God"** (Eph. 2:8) and **"The gifts and the calling of God are irrevocable [for He does not withdraw what He has given** (*salvation falls under this category, it's a gift*) **nor does He change His mind about those to whom He gives His grace or to whom He sends His call]."** The faith in Christ's priestly works is what gives us the power to move ahead (Rom. 11:29). The believer walks in a power/faith in this forgiveness, and by this conscious acceptance, they go on reducing to almost nothing their evil conducts each day by the authority of truth acquired from Scripture. Therefore, what the God BEING stated is what we must believe and walk in its power. Why add to it? Everything He has said is perfect. Sanctification by position is established so that sanctification in practice can be activated through our faith in the merits of God Jesus. We walk looking at reality through the eyes of God, according to His written word (*she possesses His attributes of omniscience, omnipresence, and His omnipotence to do what He says must be done*). This is also why God does not want you to give His word to dogs or pigs. Neither does He spends a drop of His blood on those whom He knows will always be dirty and unfaithful. This is also why He elected (*handpicked*) His chosen in the first divine, heavenly summit and prepared their works beforehand that they would walk in them (Eph. 1:3–4; Matt. 7:6).

It is by the promise of the given Holy Spirit we receive that tangible salvation and know that we belong. It is said: "**Where can I go from Your Spirit? Or where can I flee from Your presence?**" (Ps. 139:7). God the Holy Spirit is omnipresent and "**being exalted to the right hand of God and having received from the Father the promise of the Holy Spirit, He poured out this which you now see and hear.**" The Holy Spirit is God, just like the Son is God. The apostolic traditions left us an incident giving light to this truth: "**Ananias, why has Satan filled your heart to lie to the Holy Spirit**" […and] "**You have not lied to men but to God.**" All the attributes of God the Father and the Son are also manifested by God the Holy Spirit (Acts 5:3–4).

The Holy Spirit also chooses who He wants to use for the gospel ministry: "**As they ministered to the Lord and fasted, the Holy Spirit said, 'Now separate to Me Barnabas and Saul for the work to which I have called them'**" (Acts 13:2). The apostles also said, "**In Him you also *trusted*, after you heard the word of truth, the gospel of your salvation; in whom also, <u>having believed</u>, you were sealed with the Holy Spirit of promise, who is the guarantee of our inheritance until the redemption of the purchased possession, to the praise of His glory.**" Then we must ask this question again: why should we add to the Word?

Everything is made perfect by God. All the attributes of God: omniscience, omnipresence, omnipotence, etc. are all activated by *His Word* in us and manifested by God the Holy Spirit because they are one, an Omni-God BEING; and He uses His attributes by the anointing inside of us, to help us in the works of our fallen nature (*in Him, we live and move and have our being*). Just like King Hezekiah who prayed in great tears after the prophet Isaiah told him that God said he was going to die, he then prayed to the God of Israel, (the God BEING) to change his future, giving him fifteen more years of life (2 Kings 20). The believers must always pray for God to change the outcome of their future, which is in eternal disorder (*condemned to a lake of fire*) before it gets to them, and now even more since we are in a new covenantal order under better promises. Then we must pray for our tomorrow today (Heb. 8:6). It is no different than to pray for a healing or a miracle.

The Word provokes us to believe, and in prayer, we can ask for our tomorrow today. Remember God Jesus's words: **"I no longer call you servants, because a servant does not know his master's business. Instead, I have called you friends, for everything that I learned from my Father I have made known to you"** [*this is why we become Bible students...and*] **"You did not choose Me, but I chose you and appointed you that you should go and bear fruit** [*through prayers*] **and** *that* **your fruit should _remain_"** [*...and* NIV] **"whatever you ask in my name the Father will give you"** (John 15:15–17). God already lives in our future, and His prophecies and promises are for us to take advantage of them. They were given in the past to be manifested from the future to our present stance. Therefore, we are called to pray without ceasing, for our life is dependent on it.

The apostle's theology teaches us these precepts: **"Behold what manner of love the Father has bestowed on us, that we should be called children of God! Therefore, the world does not know us, because it did not know Him"** [*...and*] **"However, when He, the Spirit of truth, has come, He will guide you into all truth; for He will not speak on His** *own authority,* **but whatever He hears He will speak; and He will tell you things to come (***the Apocalypse***). He will glorify Me, for He will take of what is Mine and declare** *it* **to you. All things that the Father has are Mine.**

Therefore, I said that He will take of Mine and declare *it* to you." Scripture elevates us into believing in Him as the only God BEING (1 John 3:1; John 16:13–15). She explains,

> For as many as are led by the Spirit of God, these are sons of God. For you did not receive the spirit of bondage again to fear, but you received the Spirit of adoption by whom we cry out, "Abba, Father." The Spirit Himself bears witness with our spirit that we are children of God, and if children, then heirs— heirs of God and joint heirs with Christ, if indeed we suffer with Him, that we may also be glorified together. (Rom. 8:14–17)

This is not saying that maybe this will be nor that this is by our effort of work. God is the one giving/tagging sanctification by position (*it's written in Scriptures: we are His sons/daughters*), and the word is producing in our spirit/soul the walk by sanctification in practice, all the days of our peregrination by the power of His Holy Spirit manifested in our lives: "**For God did not call us to uncleanness, but in holiness**" (*separation*), which is a work of God while here on earth and until our transformation from this fallen nature to His new body in flesh and bones (1 Thess. 4:7). The apostles assured us that "**we are His workmanship, created in Christ Jesus for good works, which God prepared beforehand that we should walk in them**" (Eph. 2:10) [...and] "**Do you not know that you are the temple of God and that the Spirit of God dwells in you?**" In this powerful affirmation, we believe and walk doing what He asks of us (1 Cor. 3:16). There are also reasons why following God's anointing by the apostles makes sense, and they explain: "**Let no one deceive himself. If anyone among you seems to be wise in this age [*world*] let him become a fool [*this world and its desires will soon perish*] that he may become wise. For the** wisdom of this world is foolishness with God. For it is written, 'He catches the wise in their own craftiness'; and again, 'The Lord knows the thoughts of the wise, that they are futile.'" That is foolishness and their so-called (*false*) science/knowledge (1 Cor. 3:18–20; 1 Tim. 6:20). The apostles advise the chosen, giving us real science/knowledge as it comes to this world by saying,

> Flee [escape, run from] sexual immorality. Every sin that a man does is outside the body, but he who commits sexual immorality sins against his own body. Or do you not know that your body is the temple of the Holy Spirit *who is* in you, whom you have from God, and you are not your own? For you were bought at a price; therefore, glorify God in your body and in your spirit, which are God's. (1 Cor. 6:18–20; Isa. 52:10–12)

Scripture states, "*For in Him we live and move and exist [that is, in Him we actually have our being]*" (Acts 17:28). We are word of God spoken/activated in this existence since birth but being born again makes us *prophecy of God manifested and witness of His testimony*, as explained in the author's first published book, *The Apostles Methodology* (1 John 5:10–12). The word of God is activated by and through us because it has been given/written for, in, and about us. Scripture provokes us to believe in its powerful content and argues:

> If we accept [as we do] the testimony of men [that is, if we are willing to take the sworn statements of fallible humans as evidence], the testimony of God is greater [far more authoritative]; for this is the testimony of [the] God [BEING], that He has testified regarding His Son. The one who believes in the Son of God [who adheres to, trusts in, and relies

confidently on Him as Savior] has the testimony within himself [anointing, because he can speak authoritatively about Christ from his own personal experience]. The one who does not believe God [in this way] has made Him [out to be] a liar, because he has not believed in the evidence that God has given regarding His Son. And the testimony is this: God has given us eternal life [we already possess it], and this life is in His Son [resulting in our spiritual completeness, and eternal companionship with Him]. He who has the Son [by accepting Him as Lord and Savior] has the life [that is eternal]; he who does not have the Son of God [by personal faith] does not have the life.

How can one not believe in Him, for His gift is eternal life, through His Omni-God's powers (*about His Son/Word*) (1 John 5:9–12). Then understand, the knowledge of theology is the fuel that ignites our worship, for through faith, the manifestation of His Holy Spirit in our hearts provokes us to believe and walk knowing this is what pleases the living God, our walking in a fallen nature but animated to live by His spirit word of truth. As we undertake reading and assimilating (*our real struggle is to believe against our carnal foolish fallen nature*) the word of God, we learn to tell others this message of redemption, peace, and salvation. The word of God directs us to walk in this path: "***worship, edification into evangelism.***" These are the columns that hold our *ekklesia*, or gatherings, healthy.

The Solemn Feasts Are God's Plan

The things of the "thereafter" are the things that spiritism, mediums, and false prophets are wanting to know. Those are the things God the Holy Spirit has already told us, by the omniscient knowledge of His word (John 16:12). They are the future things God Jesus said the Spirit of Truth would let us know (*including the gift of discernment, wisdom/knowledge, and prophecy by God the Holy Spirit*). Then we mainly see them not just in the book of Revelation, but throughout the Bible scriptures as confirmation as we understand that the apostles' theology is preparing us for the apostles (*biblical*) eschatology. The backbone of the apocalypse are the solemn festivities in Leviticus (23) and are the things the apostles drafted for us to see. They are the Bible's spinal cord (*God's plan*) of future events, which we are prepared to escape the horror of the apocalyptic disaster. The Lord commanded us: **"Watch ye therefore, and pray always, that ye may be accounted worthy to escape all these things** [*prayer is the key*] that shall come to pass, and to stand before the Son of man." (KJV is very blunt [Luke 21:36]). God Jesus is preparing us for the next solemn festivity of the trumpet, and it is through praying for our tomorrow today, in accord with God's holy word.

Scripture also states, **"For God hath not appointed us to wrath, but to obtain salvation by our Lord Jesus Christ,"** and Christ also assured us, **"Because you have kept My command** [*apostles' theology, sound doctrine*] **to persevere, I also will keep you from the hour of trial which shall come upon the whole world** [*apocalyptic disaster*] **to test those who dwell on the earth."** It is clear that bad things are coming to earth, and they have been foretold as into "Heads up, guys" (1 Thess. 5:9; Rev. 3:10). By the solemn festivities in Leviticus 23, you can place all the events God the Father revealed to His Son in scripture (*to make it known to His believers*), for it is all predestined (Rev. 1:1, 5:7). As we

229

contemplate the first two solemn feasts accomplished (*Passover and Pentecost*), we know what is expected to happen next. The apostles' theology prepares us to achieve this next event. They were established by God the Father and written by Moses:

> The Lord spoke again to Moses, saying, "Speak to the children of Israel and say to them, 'The appointed times (established feasts) of the Lord which you shall proclaim as holy convocations—My appointed times are these.'" The Lord's Passover [*Christ Jesus fulfills this feast in His death and resurrection*]. You shall count fifty days [...*Pentecost when Jesus received the promised Holy Spirit and poured it down for the church to be born (Acts 2:4, 32–33)*] then you shall present a new grain offering to the Lord [*Christian converts*]. On the first day of the seventh month, you shall observe [...*we are waiting for this one now*] memorial day by the blowing of trumpets, a holy convocation [*notice as one feast marks its end, it begins the event of the other*]. The tenth day of this seventh month is the Day of Atonement [*seven-year great tribulation for those who did not prepare at Pentecost and the preparation for those who will be rescued by God: Israel and the beheaded*]. Say to the children of Israel, "On the fifteenth day of this seventh month, the Feast of Booths (Tabernacles) to the Lord."

The last one is the *second coming of Christ* to the land of Israel as the prophet Zachariah announced it and will be the second coming of Messiah, Jesus of Nazareth, into Israel, who did not believe Him the first time (Lev. 23:1, 4, 16, 24, 34 [Zech. 14:4]). These events are part of what God said through the prophet Isaiah: "Remember [carefully] the former things [which I did] from ages past; for I am [*the*] God [BEING] and there is no one else; *I am* God, and there is no one like Me, declaring the end and the result from the beginning." God is the only BEING/Potter with sovereign right, and Jesus of Nazareth is His Word/Son (Isa. 46:9–10). Scripture says about Israel,

> **They shall look on Him whom they pierced. [...***John*** *Apostle took these words up from the Prophet Zachariah, for it will happen*] I will pour out on the house of David and on the people of Jerusalem, the Spirit of grace (unmerited favor) and supplication. And they will look at Me whom they have pierced; and they will mourn for Him as one mourns for an only son, and they will weep bitterly over Him as one who weeps bitterly over a firstborn.**

Israel will mourn at the sight of God Jesus, Son of God, just as the eleven brothers (*Jacob's sons*) wept at the sight of Joseph (*and their betrayal*) who they sold into slavery in Egypt. This is a chosen historic event by God (John 19:37; Zech. 12:10; Gen. 37:18–36).

The apostle's tradition prepares us for the apostle's eschatology (*doomsday*), for they said, "**For God has not destined us to [incur His] wrath [that is, He did not select us to condemn us], but to obtain salvation through our Lord Jesus Christ.**" Paul assured us of this heavenly purpose (1 Thess. 5:9). In this same understanding, God Jesus told John of His purpose about His extended theology through the apostles: "**Because you have kept the word of My endurance [My command to persevere], I will keep you [safe] from the hour of trial, that *hour* which is about to come on the whole [inhabited] world, to test those who live on the earth.**" This is the one and the same hour of God's judgment upon this world (Rev. 3:10, *the solemn feast of Israel atonement, Jacob's* *trouble*). Then in God Jesus's extended theology of grace through the apostles, He assures us, "**Therefore being justified by faith, we have peace with God through our Lord Jesus Christ**" (Rom. 5:1).

This is a gift from God: "**Being justified freely by his grace through the redemption that is in Christ Jesus.**" There is no work or purchase to acquire this gift (Rom. 3:24). The believer must remember how this gift must be placed with the others: "**God's gifts and his call are irrevocable**" (Rom. 11: 29). Even the prophet announced it, saying, "**Come, buy wine and milk without money and without price.**" Isaiah was given to write this about our (*sacrificial, pure blood/lamb scent*) salvation through grace (Isa. 55:1 KJV). This is also why the apostle advised: "**Fear God and give glory to him; for the hour of his judgment is come: and worship him that made heaven, and earth, and the sea, and the fountains of waters**" (Rev. 14:7).

When scripture speaks of the last trumpet, it is referring to the last trumpet solemn feast to be sounded in the heavenly temple (*Moses, tabernacle is a copy of the heavenly one*), where they are celebrated but once and in its due season, proclaimed by God the Father (Heb. 8:5, 7:22, 9:11–12, 14–15). This is also why God the Father's testimony of Christ is to be taken seriously. We must understand the love of God the Father, who made a temple around His throne that speaks about our redemption. It is said, "**And another angel came and stood at the altar, having a golden censer; and there was given unto him much incense, that he should offer it with the prayers of all saints upon the golden altar** [*in the holy place as Moses's desert tabernacle teaches*] **which was before the throne.**" God made around His throne a temple that speaks about our redemption. How romantic of Him (Rev. 8:3). A man once asked me in a sarcastic tone, "*Save from what!*" Well, he will find out one day and in a bad way if he doesn't heed the Word. Then John continues, "**An angel took the censer, and filled it with fire from the altar, and cast it into the earth: and there were voices,**

and thunderings, and lightning, and an earthquake." And this is right after the church was snatched away, saved into the City of Light, the New Jerusalem (Rev. 8:5).

A lot of people think God is going to use a nuclear holocaust to show His wrath, but the God BEING does not need man's weapons to pour His wrath. It has been written; and the believer, Bible student/disciple, must realize it from the revelation given. God is the source, fabric of life.

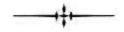

Answer the questions from this chapter to interact with others in a book club:

1. What are at least three church columns the apostles taught about, that holds the church together?

2. What prepares us for the wrath of God, mentioned in this chapter, and what are the three terms/tools used, that expresses the power to practice the sound doctrine?

3. What is sanctification by position? What does it lead us to? Give at least three verses that point them out.

FIFTH LESSON

The Armor of God to Plunder the Enemy's House/Den

L et us do a recompilation of what we have written. Everything said in the word of God is unchangeable, all of it. The seal of its coded mystery is broken/open when a believer is sealed/touched and born again by God Jesus. God has given His attribute of immutability to His word, for she is the testimony the Father gives of His Son. Until He touches a person, they will only see the door and an invitation to come through. Only once they are touched by the word (*provoked to believe*), this is when the power of God reveals itself to the believer by its true authority, and the word becomes alive to them. God's word is the door for the revelation of Himself.

Through it, God reveals His godly BEING to His born-again believers. Then they become disciples through studying His word. The word of God is empowered by the LORD's Spirit, for she reflects His omniscient, omnipresent, and omnipotent attributes as she works in our lives its knowledge of truth (Rom. 8:11). Through the written word, God proclaims redemption for all men (*and women*) that will heed the call. God Jesus is the One creating a body of born again, believers, whom He calls a kingdom of kings and priests (Rev. 5:10). God Jesus is the Word that comes out of the abundance of the heart of the God BEING, and He is now the image of that invisible BEING. Before they created all things, they got together in a divine, heavenly summit and brainstormed everything they were to do. They saw the future; and God so loved the world that He gave His only unique son, His Word, to give us salvation from the death/conflict that was to distort all things (*He predestined what He wanted*). By creating us, He has given us significance, and by His becoming like one of us and dying for our eternal restoration, He has doubled up given more significance to us. God is love.

At the end, God the Father predestined all things in a book of seven seals that proclaims the end of the rebellion, conflict of death (Rev. 1:1). He started by creating a body of born-again believers, and here on earth Christ calls them His church. He said, "**I will build my church; and the gates of hell shall not prevail against it**," as He made a spectacle of His (*and their*) enemies. Today, He lives in a body of *flesh and bones*, letting us know (*as all creation*) that this is from everlasting to everlasting (Matt. 16:18). The building of the church has not been the work of men or women in ministry, for the church has been constructed by God Jesus Himself. It is His ministry, and we are His collaborators.

It is written: "**And the Lord added to their number daily those who were being saved**" and "**After two days he will revive us; on the third day he will raise us up, that we may live before him.**" He has been reviving the church for two thousand years now. This is also why this has gone viral from generations to generation (Acts 2:47; Hos. 6:2). God Jesus created the church to *worship* God; to be *edified*; and to go out to the world and *evangelize*, sharing the grace received as collaborators. These three columns are what maintain the church standing, but it is through God the Holy Spirit in its three phases that this gets done. It has been through the revelation God has given us of Himself that the church stands.

First, God reveals Himself through His general grace by the things created (*this reality*) including all and us in it. Scripture states, "The LORD **has made everything for its purpose, even the wicked for the day of trouble**," (Rom. 1:20; Prov. 16:4). Then He reveals Himself through His special revelation as He washes us with His blood and seals our hearts with His Spirit (Eph. 1:11–14, 4:30; Rom. 8:11).

Finally, God reveals Himself through His written word as He washes us with pure water from our mind's stains and spirit/soul's wrinkles, through the knowledge of knowing His persona (Eph. 5:26–27; Jer. 9:23–24). It is by these three revelations of God that we stand upon the rock, which is His word. And once we do, we begin to look at reality through the eyes of God, according to His written word, as we are also dressed in the armor of God. It's been established: "**Without faith no one can please God. For anyone who comes to God must believe that he is real and that he rewards those who truly want to find him.**" The tools are faith, hope and love.

This is a provocation to believe (Heb. 11:6 AMP). The word of God explains to us that justification is an act of God and sanctification is a work of God, and therefore, she explains that we are of God by His will and not ours. It is through sanctification by position that we have our faith/hope stand, which produces sanctification in practice through that powerful anointing in the word's sound doctrine. It gives us the authority of truth as God's light shines in us. He brought us out of darkness and into the kingdom of light in Christ, and this by a process in which we learn and mature as we understand we are plundering the house of the evil one our very treasure stolen from the first Adam.

Scripture teaches of God's promises: "**I will restore** [*give or pay you back, compensate*] **to you the years that the** [*evil one*] **swarming locust has eaten.**" These are promises to the born-again citizens of the New Jerusalem (Joel 2:25). After this verse in Joel, it's explained how: "**And it shall come to pass afterward That I will pour out My Spirit on all flesh** [*the One whose greater than all*]; **Your sons and your daughters shall prophesy, Your old men shall dream dreams, Your young men shall see visions.**" The apostle Peter used this prophecy to make it known what had happened at Pentecost, after God Jesus resurrected (Joel 2:28; Acts 2:32–33). Scripture teaches us that "***the way of the good [just] person is like the light of dawn, growing brighter and brighter until full daylight.***" And this has been possible by the victory of God Jesus for us all (Prov. 4:18 NCV). His priestly work establishes as He said, "**How can one enter a strong man's house and plunder his goods, unless he first binds the strong man?** [*Which He did at the forty-day retreat in the desert and by His resurrection*] **And then he will plunder his house.**" This is a powerful statement by Jesus of Nazareth (*the Second Adam*), and He fulfilled it for us, for after fasting in the desert retreat, He started His ministry on earth proving His statement (Matt. 12:29). The LORD made a spectacle of the evil one and his forces as scripture tells us:

> **And you, being dead in your trespasses and the uncircumcision of your flesh, He has made alive together with Him** [*God raised us up with Christ and seated us with him in the heavenly realms in Christ Jesus, as members of His body (Eph. 2:6)*] **having forgiven you all trespasses** [*God means this in His omnipresent stand*] **having wiped out the handwriting of**

requirements that was against us [*the law (1 Cor. 15:56)*] which was contrary to us. And He has taken it out of the way, having nailed it to the cross. Having disarmed principalities and powers, He made a public spectacle of them, triumphing over them in it.

The death and murder of God's Son has not been taken lightly by the Father at all (Col. 2:13–15). In Zachariah (3:2), it is written, "And the Lord said to Satan, 'The LORD [the God BEING] rebuke you, Satan!'" In other words, the voice that said, "*Let there be light*" is now rebuking in harsh disapproval, criticism, and punitive action a creature He created because of a violent behavior daring to harm the Anointed One, God's Chosen. It used to be said in the Old Covenant about the evil one: "[*Whom*] did not open the house of his prisoners." He has no love for his prisoners at all, but that was changed when the day for humanity's freedom came. The prophet wrote of Christ:

> The Spirit of the Lord God is upon Me, because the Lord has anointed Me to preach good tidings to the poor; He has sent Me to heal the brokenhearted, to proclaim liberty to the captives, and the opening of the prison to *those who are* bound.

It was this last that God Jesus accomplished for us all, and He did it by opening the prisons of His elect bound by Satan (Isa. 14:17, 61:1). Now the born again walks in freedom of guilt and condemnation, for we have peace with God (Rom. 5:1).

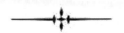

The Abundant Riches of His Mercy and Grace

It is true we are not worthy of God's grace and mercy or anything He has to offer, but it has pleased Him to visit and reveal Himself to us from His reality and attribute of invisibility. He loved us since before He created us. This was one of the resolutions in God's first divine, heavenly summit before creation, and it can be captured, as Scripture states, "**For God so loved the world, that He gave** [*at Their first divine, heavenly summit*] **His only begotten Son, that whoever believes in Him shall not perish, but have eternal life.**" This love of God for us started before the foundation of the world (John 3:16). God saw His creation, for He is omniscient (*and omnipresent*), and the preparation of all creation started with this agenda: "**He indeed was foreordained** [*God Jesus*] **before the foundation of the world but was manifest in these last times for you.**" This is how we know God so loved the world before He created angels and humans (*He foreordained His Word*). God knows everything, and everything is fresh in His eyes always. The God BEING works from that platform (1 Pet. 1:20; Isa. 46:9–10).

It was at that divine summit that God so love the world (*man and woman before creating them*) He decided (*gave and foreordain His only begotten Son*) to make the greatest investment ever made in His existence (*reality*); and that was to save us from this evil age, *death time zone*, and eternal damnation. The apostle John announced that "**God is Love.**" In the middle of His unlimited power and sovereign rights toward His subjects, God is love. At a time when we were dead by our crimes and sins, departed from the grace of God forever, He loved us and gave out of His heart the most precious thing of all, His only unique son. Paul explained,

> **And you [He made alive when you] were [spiritually] dead and separated from Him because of your transgressions and sins, in which you once walked [***a***

dead person cannot: think, move or talk, for he/she are dead]. You were following the ways of this world [influenced by this present evil age], in accordance with the prince of the power of the air (Satan), the spirit who is now at work in the disobedient [the unbelieving, who fight against the purposes of God (*you were a slave*)]. Among these [unbelievers] we all once lived in the passions of our flesh [our behavior governed by the sinful self/fallen nature], indulging the desires of human nature [without the Holy Spirit] and [the impulses] of the [sinful] mind. We were, by nature [*animals*] children [under the sentence] of [God's] wrath, just like the rest [of mankind] (*This is why we did not choose Him, we couldn't, but He chose us, John 15:16*). But God, being [so very] rich in mercy, because of His great and wonderful love with which He loved us, even when we were [spiritually] dead and separated from Him because of our sins [*amazing grace*], He made us [spiritually] alive together with Christ (for by His grace, His undeserved favor and mercy—you have been saved from God's judgment). And He raised us up together with Him [when we believed] and seated us with Him in the heavenly *places* [because we are] in Christ Jesus, [and He did this] so that in the ages to come He might [clearly] show the immeasurable *and* unsurpassed riches of His grace in [His] kindness toward us *in* Christ Jesus [by providing for our redemption].

How can anyone miss this? (Eph. 2:1–7 AMP). Many preachers and believers today speak of salvation as if they were the ones that accepted Christ by saying, "*When I embraced the gospel,*" "*When I converted,*" or "*When I accepted Christ*" (*really*), as if they had something to do with the decision and as into doing the gospel a favor. The truth is, it was God who resurrected us when we were dead. We were allowed to hear the words of the gospel in the time of God and our urgent need, as scripture states, **"You have not chosen Me, but I have chosen you and I have appointed, *and* placed, *and* purposefully planted you."** This was a bold statement by God Jesus (John 15:16). Scripture also states, **"But God demonstrates His own love toward us, in that while we were still sinners, Christ died for us."** Our faith/hope is based on the merits of Christ (Rom. 5:8). God never said, "Wow! Those people are so good, let me go and save them." No! The word of God produces the faith/hope of salvation in our spirit/soul when we were brought to listen (*by Him*) the word of the gospel. This was the only way toward our salvation. *He decided for you and me,* for we were dead running the other way.

Even now after being saved, Paul declares this, saying, **"Although I want to do good, evil is right there with me"** [...*and*] **"What a wretched man I am! Who will rescue me from this body that is subject to death?"** And his answer to us is, **"Thanks be to God, who delivers me through Jesus Christ our Lord!"** (Rom. 7:21–25). In this same understanding, Paul quotes the prophets, who wrote from God, saying, **"There is no one righteous, not even one [...] there is no one who seeks God. All have turned away they have together become worthless."** And God, who is the One saying this, being omnipresent, He looked yesterday, today, and tomorrow and found not one righteous, nor looking for Him, because we were all dead. We needed a redeemer, even in this fallen nature (Rom. 3:10–12). It is a legal act on God's behalf for us, and He designs the terms that you must walk in.

Remember and understand, it is about the God BEING's nature. These verses explain: **"[The] God, who made the world and everything in it, since He is Lord of heaven and earth [*sovereign*] does not dwell in temples made with hands. Nor is He worshiped with men's hands, as though He needed anything** [*these are God's attribute of freedom and independence*] **since** **He** **gives to all life, breath, and all things**," that is, to all our needs daily (Acts 17:24–25). The Bible student must remember: "*He* *chose us in Him before the foundation of the world,*" and He said to Jeremiah, "**Before I formed you in the womb I knew [or chose] you, before you were born, I set you apart.**" Remember, we are dealing with an Omni-God in scripture (Eph. 1:4; Jer. 1:5). The apostle Paul explains this legality:

> But what does it say? "The word is near you, in your mouth and in your heart" [*a rider, Deut. 30:14*]— that is, the word [the message, the basis] of faith which we preach—because if you acknowledge *and* confess with your mouth that Jesus is Lord [recognizing His power, authority, and majesty as God], and believe in your heart that God raised Him from the dead, you will be saved [*you are brought to believe*]. For with the heart a person believes [in Christ as Savior] resulting in his justification [that is, being made righteous—being freed of the guilt of sin and made acceptable to God]; and with the mouth he acknowledges and confesses [his faith openly], resulting in and confirming [his/her] salvation." For the Scripture says, "Whoever believes in Him [whoever adheres to, trusts in, and relies on Him] will not be disappointed [in his expectations]." (Rom. 10:8–11; Joel 2:32)

From a historical covenantal point of view, this is a legal matter on God's behalf and is the only way He intervenes in a person's life (*as we explained in our first published book*). Being "just" or righteous practically means being right with God, and we are made just (*right*) with God in His own terms, according to His norms and design. Think of this: God is the only BEING in the universe, and *"He cannot deny Himself."* He had to provide the justice that we cannot provide by our own selves. We cannot be saved by our own perfection for God Himself would have to demand it, and you and I are incapable of providing it. We are His creation (*clay*). Neither can He accept us by our imperfection because of who He is, the only God BEING in perfect nature. This is also why God provides for us a justice as it was explained in *The Apostle Methodology to Interpret Scripture*. God provides for us a justice, but to understand and acquire this justice, we must ask our carnal selves, "What is justice?" The justice of God can only be defined not like the character of God (*love*) nor as our own justice (*flaw*) by the works of the law, but by His Own absolute BEING of perfection. In the merits of Christ.

Scripture states, **"This [the law] stops all excuses and brings the whole world under God's judgment, because no one can be made right with God by following the law. The law only shows us our sin"** (Rom. 3:19–20 NCV). Then this justice of God can only be defined and reached by our faith in the merits of Jesus Christ (*an omni-absolute sacrifice*), for the justice of God is the justice that the absolute justice of God requires of Him. This justice is approved, designed, and sealed as righteousness by the God BEING's nature. Jesus of Nazareth (Christ) made Himself that justice (*before the foundation of creation*); and God the Holy Spirit declares to us, through His written word, the legality of it. It's *a God thing*, and its value belongs to Him alone, the only God BEING. This justice is the totality of what the God BEING approves, orders, demands, and that only He can provide.

In God's BEING, all the absolutes are manifested—that is, absolute authority, absolute power, and absolute justice. And He is all this absolute because He is the only *absolute* BEING. The absolute authority of God was broken by angels (*one-third)* and men (*all*), and she demands an absolute justice in which an eternal sentence has been declared and remember Paul's insight of the God BEING: "*He cannot deny Himself*" (2 Tim. 2:13). The apostle Paul wrote from God the Holy Spirit's foresight: "**For it pleased *the Father that*in Him [Christ] all the fullness should dwell, and by Him to reconcile all things to Himself, by Him, whether things on earth or things in heaven, having made peace through the blood of His cross.**" An absolute cannot be broken, for if it were, then it would not be what it's said to be (*absolute*), where God cannot deny Himself on the demands of Himself (Col. 1:19–20). The word of God was disobeyed, and by that very Word, God dealt with His creation. When you felt in your spirit/soul that *zap, jolt, rush* of light by the faith of Christ revelation running within, that is the power of the word of God in you and the power that resurrected Christ (Rom. 10:8–11; Eph. 1:19–20 AMP).

We must understand God's attributes as we read His word, for it gives us the reality of His message, and that is how we can perceive the riches of His grace and mercy that bring us into His presence. Nathanael's conversion with Christ was like this, and he exclaimed after asking, "**How do You know me?**" **Jesus answered and said to him, "Before Philip called you, when you were under the fig tree, I saw you." Nathanael answered and said to Him, "Rabbi, You are the Son of God! You are the King of Israel!**" (*You must guess Nathanial was alone under that fig tree, praying, and Christ's confession was omniscient, but it really was as the Second Adam's stamina and right to stand with God*). **Jesus answered and said to him, "Because I said to you, 'I saw you under the fig tree,' do you believe?**" Only when God Jesus talks to you can you believe in Him, remember that, for He said, "***You did not choose me, I chose you***" (John 1:48–50). When God speaks, He does it with an omniscient and omnipresent knowledge/attribute. In other words, He knows everything, always, which is fresh at His sight and/or spirit/soul. And yes, scripture teaches that God the Father has a soul and He is spirit. We read about it from the King James Version in the following words: "**Behold my servant** [Jesus of Nazareth] **whom I uphold; mine elect, in whom *my soul* delighteth; I have put *my spirit* upon him: he shall bring forth judgment to the Gentiles.**" The power of the KJV is that it was derived from the oldest known Hebrew and Greek version. This is in difference to many other translations today, including the Latin Vulgate Vaticana version (*not original*). She is a translation from the Greek into a Latin standpoint. It has many flaws in comparison to the Greek original text (*a topic to be researched on the Internet*) (Isa. 42:1; John 4:24 KJV). This verse was speaking about His Chosen, God's Son, appointed to come to earth as the woman's Seed, and was no other than Jesus of Nazareth, explained by His Jewish disciples called apostles (Isa. 42:1; John 4:24).

God's justice is needed to stand on His trial. And remember, here on earth a person is innocent until proven guilty, but in the courts of heaven, everyone is guilty, and a price/payment must be place, which good works cannot cover/provide for "**everything is uncovered and laid bare before the eyes of him to whom we must give account,**" and the price is high. No one on earth can meet the value of it, but God provided His Son's blood for you and me by faith in His word. "*Can you believe it?*" (Heb. 4:13).

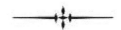

We Are Not Worthy of God's Blessings

As Bible students, we must understand the *anthropomorphic language* used by the writers to tell us about the I AM, for it is how God wanted for us to know Him, and we have the apostle's tradition that testified to this understanding. The LORD's nature as an Omni-God is different from ours, who are creatures (*created, and now in a fallen condition*), and He speaks to us in a way so that we may understand that He alone is God and there is no other. He has not found another BEING like Him. God told the prophet, "Indeed *there is* no other Rock; I know not *one*" (Isa. 44:8).

The apostle Matthew testifies about John the Baptist declaration, and in it we see the God BEING baring His holy arm, as Isaiah the Prophet mentions, "**The Lord will lay bare his holy arm in the sight of all the nations, and all the ends of the earth will see the salvation of our God.**" I like to say of this "*baring His holy arm*" as into rolling up the cuff of His shirt sleeves to work out our redemption as *Father, Son, and Holy Spirit*, my version (Isa. 52:10). Matthew mentions of the God BEING: "**When He [Jesus of Nazareth] had been baptized, Jesus came up immediately from the water; and behold, the heavens were opened to Him [Jesus] and He saw the <u>Spirit of God</u> descending like a dove and alighting upon Him. And suddenly <u>a voice came</u> from heaven, saying, 'This is My beloved Son, in whom I am well pleased.'**"

In these verses, the apostle points out that, though talking about John the Baptist's testimony, it must have been Jesus who told him about this (*if you can capture the verses' content, Matthew wasn't yet a disciple*). Then we conclude, salvation is on God's terms and design He provided (Matt. 3:16–17 KJV). We can understand through scripture as we perceptively sense the anointing God has placed in us (*by His riches in glory*) that He gives more than we can expect of His abundance because He possesses all things. The apostle Paul continues to share this to the Ephesians in chapter 3, saying,

> **For this reason [grasping the greatness of this plan by which Jews and Gentiles are joined together in Christ] I bow my knees [in reverence] before the Father [of our Lord Jesus Christ], from whom every family in heaven and on earth derives its name [God—the first and**

ultimate Father]. [There is no other God.] **May He grant you out of the riches of His glory [*limitless*] to be strengthened and spiritually energized with power through His Spirit in your inner self [indwelling your innermost being and personality (*which riches are knowing and understanding Him, Jer. 9:24*)], so that Christ may dwell in your hearts through your faith. And may you, having been [deeply] rooted and [securely] grounded in love, be fully capable of comprehending with all the saints (God's people) the width and length and height and depth of His love [fully experiencing that amazing, endless love]; and [that you may come] to know [practically, through personal experience] the love of Christ which far surpasses [mere] knowledge [without experience], that you may be filled up [throughout your being] to all the fullness of God [so that you may have the richest experience of God's presence in your lives, completely filled and flooded with God Himself (*abundance, and remember: in Him we move and live and have our being, Acts 17:28*). Now to Him who is able, to [carry out His purpose of salvation and] do superabundantly more than all that we dare ask or think (*surpass*) [infinitely beyond our greatest prayers, hopes, or dreams], according to His power that is at work within us, to Him be the glory in the church and in Christ Jesus throughout all generations forever and ever. Amen.**

God has given us more than what we have asked for. Let's worship His name in love and reverence: "**Through Him [God Jesus], therefore, let us at all times offer up to God a sacrifice of praise [which is], the fruit of lips that thankfully acknowledge *and*** confess *and* glorify His name" (Eph. 3:14–21; Heb. 13:15). The faith in the merits of Christ alone makes us work His sound doctrine in the order of Melchizedek.

The apostle Paul, writing to the Romans in chapter 3 (*after in one and two*), accuses Jews and Gentiles alike and includes believers of being in bad standing with God, that is the condemnable type. Paul mentions there are fourteen accusations by God, six in judgment and eight as a medical prognosis, against humanity. These accusations are including all (*we must also observe that Paul is quoting the prophets on God's behalf*) saying,

> **What then? Are we better than they?** (*asked believers*) **Not at all. For we have previously charged both Jews and Greeks** (*Rom. 1 and 2*) **that they are all under sin. As it is written: "There is none righteous, no, not one; there is none who understands; there is none who seeks after God. They have all turned aside; they have together become unprofitable; there is none who does good, no, not one."**

These are six accusations of God in judgment toward humanity. Then Paul speaks of God as if being a doctor bringing us (*humanity*) to his office and, with a mouthpiece on his hand, says, "Open your mouth," and makes a prognosis, projecting an ailment and a terrible disease.

> **Their throat is an open tomb; with their tongues they have practiced deceit; the poison of asps is under their lips; whose mouth is full of cursing and bitterness. Their feet are swift to shed blood; destruction and misery are in their ways; and the way of peace they have not known. There is no fear of God before their eyes.** [*God points out these eight signs to tell us how dead we*

are]. Now we know that whatever the law says, it says to those who are under the law, that every mouth may be stopped, and all the world may become guilty before God [*all things are naked on front of whom we must give account* (Heb. 4:12–13)]. Therefore, by the deeds [*of works*] of the law no flesh will be justified in His sight, for by the law is the knowledge of sin.

This last takes away from all humanity any form of self-justification or goodness (Rom. 3:9–20). Then the plan of God is clearly revealed by His richest in abundance toward those who believe, confessing their inability to become saved. Scripture, after the fact, states,

But now the righteousness of God has been clearly revealed [independently and completely] apart from [*our works of*] the Law, though it is [actually] confirmed by the Law and the [words and writings of the] Prophets. This righteousness of God comes through faith in Jesus Christ [*Messiah*] for all those [Jew and Gentile] who believe [and trust in Him and acknowledge Him as God's Son]. There is no distinction, since all have sinned and *continually* fall short of the glory of God and are being justified [declared free of the guilt of sin, made acceptable to God, and granted eternal life] as a gift by His [precious, undeserved] grace, through the redemption [the payment for our sin] which is [provided] in Christ Jesus.

The NKJV (vs. 24) says, "Being justified freely [*without any cost (Isa. 55:1)*] by His grace through the redemption that is in Christ Jesus" (Rom. 3:21–24 AMP). There is a reason God has done this, and this is because He is omnipresent/omniscient. He looks, knows, and finds not one just or one looking for Him, yesterday, today, or tomorrow. This also tells us that man and their religions that say they are looking for God are lying unto themselves. Again, yesterday, today, and tomorrow, God's omniscient knowledge is fresh in His eyes at all times; therefore, He cannot be mocked (Gal. 6:7).

This reality, in the God BEING's existence, is ordained by Him; and we see it in Revelation (5:5) (*a future predestination*) about to happen: "**The Lion of the tribe of Judah, the Root of David, has triumphed. He is able to open the scroll and its seven seals.**" This is also why God had to reveal Himself to us, and He has done it in His three chosen forms: first through His creation: "**[By] the creation of the world His invisible *attributes* are clearly seen, being understood by the things that are made, even His eternal power and Godhead, so that they are without excuse**" (Rom. 1:20); second by His special revelation: "**In Him, you also, when you heard the word of truth, the good news of your salvation, and [as a result] believed in Him, were stamped with the seal of the promised Holy Spirit [the One promised by Christ] as owned and protected [by God]**" (Eph. 1:13–14); and finally, through His written word: "**For no prophecy [*written word*] was ever made by an act of human will, but men moved by the Holy Spirit spoke from God**" [...and] "**But in these last days he has spoken to us by his Son [***His Word that flows, from the abundance of His Heart***] whom he appointed heir of all things, and through whom also he made the universe**" (Heb. 1:2) [...also] "**Sanctify them by the truth; your word is truth**" (John 14:6). This is how we get the anthropomorphic language from the Bible by the will of God (*that is God who is light with nothing to hide*), revealing Himself to us, giving us His richest of grace in abundance, through these three forms mentioned (2 Pet. 1:21). The apostle Paul declared in his revelation of this truth the following:

For God has committed them all to disobedience, that He might have mercy on all. Oh, the depth of the riches both, of the wisdom, and knowledge of God! How unsearchable are His judgments and His ways past finding out! "For who has known the mind of the Lord? [*He is a* BEING, *not a creation*] Or who has become His counselor?" "Or who has first given to Him and it shall be repaid to him?" For of Him and through Him and to Him are all things [and in Him all things hold together] to whom be glory forever. Amen. (Rom. 11:32–36)

The Creator and Founder of all things, the *I AM*, is conscious of your existence and everything pertaining to your life. Some people have accused, saying, "Where is He when all the evil and bad things in this world are happening?" And the answer is, right in the same place He was when they were killing His Son for you and me: at His very throne of mercy. Would you have done the same, sacrificing your kids for all of us?

The Bible Is Filled with Promises and Prophecies for the Believer

The knowledge of the destruction of the evil one (*and his forces that are now bound*) has been a greater blessing given to the believer after being chosen, and we must remember this was a promise by the LORD, God Almighty. This was the first promise of redemption recorded given in the land of Eden:

The Lord God said to the serpent, "Because you have done this [*the devil is blamed for our falling into sin and also is blamed for the one-third of the fall of the angels in heaven*]. **You are cursed more than all the cattle** [*the world and all in it that got cursed*]. **And more than any animal of the field; on your belly you shall go, and dust you shall eat all the days of your life.** [*This is God's sovereign right in action, predestination.*] **And I will put enmity (open hostility) between you and the woman** [*the church*] **and between your seed** [*offspring, Nephilims, the goats/tare*] **and her Seed** [wheat/lambs]; **He shall [fatally] bruise your head, and you shall [only] bruise His heel."**

The church and its struggles, she has been bruised but still standing (Gen. 3:14–15). The Seed of the woman coming was revealed by the prophets to the people of Israel, saying, **"Therefore the Lord Himself will give you a sign: Behold, the virgin shall conceive and bear a Son, and shall call His name Immanuel."** This means, *"God is with us"* (Isa. 7:14). This promise was well-known until the prophet John the Baptist re-announced it to the people of Israel, written by the apostle, declaring, **"The next day John saw Jesus coming toward him, and said, 'Behold! The Lamb of God who takes away the sin of the world!** [*...Gen. 3:15 was describe by Moses and the temple sacrifices*] **And I have seen and testified that this is the Son of God,'"** words of testimony but were not received, understood, nor accepted by all the people of Israel those days, just a handful of them (John 1:29, 34). As the Lamb of God, you must understand what the prophet was saying, that He was to give His life like the animal sacrifice used in the altar of sacrifice at the exterior part of the tabernacle of Moses and/or their temple; but as Son of God, they we're talking about the Creator of this reality: "**The Word was in the world, and the world was made by him, but the world did not know him,**" it is said (John 1:10). He was going to do this sacrifice for all of us—that was, to have His Soul pierce as a payment for our redemption.

This reality is upheld by the power of *God the Word,* for there is no Mother Nature. This is just the sinful statements of women and men whose minds are blinded by death. It has been written: "**And that same word of God is keeping heaven and earth that we now have in order to be destroyed by fire. They are being kept for the Judgment Day and the destruction of all who are against God**" (2 Pet. 3:7). As you accept God's word, you'll see how they ridicule the truth (*as we all once did*), but this was then because death by sin blinded our sight. This habitat, fauna, and/or ecosystem were created by God for people with His image and likeness to live in it; and it all reacts to our very needs in this fallen nature. At this present moment, creation is in sinful ruin, but this happens for a very good reason as we look at reality through the eyes of God. According to His word, we can understand:

> **The sufferings we have now are nothing compared to the great glory that will be shown to us. Everything God made is waiting with excitement for God to show his children's glory completely. Everything God made was changed to become useless, not by its own wish but because God wanted it and because all along there was this hope: that everything God made would be set free from ruin to have the freedom and glory that belong to God's children. [*The promise in Genesis 3:15, God predestined it.*] We know that everything God made has been waiting until now in pain, like a woman ready to give birth. Not only the world, but we also have been waiting with pain inside us. We have the Spirit as the first part of God's promise. So, we are**

waiting for God to finish making us his own children ["*Until the fullness of the Gentiles has come into the church,*" *(Rom. 11:25)*], which means our bodies will be made free. We were saved, and we have this hope. If we see what we are waiting for, that is not really hope. People do not hope for something they already have. But we are hoping for something we do not have yet, and we are waiting for it patiently [as we see reality through the eyes of God according to His prophecy/promises]. (Rom. 8:18–25)

The apostle Peter wrote: "By His word the present heavens and earth are being reserved" (2 Pet. 3:7). This is why it is written: "[By] The creation of the world His invisible attributes, His eternal power and divine nature, have been clearly seen, being understood through His workmanship [all His creation, the wonderful things that He has made], so that they [who fail to believe and trust in Him] are without excuse and without defense." This last speaks about a final judgment, God reveals Himself through His creation, which is right in front of our eyes (Rom. 1:20 AMP). A person cannot miss it: "For in Him we live and move and exist [that is, in Him we actually have our being]." He is not far from each one of us, and He has given us His image and likeness—that is, a spirit/soul like He has—so we can understand the God BEING by believing, knowing, and accepting His revelation: there is no other being like Him. He is God Almighty, and we are His creation. There is no other Rock, He said (Acts 17:28). Scripture shows God's intention in this fallen creation:

For [even the whole] creation [all nature] waits eagerly for the children of God to be revealed. For the creation was subjected to frustration *and* futility, not willingly [because of some intentional fault on its

part], but by the will of Him who subjected it, in hope that the creation itself will also be freed from its bondage to decay [and gain entrance] into the glorious freedom of the children of God. (Rom. 8:19–21)

This is the biggest promise and prophecy to our redemption, and God is at the forefront. It is His sovereign right as Creator and the One holding it all together.

The Priestly Works of our High Priest

The evil one has been destroyed by Jesus of Nazareth, scripture states. Believe it. *Destroy* means to demolish, made of no use, dethrone, ruined, broken into small pieces, like the demolishing of a building or a tower. Scripture points to this fact and characteristic by the priestly work of Jesus Christ, for it is written/revealed in the New Testament: **"[Since] the children have partaken of flesh and blood, He Himself likewise shared in the same [Rom. 8:3] that through death He might _destroy_ him who had the power [*or empire*] of death, that is, the devil"** (Heb. 2:14). (*This is explained in* The Apostles Methodology to Interpret). We can see by scriptures how the evil one entered Adam and Eve's reality and stole it because he wanted to be king. The evil one fooled them (*his lying power [spirit of the world] is in his mouth, for we see an angel:* **"Set a seal on him, so that he should deceive the nations no more,"** *[Rev. 20:3]*). He stole Adam's title as a prophet knowing God (*sin does not let us see God physically nor in our spirit/mind*), a priest of his home (*marriage dissension, as*

Adam accused Eve), and as the king of his world (*earth's power in strength is no more, Gen. 4:12*). It all seemed to have been lost, but this reality was created for creatures with image and likeness of God, and the evil one only had at one time (*like all the angels do*) likeness of God in heaven, which likeness he lost once kicked out of heaven for his rebellion (Isa. 14.12; Ezek. 28:13–19; Job 1:6).

As the evil one encounters himself in this stolen reality, he is unable to see its beauty, absorb its energy; for this is not his habitat. But God Jesus took a body like ours, becoming the *second and last* Adam. The evil one did not understand the covenant God made with man in this reality, where the wage of sin is death (Gen. 2:17; Rom. 6:23). When the evil one killed an innocent man with no sin (God's chosen), he sinned against the God BEING and lost everything he stole from Adam into the hands of the Second Adam and more; for by his evil act, God assigned all his followers, fallen angels and their human-born offspring alike (*Nephilims [Gen. 6:1–2]*), unto the lake of fire eternally with him (Matt. 25:41). The consequences of his action condemned all his followers.

Let us do a recount of what Jesus of Nazareth took away from the evil one: "**All authority has been given to Me in heaven and on earth.**" He declared this after resurrecting (Matt. 28:18). The Lord already owned the title to this creation because He created it and sustains it, but He entered the creation of man (*whom He gave this creation to*) as a man and did what He did to buy it back (*from God the Father's real estate title*). Its price was the price of His blood, (Rev. 5:9). This now means the kingdom of Adam on earth belongs to God Jesus (Second Adam) from beginning to end, and He acquired it as the *son of man in a* body of flesh and bones.

When He appeared to the disciples, He told them that all power was given to Him, and so "**Do not be afraid. I am the First and the Last. I am the Living One; I was dead, and now look, I am alive for ever and ever! And I hold the keys of death and Hades**" because He went into the bosom of Abraham and released all those waiting for His arrival in the regions of death. Scripture states of this place, that a person burning in hell: **"lifted up his eyes and saw Abraham afar off, and Lazarus in his bosom."** And scripture also says, **"He [Christ] who descended is also the One who ascended far above all the heavens."** Christ saved all of those who were waiting for Him on a *faith/hope credit* of the Old Covenant, at Abraham's bosom (Luke 16:19–31; Eph. 4:7–10). He also took the keys from the evil one, those of death and hell as He proclaims His reign (Rev. 1:17–18). But there is much more of His victory at the cross, for God the Father declared, making Him *head* of all His enemy's forces; therefore, the evil one was kicked out of his office when the Father made God Jesus head over all things. Paul mentions,

> **For God was pleased to have all his fullness dwell in him [the Son] and through him to reconcile to himself all things, whether things on earth or things in heaven, by making peace through his blood, shed on the cross [...and] He raised Him from the dead and seated Him at His right hand in the heavenly** *places,* **far above all rule and authority and power and dominion, and every name that is named, not only in this age but also in the one to come. And He put all things in subjection under His feet and gave Him as head over all things to the church, which is His body, the fullness of Him who fills all in all [...*and now is said of*] Him [Christ], who is the** *head* **of all principality and power [meaning, all the evil one powers have been given to Christ]."** (Col. 1:19–20, 2:10; Eph. 1:20–23)

Jesus of Nazareth, the Messiah, has been made, as declared by scripture, for all to know:

He is [the] exact living image [the essential manifestation] of the unseen God [the visible representation of the invisible], the firstborn [the preeminent one, the sovereign, and the originator] of all creation. [*It is not business as usual for the evil one and his fallen forces.*] **For by Him all things were created in heaven and on earth, [things] visible and invisible, whether thrones or dominions or rulers or authorities; all things were created and exist through Him [that is, by His activity] and for Him.**

He really had no need to do what He did for us, but this is also why He is so awesome. He became an intricate part of creation, its centerpiece. This is where He has given meaning and significance to us for Himself.

And He Himself existed *and* is before all things, and in Him all things hold together. [He is the controlling, cohesive force of the universe.] He is also the head [the life-source and leader] of the body, the church; and He is the beginning, the firstborn from the dead, so that He Himself will occupy the first place [He will stand supreme and be preeminent] in everything. (Col. 1:15–18 AMP)

The reason for this has been written in scripture, saying, "**For it was fitting for Him, for whom *are* all things and by whom *are* all things, in bringing many sons to glory, to make the captain of their salvation perfect through sufferings.**" Now this is how we have learned to follow God Jesus (Heb. 2:10). But you must now understand this saying: "*To whom are all things*" this "Man" lives in *flesh and bones (from everlasting to everlasting)* and "[God the Father] has in these last days spoken to us by [this "Man"] His Son, whom He has appointed heir of all things, through whom also He made the universe [*heavens and earth and all that's in them*]; who being the brightness of *His* glory and the express image of His person, and upholding all things by the word of His power, when He had by Himself purged our sins, sat down at the right hand of the Majesty on high, having become so much better than the angels, as He has by inheritance [*Christ lives in a body of flesh and bones*] obtained a more excellent name than they" (Heb. 1:1–4). And when He did, He said, "I have the keys of Hades and of Death" […and] "All power in heaven and on earth is given to me" (Rev. 1:18; Matt. 28:18 NCV). And scripture continues to say of Him: "[In] Him dwells all the fullness of the Godhead bodily" (Col. 2:9–10) and "[God the Father] raised Him from the dead and seated Him at His right hand in the heavenly places [*a Man in flesh and bones*] far above all principality and power and might and dominion, and every name that is named, not only in this age but also in that which is to come. [*God Jesus took the devil's office and now He is head over all.*] And He put all *things* under His feet and gave Him *to be* head over all *things* to the church" (Eph. 1:19–22). There is more from this outcome: "For in Him all the fullness of Deity (the Godhead) dwells in bodily form [completely expressing the divine essence of God]. And in Him you have been made complete [achieving spiritual stature through Christ], and He is the head over all rule and authority [of every angelic and earthly power]." He is head of them, kicking the evil one out of office and subduing all principalities and powers of darkness under Him and His church/body. He has set us up over the top in Him as He is sovereign, God Almighty (Col. 2:9–10). And "[God the Father] raised *us* up together and made *us* sit together in the heavenly *places* in Christ Jesus [*who is at the right and of God the*

Father] that in the ages to come He might show the exceeding riches of His grace in His kindness toward us in Christ Jesus," these riches started two thousand years ago (Eph. 2:6–7). Finally, it is stated unto the church:

> [For God's] intent that now the manifold wisdom of God might be made known by the church to the principalities and powers in the heavenly *places,* according to the eternal purpose which He accomplished in Christ Jesus our Lord, in whom we have boldness and access with confidence through faith in Him.

In other words, the victory of God Jesus is for Him as the "Head-Man" in flesh and bones to rule over all, from everlasting to everlasting, and we must let everyone know, specially the principalities and powers of darkness in the air about, who is boss in command: Jesus of Nazareth, Israel's triumphant Messiah (Eph. 3:10–12).

The destruction of the evil one was for Christ to start building His church, and He said of her: "I will build my church, and the power of death will not be able to defeat it" (Matt. 16:18). The King James Version states, "The gates of Hades shall not prevail against it," speaking of a central power by the empire of death. The Spanish (DHH) version says, "Y ni siquiera el poder de la muerte podrá vencerla," and the phrase *ni siquiera* is an adverb meaning in English "not even." My point is that, not even the power of death, meaning its *principalities, powers, authorities, and host of death in the region of darkness* cannot prevail against those who are members of the body of Christ, named the invisible church chosen. Then we continue to use the word's power as a legal written statement of our Omni-God, and say as written:

> What then shall we say to these things? If God *is* for us, who *can be* against us? [...and] Yet in all these things we are more than conquerors through Him who loved us. For I am persuaded that neither death nor life, nor angels nor principalities nor powers, nor things present nor things to come, nor height nor depth, nor any other created thing, shall be able to separate us from the love of God which is in Christ Jesus our Lord.

And that love gives us the victory to live in peace (Rom. 8:31, 37–39). This is also why we walk in this confidence created by God's (Word) love and acceptance. God Jesus, by His omniscient knowledge, said, "**Whatever you ask in my name the Father will give you.**" And scripture abundantly explains of this:

> Christ may dwell in your hearts through faith; that you, being rooted and grounded in love, may be able to comprehend with all the saints what *is* the width and length and depth and height—to know the love of Christ which passes [all] knowledge; that you may be filled with [all] the fullness of God. Now to Him who is able to do exceedingly abundantly above all that we ask or think [*Wow!*] according to the power that works in us, to Him *be* glory in the church by Christ Jesus to <u>all</u> generations.

And all of you have experienced this love. God so loved that He gave; and that is something precious to His Heart, His own family member, His Unique Son. When God gives, He does and more than expected (John 15:16; Eph. 3:17–21). This is also why when the enemy's forces (*any*) dares to overstep their boundaries of the written word of God against you, the believer, then has authority over them to cast them into hell until the day of judgment; and that is a legal written statement in heaven's court, by God's word stated by the Father of His Son's testimony to the church members. God Jesus said so:

> **I will give you the keys (authority) of the kingdom of heaven; and whatever you bind [forbid, declare to be improper and unlawful] on earth will have [already] been bound in heaven, and whatever you loosen [permit, declare lawful] on earth will have [already] been loosed in heaven.**

Do not let anyone fool you; God Jesus is on your side (Matt. 16:19). The word of the God BEING, all of Him, makes us walk in the victory of His Son, of whom He gives testimony. Then how can you not believe Him? The evil one has enslaved all the peoples (*minds*) of the world into darkness of sin and death (*by their worldviews*), those who have not believed God's word, and that's the only power he has got over humanity today. But all who receive Christ are unbound, unshackled from the dragon's claws. When the enemy tries to remind you of your fallen nature's constant slips into sin, remind him of his present near future: guilty as charged of all condemnation from all the sins committed in existence. The evil one has been destroyed by God Jesus, and God the Father made a *spectacle of him* and his demons. It is written:

> **[For] having canceled the charge of our legal indebtedness** [*that is all of them from beginning to end, for God is speaking as an omnipresent God*]**, which stood against us and condemned us; he has taken it away, nailing it to the cross. And having disarmed the powers and authorities, he made a public spectacle of them, triumphing over them by the cross.**

This means all our sins, past, present into our future, (*for if not, this verse would be a contradiction*). Therefore, remind the evil one of the cross, where all the charges of our indebtedness are hanged and his guilty sentence as charged, from beginning to forever of all the sins committed (Col. 2:14–15 NIV). Spiritual victory is marked by the same principle (*faith/hope*) that was used to acquire salvation of your fallen (*spirit/soul*) state, and that is by listening and believing the word of God and its immutable attribute, which produces the faith of your victory in Christ. Salvation out of God's BEING's wrath is a God thing, and we are just bystanders, and so we must listen and receive the promises and prophecies to our salvation today. We were dead people living in darkness in a fallen nature and could not see the truth of light, as we see it now as *elect*.

The First Two Solemn Festivities Marks the Lord's Victory

The solemn festivities already fulfilled are the *Passover*, Jesus of Nazareth's death and resurrection, and *Pentecost*, where a Holy Man/God goes to the Holy Heavenly/God the Father (*they are both holy*) and makes an exchange with His holy blood for the promised Holy Spirit for us as the Father had predicted in Their first divine, heavenly summit (Acts 1:8, 2:32–33; Gen. 3:15). We have explained these solemn feasts found in Leviticus 23 and said they are the spinal cord not only of the apocalypse but of the whole biblical story line about our redemption (*as Israel's restoration*), ending in God's millennium into making all things new. As our High Priest according to the order of Melchizedek, God Jesus fulfilled these two first solemn feasts, and as High Priest, scripture says,

> Therefore *it* was necessary that the copies of the things in the heavens [*like Moses, tabernacle of the desert with blood*] should be purified with these, but the heavenly things themselves with better sacrifices than these. For Christ has not entered the holy places made with hands, *which are* copies of the true, but into heaven itself [with His own blood] now to appear in the presence of God for us; not that He should offer Himself often, as the high priest enters the Most Holy Place every year with blood of another—He then would have had to suffer often since the foundation of the world; but now, once at the end of the ages, He has appeared to put away sin by the sacrifice of Himself.

By His own blood, He put sin and death away and destroyed the devil (Heb. 9:23–26). This means that to those who have accepted, their sins have been put away, forgiven. In this passage, we understand God Jesus presented Himself in the holy of holies in the celestial temple to celebrate the solemn feast of the Passover and Pentecost, which have already been celebrated. Now these feasts are to be celebrated once and in its due season in the heavenly temple, and two of them have been celebrated by our High Priest. At the present time, He sits in the heavenly throne by the right hand of the throne of God, waiting for the Father to tell Him, "Now is the time to celebrate the feast of the church wedding at a trumpet sound." These are sacred divine festivities in heaven, and those (*feast*) on earth are designed to resemble the ones in heaven. The writer of Hebrews explains, like Moses celebrated his first priestly work in the tabernacle of the desert, they were done as an image of those celebrated in heaven, in the Temple made not by man's hand. It was determined at the first *divine, heavenly summit* that these festivities in heaven were to be celebrated once and in its due season by God the Father's consent. These solemn feast works explain the priestly works God Jesus did here on earth where the Leviticus priestly works were an imitation of those originals in the order of Melchizedek. It is written:

> For when Moses had spoken every precept to all the people according to the law, he took the blood of calves and goats, with water, scarlet wool, and hyssop, and sprinkled both the book itself and all the people, saying, "This *is* the blood of the covenant which God has commanded you." Then likewise he sprinkled with blood both the tabernacle and all the vessels of the ministry. And according to the law almost all things are purified with blood, and without shedding of blood there is no remission.

This is also why the blood of Christ's sacrifice is so sublime and powerful, it's moving God the Father, omniscient and omnipresent stand, forever (Heb. 9:19–22). The first two solemn feasts have been celebrated by God Jesus, and He sprinkled with His own blood the instrument of the celestial temple, the Book of Life. And everyone who accepts Him is washed by His blood and their name written in the Book of Life forever. The omniscient God BEING does not spend His blood in those He knows will not accept His word; therefore, He told us not to throw the seed/pearl to the dogs/pigs. Now those who do not get it: all things are fresh at the eyes of Him whom we must give account to, and in His omniscient stand, the death of His Son is present/fresh always and grace or wrath is upon those who listen or won't, to obey or disobey God in His dealing. This dealing is for all who have listened to God's word, for all are included for salvation. The third solemn feast is the feast of the (*trump*) wedding of the Lamb. This one is the most exciting one, but also is the beginning of the wrath of the God BEING upon this earth. The apostle Paul explained it to the Thessalonians, for there were (*like in these days*) people speaking false doctrines of the gospel. Paul told them:

> But I do not want you to be ignorant, brethren, concerning those who have fallen asleep [*they were being taught a false message*] lest you sorrow as others who have no hope. For if we believe that Jesus died and rose again, even so God will bring with Him those who sleep in Jesus [*see how it was a false teaching*]. For this we say to you [*now this is correcting them*] by the word of the Lord [*God Jesus told him*] that we who are alive and remain until the coming of the Lord will by no means precede those who are asleep. For the Lord Himself will descend from heaven with a shout, with the voice of an archangel, and with the trumpet of God [*as a High Priest and His priestly works*]. And the dead in Christ will rise first. Then we who are alive and remain shall be caught up together with them in the clouds to meet the Lord in the air [*an almighty event*]. And thus, we shall always be with the Lord. Therefore comfort one another with these words.

This is not the Second Coming (1 Thess. 4:13–18). This third solemn feast will be celebrated at a trumpet sound, and only the church of Christ (*those who spirit/soul is living in light, the ninety-nine of this generation waiting for the last one [1 percent] lost to enter the flock*) with those who slept will hear the call as they are transformed into the likeness of Christ to meet the Lord in the clouds. As the lector notices, God Jesus as High Priest is going to come with these powerful instruments: with a shout, with the voice of an archangel, and with the trumpet of God (three things) to pick up His complete 100 percent of His sheep. The disciple must remember God Jesus's words: "**Here is what the One who sent me wants me to do: I must not lose even one whom God gave me** [*see how we are chosen/elect*] **but I must raise them all on the last day.**" This has nothing to do with us. It's a deal between the God BEING: the Father, His Son, and Holy Spirit (John 6:39). We must look at this event as the words of God are telling us of it, and the prophet Habakkuk saw it: "**God came from Teman, the Holy One from Mount Paran.** [*Selah*] **His glory covered the heavens, and the earth was full of His praise.** *His* **brightness was like the light** [God is light]**; He had rays** *flashing* **from His hand, and there His power was** *hidden.*" Must add on the other hand, He had God's trumpet of victory. What a glorious moment (Hab. 3:3–4). The heavens will be reaped open in two, and He will lift us up, His chosen, the church of ages and the dead in Christ are first (*resurrected/transformed*). Then we who are still alive on earth will be transformed in the same twinkling of an eye and snatched away to meet the Lord in the air as the dragon and his angels are cast out into earth (Rev. 12).

The first two solemn feasts have been fulfilled, and we are waiting for this third one. It will be something like what God told Moses:

> **The Lord also said to Moses** [*he was a type of the coming Messiah*] "**Go to the people and consecrate them today and tomorrow** [that is, **prepare them for My sacred purpose**] **and have them wash their clothes** [*to us by the sound doctrine anointing and we must remember:* "*Just as Christ loved the church and gave himself up for her to make her holy, cleansing her by the washing with water through the word,*" *so did Moses, as God Jesus cleanses us (Eph. 5:25–26)*] **and be ready by the third**

day, because on the third day the Lord will come down on Mount Sinai [in the cloud] in the sight of all the people."

How is this not different from what the apostles' theology taught us? Let us be ready living by the faith/hope presented to us, using it to cleanse our spirit/soul and flesh by the anointing of God the Holy Spirit and the apostles' sound doctrine (Exod. 19:10–11). They said, **"Therefore, having these promises, beloved, let us cleanse ourselves from all filthiness of the flesh and spirit** [*our spirit also gets dirty, it's cleanse through prayer quoting the word*] **perfecting holiness in the fear of God."** The apostle's theology prepares us for the apostle's eschatology (1 Cor. 7:1). The next solemn feast is the trumpet sound as these verses are teaching, and it has also been two days or two thousand years, and the church members have been getting cleansed/ready using fine white linen, the acts of faith/hope that were given to us by God Jesus's merits. We must use this second look from scripture, for she is immutable: **"After two days <u>He will</u> revive us; on the third day <u>He will</u> raise us up, That we may live in <u>His sight</u>."** The prophet Hosea was given to confirm the words of Moses, and this is a God thing: *"He will"* (Hos. 6:2). This was said to Israel, but we are just following what was planned by the God BEING, and it has been two days now, and the New Testament is the continuation/fulfillment of the Old. God Jesus also spent *two days* in Samaria (*with a mix Gentile/Jews, Samaritans*) and then headed to Jerusalem. This is a chosen historic event to teach us this truth (John 4:43). After the rapture, God will deal with Israel, Abraham's descendants (Zech. 11:10; Rom. 11:25–27). John the Apostle was also told to write about this church event:

She has been permitted [*given*] to dress in fine linen, dazzling white and clean—for the fine linen signifies

[*the written word which produce faith, sanctification by position, which creates sanctification in practice*] **the righteous acts of the saints [the ethical conduct, personal integrity, moral courage, and godly character of believers** (*sanctification in practice produces this by the word's faith/hope*)].

God the Holy Spirit gives testimony to your spirit/soul that you are living in His holiness (Rev. 19:8). Immediately, as the snatching away of the church happens, the atonement or expiation solemn feast starts. That's seven years of great tribulation, and/or Daniel's seventh week for those who did not believe. It starts with the rapture/snatching away event, and you must understand, millions of people will vanish from earth. The chaos will be extreme, but that is for my next (*first unpublished book*) *Terminal Damage* to be explained.

The point to understanding the solemn feasts is that God is letting us know everything is prepared, ready to happen, and the LORD has gone from generation through generation of the people He chose to save and begin their eternal life (1 John 5:10–12; Eph. 1:3–4). Predestination sounds to some like God will leave some people behind, but that is not the case, for predestination also determines the end of evil and death into the lake of fire—that is, the whole package of salvation. And He is offering it to all the chosen (*for they will accept it, no doubt*), and once they receive it, there is no turning back, for you are bought at a price of blood, and God knows who will answer the call. King David wrote in one of his songs (*psalms*) an insight that pointed to this true nature of God. He said, **"Your eyes have seen my formless substance; and in Your book were written All the days that were ordained *for me*, When as yet there was not one of them."** We must understand predestination not as a human thing but as an act (*programmed/*

coded destination) of the God BEING, the Potter, as Jeremiah and the apostle Paul would say (Ps. 139:16; Jer. 1:5; Eph 1:4).

In God's behalf, He started with one hundred sheep, and let us say, 1 percent through the generation backslid or needed to be brought newly save, but He (*the Son*) puts the ninety-nine aside and seeks those astray and brings them to Him, telling us that He started with one hundred sheep and when the trumpet sounds, He is taking one hundred sheep with Him. This is the story of the gospel. Jesus said,

> **What do you think?** [*He starts with a question.*] **If a man has a hundred sheep, and one of them goes astray** [*she was saved before stranded*], **does he not leave the ninety-nine and go to the mountains to seek the one that is straying?** [*God's love and mercy for us all*]. **And if he should find it, assuredly, I say to you, he rejoices more over that sheep than over the ninety-nine that did not go astray** [*it's a godly job*]. **Even so it is not the will of your Father who is in heaven that one of these little ones should perish.**

The ninety-nine should stop gossiping among each other and stop judging those who have gone astray (Matt. 18:12–14). We must understand God Jesus's responsibility and God the Father's agenda toward all of humanity, even though there will be those who refuse to heed the call and those who slip and fall. The apostle John captured this from Christ and wrote: "**This is the will of the Father who sent Me, that of all He has given Me I should lose nothing but should raise it up at the last day**" (*one hundred sheep*). This was determined at the first divine, heavenly summit before the foundation of the world (John 6:39; Eph. 1:4).

Predestination by God the Father starts in the life of those He created before He created them: **"Before I formed you in the womb, I knew you, And before you were born I consecrated you; I have appointed you as a prophet** [*speaker*] **to the nations,"** and how can anyone say no to that (Jer. 1:5). The Son does not accept anyone else but those sent by the Father, as He explains, **"All that My Father gives Me will come to Me; and the one who comes to Me I will most certainly not cast out** [I will never, never reject anyone who follows Me]**."** Then predestination is a God thing and an accept-it-by-us thing (John 6:37). The life of the last Adam was predestined (*prophesied*) as He mentioned it is about Himself and Isaiah prophesied it (Luke 24:44/Isa. 53)

Through the centuries people have argued about this topic, which is a simple matter as the apostle Paul taught us, and it's just a matter of accepting that God knows what He is doing, and it is about His BEING'S nature. The apostle wrote:

> **What shall we say then? Is there injustice with God? Certainly not!** [...] **You will say to me then, "Why does He still blame me** [for sinning]**?"** [...*and Paul answers by stating*] **"On the contrary, who are you, O man, who answers** [arrogantly] **back to God and dares to defy Him?** [*He is sovereign, and we are just animal creatures in a fallen nature.*] **"Will the thing which is formed** [*and sustained alive*] **say to him who formed it, 'Why have you made me like this?' Does the potter not have the** [sovereign] **right over the clay, to make from the same lump** [of clay] **one object for honorable use** [something beautiful or distinctive] **and another for common use** [something ordinary or menial]**?"** [...and] **"What if God, although willing to show His** [terrible] **wrath and to make His power known, has tolerated with great patience the objects of His wrath** (*there are those who*

will refuse to accept as they listen to these words, because they are born Nephilims, tare/goats) [which are] **prepared for destruction?** (Rom. 9:14–22).

(*My take*): what if God (*in His mercy*) prepared those vessels for wrath with the stamina to live in that lake of fire in darkness and those of us chosen to live with joy in the City of Light? We all must remember that God is a BEING, the only BEING (*He said, "I know of no other god."*) in that matter, not a creation as we are of Him. At the end, this is saying that we are creatures, created people (*angels and humans alike*), with no moral say so since we (*humans*) can't even stay alive by our own powers, if we really have any, like taking our next breath of air.

The principal point of the prophecy is for the believer to understand in God's omniscient, omnipresent stand, by His omnipotent BEING, He has lived and seen all things that have happened already (*its development*) and has fixed them in His ways and terms. It has been written: **"All things have been created through Him and for Him. He is before all things, and in Him all things hold together."** Then looking at reality through the eyes of God, it's not difficult, **"for in Him we live and move and exist [that is, in Him we actually have our being]."** What can we say of that? (Col. 1:16–17; Acts 17:28).

We must walk in His word believing its outcome, for He is working out the details: **"And we all, with unveiled face, continually seeing as in a mirror the glory of the Lord, are *progressively* being transformed into His image from [one degree of] glory to [even more] glory, which comes from the Lord, [who is] the Spirit."** By His and through His written word, this is where we begin to see reality through the eyes of God. Again, according to His written word, it has all been established (2 Cor. 3:18).

The apostle's theology is the supplement preparing us for the apostle's eschatology. Their sound doctrine's living anointing is preparing us for the future event of the wedding of the Lamb. When you hear the word provoking you to believe, she produced the faith that lit up the real meaning of the word of God. Without that special anointing, no one can understand God's truth revealed. This is the reason God the Father reveals Himself to us, to prepare us by believing in His word: the testimony He has given of His Son, God Jesus our Messiah. This is where we know and understand that not all are wheat/sheep and will obey and so does *the God Being*.

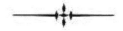

Answer the questions from this chapter to interact with others in a book club:

1. What two main events happened after God Jesus's resurrection? Name them.

2. What did God Jesus take from the evil one in His victory over death?

3. What is the backbone of the Bible teaching us of God's agenda through His word?

A Recap on Systematic Theology in This Book

The word *theology* is a compound word that comes from the Greek language where *theo* means "God" and *logy* surges from *logos*, or "word," and so we get the contemporary meaning in theology "*the God word*," and/or the study of God's word. The study of theology is the fuel that ignites our worship because the word of God provokes us to believe in Him and this was His intent when He gave us His written word. God Jesus said, "**Do not let your heart be troubled (afraid, cowardice). Believe [confidently] in God and trust in Him, [have faith, hold on to it, rely on it, keep going and] believe also in Me.**" This gives us the first tool, *faith* into His prophecies and promises, and that's our hook. Then comes the *hope*, which anchors our heart by His promises/prophecies:

In My Father's house [*His invisible reality*] are many
dwelling places [Mansions]. If it were not so, I would
have told you, because I am going there to prepare a
place for you [*His word promises, provoke us to believe
in Him*]. And if I go and prepare a place for you, I will
come back again and I will take you to Myself [*this
provokes our faith/hope into love*] so that where I am
you may be also [*that's in His natural reality of
invisibility, for the created ones cannot withhold Him*]
And [to the place] where I am going, you know the way
[through the faith/hope produced by His merits].

This is also looking at reality through the eyes of God,
according to His written word (John 14:1–4). The apostle's
theology explains our faith/hope in this fashion:

And we desire that each one of you show the same
diligence to the full assurance of hope until the end, that
you do not become sluggish, but imitate those who
through faith and patience inherit the promises. For
when God made a promise to Abraham, because He
could swear by no one greater, He swore by Himself,
saying, "Surely blessing I will bless you, and multiplying
I will multiply you." And so, after he had patiently
endured [the sacrifice] he obtained the promise [*He
obtained and then share them with us, for they were
meant for us*]. For men indeed swear by the greater,
and an oath for confirmation is for them an end of all
disputes. Thus God, determining to show more
abundantly to the heirs of promise the immutability of
His counsel, confirmed it by an oath, that by two
immutable things [*His Promise Holy Spirit, received by
His sacrificial payment*] in which it *is* impossible for

God to lie, we might have strong consolation, who have fled for refuge to lay hold of the hope set before *us*. This *hope* we have as an anchor of the soul, both sure and steadfast, and which enters the *Presence* behind the veil, where the forerunner has entered for us [*in Flesh and Bones to assures us this is from everlasting to everlasting*] *even* Jesus, having become High Priest forever according to the order of Melchizedek.

And scripture adds, "**For we are members of His body, of His flesh and of His bones.**" We belong to Him (Heb. 6:11–20; Eph. 5:30 NKJV). The LORD's word has His attribute of unchangeableness, confirming the testimony of His Son's account (1 John 5:10). The believer must wholeheartedly receive, as theist, the word of God; for His word possesses His attribute of unchangeableness. It is written, "**So shall My word be that goes forth from My mouth; it shall not return to Me void, But it shall accomplish what I please, And it shall prosper in the thing for which I sent it.**" The Word of God is part of the God BEING. She is an intricate part of His BEING, which comes from the depth of His heart, giving us authority of truth. *And He the Word stated,* "**Heaven and earth will pass away, but my words will never pass away.**" And this gives His word an attribute of unchangeableness. The word of the God BEING does not change, for she is immutable (Isa. 55:11; John 1:1–4; Mark 13:31).

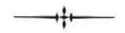

We Have Learn How to Follow Scripture's Thematic

For the general teachings in systematic theology, we've pointed to at least seven, and their in-depth subdivisions (*which we did not touch for you to research*) contains the complete knowledge as the scripture exposes its truth. We have slightly touched their veins, and it is for the lector to research on their own the complete work of that topic. This book's goal is to get the reader interested in this broad thematic and have them research the depth of its content for knowledge:

- *The teaching of what is the Word of God*: The reader must understand and grasp deep in their hearts that Scripture has God's attribute of unchangeableness. This is what she is proclaiming by Him, that she is the immutable will of God. The reader might ask, "What part?" And the answer is all of it. For she reveals herself to be spirit and life to those who are chosen by Him. When they become sealed, they encounter the power of the word of God, then it's true authority, as scripture's work is revealed plainly to them. She represents/possesses God's attributes of omniscience, omnipresence, and omnipotence to accomplish what she is sent to do. The believer becomes the prophecy of God manifested and witness of His testimony. In her statement by the "I AM, the Word, and the Spirit," the God BEING attributes are the basis to upload their authority of truth. She reveals God as she produces faith and hope in our spirit/soul that lights us up in this *death time zone* and our fallen nature. God is in control of all things; for in Him, through Him, and by Him, all that exists is also upheld. Therefore, there is no Mother Nature. That is just a lie (*ignorance*) of sinful men. God Jesus explains clearly that the word of God came to those who are created to His image and likeness (*spirit/soul*) and argues, "He called them gods, to whom the word of God came (and Scripture cannot be broken)." This is also why we (*the born again*) must look at reality through the eyes of God according to His written word (*true reality*), for she cannot be broken. Scripture states of itself to come from God's Inner Self: "For the word of God is living and powerful, and sharper than any two-edged sword, piercing [cuts] even to the division of soul and spirit, and of joints and marrow, and is a discerner of the thoughts and intents of the heart [*both verses (Heb. 4:12–13) are one*]. And there is no creature [*person*] hidden from His sight, but all things *are* naked and open to the eyes of Him to whom we *must give* account." God makes His Word one with Him and says of us that: "In Him we live and move and have our being." And so we are God's word activated (*with this reality*). We must accept God Jesus's words, for He explains, "The word that I speak to you are spirit, and they are life" [...and] "Out of the abundance of the heart the mouth speaks." This last we must apply its meaning to God the Father and His Word/Son who comes from the depth of His heart (Matt. 12:34; Luke 6:45). A dead person cannot and will never understand God's words of life unless they are awakened by Him. This is also why a disciple doesn't only know the Bible's canon (*the order and format of Scriptures*), but as he/she read the Bible, they reach a mature comprehension of its content, for we (*humanity*) are God's word "manifested/activated" and what is written is fashioned for us to awaken into a born-again status. In its format fashion, we will perceive at least four main characteristics projecting a superior conception of the Bible's content, and we define them by its *authority, capacity, realization,* and *dependence.* We are a living manifestation (*prophecy*) of the word of God spoken by Him, and we are also witness of His testimony in us (1 John 5:10–12). We begin to sense an awakening, an upheld maturity, as we walk as living spoken word of God. We are transcended unto Him as a living stone.

- *The teaching of who is God*: It is by Scripture we acquire the knowledge of knowing and understanding the God BEING and Creator of all things. His name is Existence, and He is "*absolute Himself*," and all the known absolutes are manifested through Him. That is absolute power, justice, and authority (limitless) to name a few. And scripture says that "**He cannot deny Himself**" that is any part of *himself* (2 Tim. 2:13). The God BEING reveals Himself to us in three ways: through that created, by His living touch (*salvation*), and by the written words content. God Jesus said, "**You err because you do not know the Scriptures or the power of God?**" Once you are touched by His power, His attributes must be understood to know what He said through His omniscient written knowledge (*Scripture*). This is how you know God. In order to understand Him, apply His attribute to what He is saying. Scripture uses, through its pages, anthropomorphic language to tell us about God's persona and His attachment to us (*His special creation on earth*). Once you know Him by His attributes, then you will understand well that redemption is His purpose for those who listen to His word. The LORD our God, the Lord is ONE, and He tells us of His invisible reality through His Word/God and their Spirit, which is also God. He is a BEING (*the only BEING for that matter*) with abilities to express Himself as He has explained in the scriptures. We are creations. He created us (*angels and men*); but to us, humanity, he gave His image and likeness, although we have become a downgraded replica of God because of sin. We understand this reality by our senses and our inner spirit/soul, but we are one body, spirit/soul. How much more the God that created us. In His reality, He can speak, saying, "**Let Us make man to our image and likeness.**" He also placed eternity in our hearts (*an animal created thing*) so that we can understand Him and said, "**Let the one who boasts boast in this, that he/she understands and knows Me [and acknowledges Me and honors Me as God and recognizes without any doubt] that I am the Lord**" (Jer. 9:24). The God BEING in His abilities as a BEING has bared His holy arm as the "I AM, the WORD and the SPIRIT," rephrased as Father, Son and Holy Spirit (*anthropomorphic language*) to make us understand His redemption and His abilities, attributes, character, and motive as the God BEING. It is written: "**All things have been created through him and for him. He is before all things, and [in him] all things hold together.**" He is the only BEING, and angels and humans are His creation, and in Him, we all live and move and have our beings (*in Him*) (Col. 1:15 –17; Ps. 119:160; John 17:17). Look around and understand the truth: His word is truth. It is for His namesake that He saves us and pardons us from guilt. It is a God BEING thing, and we must understand Him (Ps. 23:3, 25:11, 31:3, 79:9).

- *The teaching of God Jesus and God the Holy Spirit:* The LORD our God manifests Himself through His living Word. "**In the beginning was the Word, and the Word was with God, and the Word was God. He was in the beginning with God.**" It is spoken of Him (*the Word*) as a He—that is, a Person. "**The Word became flesh and dwelt among us.**" Who can say that He (*God*) cannot do that? His sacrifice brought about the promised Holy Spirit from God the Father, or the LORD. The Hebrew capital letters differentiates the Father from the Son, as is written, "**The LORD said to my Lord.**" But to tighten things up in the Person of God, the Holy Spirit is also God and "**The Lord is the Spirit.**" In other words, the Son is the Spirit, and the Son is also the image and substance of the invisible God (*the Father*), but God the Holy Spirit is also a Person and intricate part of God. In their redemptive worked, it is said, **"And if the Spirit of Him who raised Jesus from the dead [that was God the Father]lives in you, He who raised Christ Jesus from the dead [*the Father*] will also give life to your mortal bodies through His <u>Spirit</u>, who lives in you."** In the mystery of God, it is said, **"The Lord our God, the Lord *is* one!"** The apostles revealed that the "I AM, the WORD and the SPIRIT" (*or* LORD, *Name, and the Angel of the Lord*) of the Old Testament are also the **"Father, Son, and Holy Spirit"** of the New Testament, the God BEING (*as we are given to understand in this Bible study*). This is called and known by theologians as anthropomorphic language in Scripture, which describes God, for us to understand Him and His relationship to us. It is how God wants to reveal Himself to us His creation. God Jesus said, **"For out of the abundance of the heart the mouth speaks."** In this language, scripture is saying that the Word of the God BEING comes out of the depths of His heart, and that ability makes the Word one with God the Father. He declared in His doctrine, **"He who has seen Me has seen the Father."** As He also said, **"All things that the Father has are Mine."** It is said that what we speak comes out of our hearts, and in the God BEING's absolute abilities, it permits Him to become Father, Son, and Holy Spirit; and they are one (Matt. 12:34; Luke 6:45; John 14:9, 16:15). Scripture teaches us the Son (*who now lives in* flesh and bones) is God Almighty. He is sitting at the right hand of God the Father, but He is also the image and substance of the invisible God BEING (*Ancient of days*), and this teaches us about the Their Spirit and His work in the church redemption. Scripture states, **"He was in the world, and though the world was made through him, the world did not recognize him."** And scripture also states, **"The Lord is the Spirit,"** and then it declares this awesome ability by saying, **"And if the Spirit of Him who raised Jesus from the dead [*God the Father*] lives in you, He who raised Christ Jesus** from the dead [*the Father*] will also give life to your mortal bodies through His Spirit, who lives in you." It is in this anthropomorphic language that scripture makes it clear to our finite spirit/soul to somehow understand the signature of His persona in us, His temple (John 1:10; 2 Cor. 3:17; Rom. 8:11; 1 Cor. 6:19).

• *The teaching of man in their fallen nature*: When man was created, he was created perfect but not complete. He was a product in process until he disobeyed the Word of God. Then he became futile, worthless, even to himself; but God had loved him before the foundation of the world (*his creation*) and prepared a way for man to climb out of the hole of mire he fell in. Man became totally depraved and completely corrupted by sin into death as into God's contrast. Because of sin, death became his god, and all his offspring, descendants were imputed and tagged with death's corruption as well. Man became a slave to the powers of death and its newly acquired emperor, the devil. He took control over their behavior forcefully. It is said in scripture of the evil one: "**Who did not open [release] the house of his prisoners.**" He has no love for humanity. The evil one has made man walk in carnal constructs (*their instincts as rational animals*), making him/her walk in ungodly madness. Because of sin the whole world (*of unbelievers*) lies "**under the sway**" (*control*) of the wicked one. Humanity is dead in trespasses and sins, walking according to the course of this world, according to the prince of the power of the air, the spirit who now works in the disobedient. Scripture does not lie. Humanity is living in a fallen nature, blinded by sin into death, where it is directed to a lake of fire, which lake of fire was determined at God's first divine, heavenly summit. Predestination is a sovereign rightful ability of God, and everything has been predestined by the God BEING before the foundation of the world. We must understand that death did not exist in the plane of existence until Adam sinned and death took a hold on all his abilities over this earth. God used this (*aberration*) as a purpose to destroy him who had the empire of death: the devil and all the fallen angels that follow him and the corrupted conception of "tares and goats" (*the Nephilim*) thrown into the lake of fire. We may ask, But will there be any descendant of Adam from Seth that will fall in the lake of fire? All we can say is that all the humans who will not accept Christ are guilty as accomplices of the killing of God's chosen; for the spirit of the world and sin, not God's Spirit, lives in them.

- *The teaching of men's redemption by the merits of Christ*: Before the foundation of the world, God so loved mankind, that knowing his future disarray, He offered His unique Son, that whomsoever believe in Him would not perish but have everlasting life. The fact that the God BEING took this route to give us extra significance is mind- boggling, and we need to take it *reverently* and *seriously*. The Son indeed was foreordained before the foundation of the world; therefore, the meditation was *for God so loved* His creation that He still decided to create it (*angels and humans*) with all its goods and all its horrors. God, knowingly in their first divine summit before creation, set up a plan for His creation to draw them near Him, that angels would worship and humans receive salvation. We must understand that because of the God BEING's godly perfection, He could not accept man as is. So He created a justice for man (*grace by faith*) to be received and enter God's mercy by the works of a perfect sacrifice by a perfect human being (*like Adam was before he sinned*). The fact that man was not a finished product gave them the opportunity to receive God's grace, though scripture points that God did not need to save man as He did not spare the angels. Therefore, it is through the faith and hope produced by scripture that we are awakened into that profound quality of our being, our spirit/soul. Scripture produces, by the content of His power in His word, the door where we can enter God's grace by the merits of (*our scapegoat*) Jesus of Nazareth, our Second Adam. He has redeemed us from our eternal disorder by accepting to pay beforehand (*at Their first heavenly, divine summit*) the works we were going to walk by after the anointing called. This was taught by the apostles' theology (*tradition*) that the sound doctrine anointing would prepare us to escape the apostle's eschatology (*God's wrath*). One cancels the other for those who accept.

- *The teaching of the church by the apostle's theology*: There was a place where the Lord God formed man from the dust of the ground and breathed into his nostrils the breath of life and man became a living soul. But there was another place where a body of people was assembled, and there came a living sound from heaven as of a rushing mighty wind and filled the whole house, and they were all filled with the Holy Spirit, and the church was born. And so it is written, **"The first man Adam became a living being. [...] The last Adam became a life-giving spirit."** This last Adam assembles a body of people/members as His spiritual body, and He calls them His church. He is said to be the head of the body, the church. The apostles also taught us that God raised us up together and made us sit together in the heavenly places in Christ Jesus, bringing us over the top with Christ. This was elaborated by God, for **"The intent [of God is] that now the manifold wisdom of God might be made known by the church to the principalities and powers in the heavenly places [ours and God Jesus enemies] according to the eternal purpose which He accomplished in Christ Jesus our Lord,"** who defeated them. And having disarmed the devil, his principalities and powers, He made a public spectacle of them throughout heaven and earth, triumphing over them at the cross of Calvary. Now those of the church and members of the body of Christ have a say so in their spiritual state: from sin's darkness into everlasting light in Christ Jesus our Lord. If the enemies overstep their boundaries (*of the word of God*) to hassle/struggle with us, we have the authority over them to rebuke, bind, and send them into hell until the day of judgment (*they are an infestation*). God Jesus said so, and the gates of hell will not prevail against the church.

- *The teaching of the predestined future by the apostle's eschatology*: The apostles theology prepares us for the apostle's eschatology (*wrath of God*), in other words, the part of theology concerned with death, judgment, and the final destiny of the condemned. The apostles taught that God did not appoint us for wrath but to obtain salvation through our Lord Jesus Christ. The Lord also told the apostle John to write: "**Because you have kept My command to persevere** [*the sound doctrine*]**, I also will keep you from the hour of trial which shall come upon the whole world, to test those who dwell on the earth.**" The apostles' eschatology is real. It's the wrath of God the Father upon those who have not believed the testimony He has given of His Chosen One (*for they are guilty as accomplices of the killing of His Son; that is their condemnation*). *God's Anointed* in Hebrew means Messiah and in Greek, Christ. But the apostles knew Him as Jesus of Nazareth, a man like us humans. The world stage is set up for the wrath of God, for His absolute justice must be satisfied by His absolute authority, which was deterred by angels and man. Once the church is snatched away (*rapture*), the wrath of God will be manifested (*for man and fallen angels*), as the apostle wrote: "**For the mystery of lawlessness** [rebellion **against divine authority and the coming reign of lawlessness**] **is already at work; [but it is restrained] only until he who now**

restrains it is taken out of the way [*the church, when God the Holy Spirit takes her*]. **Then the lawless one [the Antichrist] will be revealed and the Lord Jesus will slay him with the breath of His mouth and bring him to an end by the appearance of His coming.**" The apostle's eschatology is already at work, for its God's omniscient knowledge and power shown in writing (*predestined*) for all to know that He is God, who knows all things as He proclaimed, "**I am God, and there is none like Me, Declaring the end from the beginning.**" In my book *Terminal Damage,* we will express the ins and out of God's revealed predestined future (*foretold*) and its authority of truth. Soon if God wills it.

Systematic theology is the study developed through the ages by the church's history champions where many men and women have elaborated (*theorized*) and fought against the enemies of Scripture, giving us a thorough understanding of the biblical content. We have acquired our knowledge of Scripture from the shoulders of God's giants, throughout church history. Scripture teaches this: "**For no prophecy was ever made by an act of human will, but men moved by the Holy Spirit spoke from God.**" He chose (*afterward*) each individual, man, and women alike, to establish the image of the puzzle in scriptures. And we are told, "**Where there is no [wise, intelligent] guidance, the people fall [and go off course like a ship without a helm], but in the abundance of [wise and godly] counselors there is victory.**" And God intended for us to know this, making us part of His written word (2 Pet. 1:21; Prov. 11:14). They translated the original scriptures from the Hebrew and Greek sources to our native languages (*started by courageous Jewish men*) while others fought to keep the teachings, doctrines, scripture (*meaning*) intact and pure, as in its original source. There are over five thousand copies of scriptures that bring those who work their content (*our Bible versions*) into close originality. The scripture's doctrines containing a trinity of one

God, as mentioned in this Bible study the "I AM, the WORD and the SPIRIT," are made known by the apostles' theology as Father, Son, and Holy Spirit and that they are "*One Holy Absolute Being.*" The Author calls Them the God BEING, for there is no other BEING like Them. Those involved in writing scriptures and those who uphold it fought the established doctrine given by the apostles, those like, "*God Jesus is fully God and fully man*" and that "*He was born into this reality from a virgin birth*" and, now resurrected, lives in a transformed body in *flesh and bones*. They taught that salvation is by the grace of God in Christ alone, based in the new priesthood order of Melchizedek, not by the works of the Leviticus priesthood (*law*) or any work therein but by the power of the word of God in His mercy and God's love toward us. These and many of the teachings that we have today by the apostle's theology derived from the prophets and the psalmist as God Jesus instructed the apostles. This was established in the author's first published book called *The Apostles Methodology to Interpret Scripture*, which method was given to them by Jesus of Nazareth and God the Holy Spirit (*the Spirit of Truth*). Then we can accept that the prophets, psalmist, apostles, the post-apostles, the fathers of the second to third century, and those heroes throughout the history of the church, to mention a few, stood up and fought to keep Scripture's doctrinal teachings pure. It is by the exposition of some of these giants such as John Hus, John Wesley, Martin Luther, Calvino, Charles H. Spurgeon and contemporaries as Billy Graham, J. Vernon McGee, Chuck Missler, and the like, who observed and follow what has been called systematic theology today that we understand the Bible's synthesis close to the original meaning it was meant to be. No one can claim their own theology (*as many folks do*), but the study of all these holy peoples' work throughout time has given us much to search about the God BEING.

These giants of the gospel taught us about the main structure of the church body that God Jesus Himself established. They taught that from within the members, Christ Himself would call some *to be* apostles, some prophets, some evangelists, some pastors, and some teachers (*some, not all*) for the equipping of the saints for the work of ministry and the edifying of the body of Christ. Also, that there are diversities of gifts, but they are operations from the same Spirit in their diversities of activities, but it is the same God who works them all in all. The manifestation of the Spirit is given to each one for the profit of all:

> **For to one is given the word of wisdom through the Spirit, to another the word of knowledge through the same Spirit, to another faith by the same Spirit, to another gifts of healings by the same Spirit, to another the working of miracles, to another prophecy, to another discerning of spirits, to another *different* kinds of tongues, to another the interpretation of tongues.**

They are one and the same Spirit working all these things, distributing to each one individually as He (*the Spirit*) wills. Scripture establishes about these gifts:

> **For the gifts and the calling of God are irrevocable** [*We have to add another gift to the bundle, for if not, we are missing out on God's authority of truth*] **for He does not withdraw what He has given, nor does He change His mind about those to whom He gives His grace or to whom He sends His call.**

And that gift is *salvation*, as it has been taught by the apostles (Rom. 11:29). Paul wrote by authority of God the Holy Spirit, **"For it is by grace you have been saved, through faith—and this is not from yourselves, it is the gift of God—not by works, so that no one can boast."** This is the NIV, but let's amplify this a bit:

For it is by grace [God's remarkable compassion and favor drawing you to Christ] that you have been saved [actually delivered from judgment and given eternal life] through faith. And this [salvation] is not of yourselves [not through your own effort], but it is the [undeserved, gracious] gift of God; not as a result of [your] works [nor your attempts to keep the Law (*or any good doing*)], so that no one will [be able to] boast or take credit in any way [for his salvation]. (Eph. 2:8–9 AMP)

The church of God Jesus has spiritual activities that characterize them as a living entity. He said of her: "**Most assuredly, I say to you, he who believes in Me, the works that I do he will do also; and greater *works* than these he will do, because I go to My Father.**" The church body of Christ is called to do the things through God the Holy Spirit, just like Jesus of Nazareth did while on earth, and He said we would do greater things through our collaboration into His ministry. Even the powers of hell will not prevail against her. This is a supernatural statement. No other church group is like the born-again, spirit-filled, Bible-believing, Holy Spirit-baptized body of Jesus Christ on earth. This is possible because the body of Christ is a living part of God Jesus Himself; and they are a visible, invisible, local, and worldwide church.

At end, it is written: "**The Lord knows those who are His**" and "**Let everyone who names the name of the Lord stand apart from wickedness and withdraw from wrongdoing.**" The LORD cannot be fooled: "**For the one who sows to his own flesh will reap destruction from the flesh, but the one who sows to the Spirit will reap eternal life from the Spirit.**" Or do you think that you are stronger than Him? Think again. Living in the Spirit is letting the Lord God Jesus's work His miraculous priestly work on your life; and James, His half-brother, said, "Show me your faith without your works and I will show you my works by the power of my faith in the merits of Jesus of Nazareth, my big brother, and God's Sent Messiah (*my version and understanding of their apostle's theology*)."

We Carry This Anointing through the Spirit Word

The sound doctrine anointing given by the written statement of the apostles teaches us that God has given us sanctification by position once we were born again, which leads us into its action of sanctification in practice. This was Pastor James's challenge to the believer because faith produces the miracle in this fallen nature into a godly behavior prepared *beforehand* by God. Faith in scripture produces natural godly works, like faith for a healing or a miracle. It's God's omni-power involved: "**Show me your faith without your works, and I will show you my faith by my works.**"

Real faith in the word produces the miracle of a powerful living (2:18). It is noticeable in the words of Paul as he mentions the conditions by this faith: "Now <u>He has</u> reconciled you in the **body of His flesh through death,** *to present you* <u>holy</u>**,** and <u>blameless</u>**,** and <u>above reproach</u> in His sight [*this is sanctification by position, God says this of us*]—if indeed you continue in the faith [*in Christ's merits as guarantee*], grounded and steadfast, and are not moved away from the hope of the gospel [here is another condition bringing you into sanctification in practice], which you heard, which was preached to every creature under heaven, of which I, Paul, became a minister." God also said, "But as many as received Him, to them He gave the right to become children of God [*sanctification by position*], to those who believe [*sanctification in practice*] in His name: who were born, not of blood, nor of the will of the flesh, nor of the will of man, but of God."

And this again is a place in which we are positioned by God (*perceptibly by His power touch*) as we were born from death by His will. Justification is an act of God, and sanctification is a work of God in the believer. His word has the power to produce both. It is because of our faith in the merits of God Jesus: "**For in Him dwells all the fullness of the Godhead bodily; [*and you*] are complete in Him.**" The outcome of this sanctification *by* position happens. He makes us walk as children, as sons and daughters of light producing what we call sanctification *in* practice, for we are doing (*by faith/hope more eagerly after being touched*) as we are moved by scripture through God the Holy Spirit, who leads us to walk in Him. God knows our future, for He also lives in it, and this is also why it is written that "**we are His workmanship, created in Christ Jesus for good works, which God *prepared beforehand* that we should walk in them** [*the faith/hope in God Jesus priestly works are real*]."

We practice sanctification by the power of the faith/hope He has given our spirit/soul, and it is a miracle in this fallen nature. The promises and prophecies He gave us in the past are manifesting from the future into our present "life stand," and we understand how God makes them happen coming from the future so that as they come into our present. They are bent by God's will, for He is an Omni-God. Therefore, we advise, pray for your tomorrow today. It is written about this:

"**No weapon that is formed against you will succeed** [*promised in the past*]; **and every tongue that rises against you in judgment you will condemn** [*God is preparing these things for us*]. **This [peace, righteousness, security, and triumph over opposition] is the heritage of the servants of the Lord, and *this is* their vindication from Me,**" says the Lord.

The God BEING means that His redemption for those who are called is by His hand's power/word (Isa. 54:17). When a man or a woman's faith pleases the Lord, He makes even his enemies to be at peace with them; and this is a promise from the past, activated in our future, to rest into our present stance (Prov. 16:7). He said, **"No disaster will come near your tent"** (Ps. 91:10).

This powerful anointing is possible by the Spirit that now lives in us (*we are His temple*). It was given to us by the washing of the blood of God Jesus (*so that His Spirit can live in us*), and this we must comprehend, for God does not live-in dirty vessels, and so He keeps us cleanse. He is in His BEING awesome in nature and omnipresent, omniscient, and omnipotent God (the *Absolute* of all absolutes]. In other words, He saw and knew all of whom we are from before birth to death and decided from before the foundation of the world (*at Their first divine, heavenly summit*) to save us. It is written: **"Before I formed you in the womb, I knew you"** and **"Your eyes saw my substance, being yet unformed. And in Your book, they all were written, the days fashioned for me, when *as yet there were none* of them."** Our days are counted and numbered, for **"indeed, the very hairs of your head are all numbered. Don't be afraid; you are worth more than many sparrows,"** and so we are assured (Jer. 1:5; Ps. 139:16; Luke 12:7).

This is also why He will not let us fall into eternal death, because He has bought us at the price of blood, and to Him, we are worth the eternal investment, for He suffered, being the biggest investment ever made in His reality. He knows and lives in our future, and He would be a bully if He saved us knowing we would not make it to Him (*and dropping us, this is a carnal thought do not let anyone fool you*). It is a godly thing between Them and Their Absolute BEING. We'll find out all of it one day, though we must know it now as scripture states. God did not need us for anything scripture implies. His attribute of freedom and of independence says it:

> The God who created the world and everything in it, since He is Lord of heaven and earth, does not dwell in temples made with hands; nor is He served by human hands, as though He needed anything, because it is He who gives to all [people] life and breath and all things.

And in the Old Testament, He said,

> Every beast of the forest is Mine, And the cattle on a thousand hills. I know every bird of the mountains, And everything that moves in the field is Mine. If I were hungry, I would not tell you, For the world and all it contains are Mine.

How simplistic is this idea: it is for us to get the memo (Acts 17:24–25; Ps. 50:10–12). The fact that God created us gives us significance, and even much more, the fact that He came to die for us (*purchasing us*) from the death dictated by God's nature of holiness. This gives us a sense of complete significance about His love for us to move ahead, and oh, that you would nest this grace into your deepest heart's entrails (Gen. 2:17). The words in the Bible let us know the warmth and love that the God BEING has felt for us to call us His sons.

Answer the questions from this chapter to interact with others in a book club:

1. What is the most important theme in systematic theology?

2. How does a believer prepare himself for the eschatology events forewarned by Scripture?

3. What are the two spiritual tools that prepare us for our eternity that grows into a third?

SIXTH LESSON

The Apostles Eschatology and the Wrath of God

G od Jesus said, "Look at [the marks in] My hands and My feet [and see] that it is I Myself. Touch Me and see; a spirit does not have *flesh and bones,* as you see that I have" (Luke 24:39 AMP). In this statement, God Jesus is telling us so much about Himself and about His Father's activities. He took a body in the likeness of the first Adam, and He came into our reality's nature like the first Adam before he sinned. He was innocent, immaculate—that is, already without sin in his spirit/soul; and His body stamina was like Adam's before sinning. Scripture states, **"[God the Father] send his own Son in the likeness of sinful flesh to be a sin offering [*it was a plan*]. And so, he condemned sin in the flesh, in order that the righteous requirement of the law might be fully met in us."** The story of the gospel is a legal work created at

God's first divine, heavenly summit at Their heavenly consul and invisible reality (*their natural reality*) before the foundation of the world, which satisfied Their absolute nature (Rom. 8:3–4). The Hebrew writer said it, explicitly detailing:

> **Therefore, since [His] children share in flesh and blood** (*Adam's sinned, imputed us with death*) **[the physical nature of mankind], He Himself in a similar manner also shared in the same [physical nature, but without sin],** *He became mortal in order to die and who dares tell God what to do?* **so that through [experiencing] death He might make powerless (ineffective, impotent) him who had the power of death, that is, the devil.** (Heb. 2:14 AMP)

This is also why now scripture states, "**He alone possesses immortality [absolute exemption from death] and lives in unapproachable light.**" He had become mortal like one of us, *the firstborn of all creation*, becoming the main part of this His created reality (1 Tim. 6:16). God's reasoning in Scripture is a heavenly legal matter on our behalf but pertaining to His awesome glorious nature of absolutes.

Scripture states that before He came to our reality:

> **He existed in the form and unchanging essence of God [as One with Him, possessing the fullness of all the divine attributes—the entire nature of deity and He], did not regard equality with God a thing to be grasped or asserted [as if He did not already possess it, or was afraid of losing it].**

Let's compare the words in this verse to the New International Version that says, "***Who, being in very nature God, did not*** *consider equality with God something to be used to his own advantage.*" We explained what this *advantage* was in *The Apostles Methodology to Interpret Scriptures*, a challenge done against the devil (Phil. 2:6 NIV). *Continuing with the AMP:*

> But emptied Himself [without renouncing or diminishing His deity, but only temporarily giving up the outward expression of divine equality and His rightful dignity] by assuming the form of a bondservant and being made in the likeness of men [He became completely human (mortal) but was without sin, being fully God and fully man (*this last is something fought by God's giants throughout church history*)]. After He was found in [terms of His] outward appearance as a [mortal] man [for a divinely appointed time (*preplanned by the Godhead in Their divine summit*)], He humbled Himself [still further] (*His prayer in the olive garden were answered, humbling Himself even further by His death on a cross*) by becoming obedient [to the Father] to the point of death, even death on a cross.

These verses are telling us a divine story so that we unearth scripture and acquire the authority of truth (Phil. 2:5–8 AMP). Unlike us, God Jesus, as the first Adam knew, lived, upheld the reality we are living in—that is, that the whole biblical tale is the truth humanity has and is living. When the born-again believer looks at reality through the eyes of God, according to His word, they are upholding reality's truth. God Jesus today is the living image and substance of the invisible God, a title acquired by His victory on the cross of Calvary. God Jesus lives in a glorified body of flesh and bones to dictate and rule over this physical plain, our reality, and the heavenly: who can say no to that?

He was given authority, glory and sovereign power [by the Father]; all nations and peoples of every language worshiped him. His dominion is an everlasting dominion that will not pass away, and his kingdom is one that will never be destroyed. (Dan. 7:14)

He also said that "whoever has seen Me has seen the Father," a statement that must be researched and understood. The Hebrew writer wrote that:

[God the Father] in these last days spoken [with finality] to us in [the person of One who is by His character and nature] His Son [namely Jesus], whom He appointed heir and lawful owner of all things [*this is a legal matter*] through whom also He created the universe [that is, the universe as a space-time-matter reality (*we read this in the Gospel of John 1:1–14*)]. The Son is the radiance and only expression of the glory of [our awesome] God [reflecting God's Shekinah glory, the Light-being, the brilliant light of the divine], and the exact representation and perfect imprint of His [Father's] essence and upholding and maintaining and propelling all things [the entire physical and spiritual universe] by His powerful word [carrying the universe along to its predetermined goal (*He is the beginning and the end*)]. When He [Himself and no other] had [by offering Himself on the cross as a sacrifice for sin] accomplished purification from sins and established our freedom from guilt [*the psalmist asked about this: "What is man that You are mindful of him, And the son of man that You visit [give attention or care for] him?" (Ps. 8:4)*], He sat down [revealing His completed work] at the right hand of the Majesty on high [revealing His divine authority],

having become as much superior to angels, since He has inherited a more excellent *and* glorious name than they [that is, Son—the name above all names].

And this His name He has given it to us, His chosen, to live by (*at the cross of Calvary*) in Their first divine, heavenly summit (Eph. 2:10; Heb. 1:2–4 AMP). In a moment of deep anointing, Stephen, martyr, said that "**he [saw] the heavens opened and the Son of Man standing at the right hand of God!**" (Act 7:56 AMP). Today many things are said about the veracity of Scripture, but through them all, God Jesus stands at the right hand of God and that cannot be contradicted, for one day we will all have a One-on-one appointment with God the Father, and whoever does not believe the testimony He has given of His Son is making Him out to be a liar (1 John 5:10). Jesus of Nazareth, who accepted to become the Son of Man and Second Adam is the cornerstone that the builders disregarded; and those builders are each one of us in our personal life and the so-called cream of humanity. Now if we do not place the Creator of all things in front of our lives, turning from our worldviews, we will pay dearly; for we would be found to be accomplices in the killing of God's Chosen One.

All those people involved in the killing of Jesus of Nazareth are now dead, but the spirit of sin and of the world (*who now stand condemned*) has passed from generation to generation into this generation, and whoever contains the spirit of the world in their life is guilty, an accomplice of the killing of Jesus of Nazareth. The death of His Son is seen by Him fresh in His eyes always (*He is omnipresent*). It happened because of us (*this is a God BEING thing that you must understand*). Then if anyone does not accept, repenting (*which means to turn*), they are guilty as accomplices of the killing of God's Son, and that is the charge humanity upholds as guilty. Here on the courts of earth, a person is innocent until proven guilty, but in the courts of heaven, it has been established:

"Nothing in all creation is hidden from God's sight. Everything is uncovered and laid bare before the eyes of him to whom we must give account" (Heb. 4:13). This verse is saying two things: first, all the things of our personal life are known by God, and second, we must give account of it. In other words, we are all guilty and a payment must be presented (*by the works of the Mosaic law no one will be found innocent*). It has been written: "Therefore no one will be declared righteous in God's sight by the works of the law; rather, through the law we become conscious of our sin" (Rom. 3:20). Finally, the payment is the faith in the merits of Christ, and if you do not believe it, then you are guilty as an accomplice of the murdering of God's Son. But be of good spirit, for "being justified through faith, we have peace with God through our Lord Jesus Christ." You see how God is merciful (Rom. 5:1). The story of the gospel is the greatest story ever told.

Foreordained before the Foundation of the World

Everything about God's story started in the rarest of places: in a manger, *a feeding trough for animals*, where not only did animals eat and sleep, but they also did their fecal/urine business. The King of the world, the Creator of the universe, the Son of Almighty God came to earth and was born in an animal stable of all places. The thought of it, an animal manger, a heinous place; but He did this, resembling His virgin birth in the heart of every man and woman that accepts His proposal. Every one of us was dead with a heart filled with disgusting sinfulness. We were doing demoralizing, demon-possessed, animalistic acts; and we can see dehumanization is what the spirit of the world dictates (*enslaves*) under the control of the evil one. Christ's virgin birth has cast out our darkness (*in this death-time-zone evil age*) and has given us a new beginning (1 John 5:19). We needed such a human savior, as it is written:

> Since [His] children share in flesh and blood [the physical nature of mankind], He Himself in a similar manner also shared in the same [physical nature, but without sin], so that through [experiencing] death He might make powerless (ineffective, impotent) him who had the power of death—that is, the devil—and [that He] might free all those who through [the haunting] fear of death were held in slavery throughout their lives. [...and] *It was essential that* He had to be made like His brothers (mankind) in every respect, so that He might [by experience] become a merciful and faithful High Priest in things related to God, to make atonement [*reparation*] *(propitiation)* for the people's sins [thereby wiping away the sin, satisfying divine justice, and providing a way of reconciliation between (*the*) God (*BEING*) and mankind]. Because He Himself [in His humanity] has suffered in being tempted, He is able to help *and* provide immediate assistance to those who are being tempted *and* exposed to suffering.

At the end, this redemption decision is between the God BEING, and it is a godly thing from their nature. (Heb. 2:14–18). Jesus grew from childhood to adulthood as all of us do on earth. It is said, "**For to us a Child shall be born, to us a Son shall be given.**" The Son is the Word/God. He has always existed, and because of the first divine, heavenly summit plan of redemption, He was born as a child on earth. His body is two thousand years old as of now, but He has always been (Isa. 9:6; John 1:1–14). As every human does, He learned to eat, talk, read, write, and be obedient to His parents Joseph (*stepfather/caretaker*) and Mary. Joseph was of the bloodline of Solomon, son of King David, and by marrying Mary, our Lord Jesus became heir of King David. Also, Mary was from the bloodline of Nathan, son of King David, making Him the full last heir.

The genealogy of Matthew and Luke show Jesus of Nazareth was of the nation of Israel through their father Abraham. It is all a legal matter. We read, after the apostle Matthew writes his research from the temple's birth archive, "**the book of the genealogy of Jesus Christ, the Son of David, the Son of Abraham.**" He finds Jesus's royal title and blood heredity (Matt. 1:1). Even the apostle Paul, in his personal research, writes, "**Now to Abraham and his Seed were the promises made. He does not say, 'And to seeds,' as of many, but as of one, 'And to your Seed,' who is [Messiah] Christ**" (Gal. 3:16). God the Father made sure that the environment where His Son was going to come was conditioned to His godly ethical nature. He chose Israel, a nation "*He made,*" and gave them a religion and taught them what to eat, a way to dress and talk, and how to conduct themselves. He conditioned them for His Word to become flesh and walk among us. Moses wrote about this God's heavenly plan and said to Israel,

> **The Lord did not love you and choose you because you were greater in number than any of the *other* peoples [*a nation from among Gentile people*] for you were the fewest of all peoples. But because the Lord loves you and is keeping the oath which, He swore to your fathers [*from the promise to Adam (Gen.3:15) established with Abraham of the Seed/Messiah (Gal. 3:16)*] the Lord has brought you out with a mighty hand and redeemed (bought) you from the house of slavery (*death*) from the hand of Pharaoh king of Egypt (*the evil one*). Therefore know [without any doubt] *and* understand that the Lord your God, He is God, the faithful God, who is**

keeping His covenant and His [steadfast] loving-kindness to a thousand generations with those who love Him and keep His commandments [which we keep by the power of God the Holy Spirit, served by the apostles' tradition (*teachings/theology)*]. (Deut. 7:7–9)

The upbringing and learning received by Jesus of Nazareth was like that of every human person who has existed. The evangelist Luke writes: **"The Child continued to grow and become strong, increasing in wisdom; and the grace of God was upon Him"** and also **"And Jesus kept increasing in wisdom and stature [*age*], and in favor with God and men."** And just like each human being has experiences while growing up in their individual neighborhood (*ghetto/barrio*: **"Can anything good come out of Nazareth?"** [*John 1:46]*), Jesus of Nazareth lived (Luke 1:80, 2:52). Scripture also states that He had hunger, that includes the whole physical human digestive system, though He had the stamina of the first Adam before Adam sinned (Matt. 4:22). He had a spirit/soul like us and also emotions.

The apostle Peter wrote that **"the prophets [...] which [had] the Spirit of Christ in them."** The Word of God was already in action on the prophets of the past, working His human mystery (*predestined life*) through them (*God is a spirit/soul, and He created us to this image/likeness in a physical body, with a spirit/soul*) (1 Pet. 1:10–12). The reader can capture this about God in the words of Isaiah (42:1) that says, **"My Chosen One *in whom* My soul delights. I have put My Spirit upon Him; He will bring forth justice to the nations."** God the Father made the redemptive plan, and it was written: **"Yet it pleased the LORD to bruise Him; He has put *Him* to grief. When You make His soul an offering for sin."** God Jesus's soul was the offering expiation for our sins (*this is personal*). It was not just the suffering of His body. This is also why this is so personal from Him to us. The God BEING made this event change His personal motives for our behalf (Isa. 53:10).

In His earthly days, Jesus declared at different times: "**Now My soul has become troubled; and what shall I say, 'Father, save Me from this hour'? But for this purpose, I came to this hour**" [...*it is also said*] "**He became troubled in spirit**" (John 12:27, 13:21). Mathews writes of Him, saying, "**My soul is deeply grieved, to the point of death.**" God Jesus as Adam had/has His own spirit/soul, scriptures states, and we also know that the Lord is the Spirit. This is another God BEING thing for us to ponder. How does this all fit in His reality of invisibility and those absolute eternal forces? (Matt. 26:38; 2 Cor. 3:17). The apostle Paul was taken into that reality and wrote about that place: "He [Paul] **was caught up into Paradise and heard inexpressible words, which it is not lawful for a man to utter.**" About these promises from God, we wrote them in our first published book, *The Apostles Methodology to Interpret Scripture* (2 Cor.12:4). It is to that heavenly reality He is preparing and taking us, as God Jesus assured,

> **In My Father's house are many mansions; if *it were* not *so*, I would have told you. I am going to prepare a place for you. And if I go and prepare a place for you, I will come again and receive you to Myself; that where I am, *there* you may be also.**

It is a snatching-away event (John 14:2–3). The God BEING's invisible reality is greater (*natural to Him*) than the heavens of the heavens, for she contains His glorious BEING; and so it's eternally infinite to the north, south, east, and west.

Completely Human, Completely God

Just like any of us, Jesus marveled at the things He experienced as a man. Matthew wrote of one of those moments: **"Now when Jesus heard this, He marveled and said to those who were following, 'Truly I say to you, I have not found such great faith with anyone in Israel.'"** The apostle John wrote of an emotional moment in the life of Jesus of Nazareth, saying, **"Jesus wept,"** being this as the shortest verse in scripture (Matt. 8:10; John 11:35). Jesus marveled at the faith of a Gentile centurion (*a Roman soldier*) and wept at the despair of Lazarus's sisters, His beloved friends (*emotion is a human election*), showing us His human emotional attachment. On another occasion, Matthew wrote of Jesus of Nazareth's responsive attachment to humanity's fragility, saying, **"When He went ashore, He saw a large crowd, and felt [profound] compassion for them and healed their sick."** In this same passage, Matthew goes on to say how God Jesus had compassion over the hunger of the rather large crowd and fed them from five pieces of loaves and two pieces of fish. He wrote: **"There were about 5,000 men who ate, besides women and children."**

The Lord has been real with us, and it's demonstrated by His acquiring our human nature (*coming as a man*) and dealing with our fallen nature and destroying our common enemy (Matt. 14:14, 21). At one time, He told us, **"Oh, you are stubborn, faithless people! How long shall I bear with you? Bring him here to me."** Looking at our fallen nature got Him out of His nerves, as we like to say (Matt. 17:17 TLB). Jesus of Nazareth was fond of the children of our world and said, **"Allow the children to come to Me; do not forbid them; for the kingdom of God belongs to such as these."** In this (*childish*) human fragility is how the God BEING sees us (Mark 10:14).

All these points out to how God Jesus became a complete human person, but He is also an intricate part of the Living God BEING (*the Word/God*). He took the form of bondservant and walked among us to bring us the knowledge of God the Father. He did this as a spirit/soul that scripture says He is and as a complete man/God in the likeness to our body (Rom. 8:3). The apostle John wrote of this: "**The Word (Christ) became flesh and lived among us; and we [actually] saw His glory, glory as belongs to the [One and] only begotten** [*meaning only and unique*] *Son* **of the Father, [the Son who is truly unique, the only One of His kind, who is] full of grace and truth (absolutely free of deception)**" (John 1:14 AMP).

As the Word/God, He did not use His godly powers to defeat the evil one, for He set aside His godly nature (Phil. 2:5–9] so that He did not have advantage over the evil one, but He came and defeated him in our likeness. We can say He challenged the evil one blindfolded. Like the first Adam before he sinned, Jesus of Nazareth was in a body— innocent, immaculate, and with no sin. His physical stamina was different from ours in this fallen nature. (*We must understand this: Jesus is the Man, and we are just falling apart.*) The first Adam lost the power he had over the earth that she (*the earth*) gave him to live of it, and it was said to him, "**Cursed is the ground because of you**" [...and] "**When you till the ground, it shall no longer yield its strength to you[because of sin]. A fugitive and a vagabond you shall be on the earth**" (Gen. 3:17, 4:12).

Adam lost all the power as a king over his nature when he sinned. A power that included naming and speaking to animals that spoke back to them, walking on water, speaking to the world's elements as the wind and the sea just as Jesus of Nazareth did. Jesus of Nazareth walked on water. He told (*talk to the earth*) the sea and the wind to calm down, and it obeyed Him. He cured the sick, cast out demons, resurrected the dead with the power extracted from the earth, and also conceded by the Father as we read that He resurrected Lazarus. He had all this ability as the Son of Man and the firstborn over all creation, (Gen. 1:26 Adam's dominion).

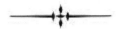

Representative of Man

The Anointed Seed of the woman, the Chosen One of God came into this world as the firstborn over all creation to make spirit people like Himself: "**The last Adam became a life-giving spirit**" (1 Cor. 15:45). Scripture teaches that the first and the Second Adam (*Jesus of Nazareth, also the last Adam*) are the representative of humanity, and the latter brought an effect to all humanity. The apostle Paul said it this way:

> **The free gift [of God] is not like the trespass [because the gift of grace overwhelms (*cancels/eliminates*) the fall of man]. For if many died by one man's trespass [Adam's sin], much more [abundantly] did God's grace and the gift [that comes] by the grace of the one Man, Jesus Christ, overflow to [benefit] the many. [...] For if by the trespass of the one (Adam), death reigned through the one (Adam), much more *surely* will those who receive the abundance of grace and the free gift of righteousness reign in [eternal] life through the One, Jesus Christ.**

In other words, one act cancels the other (Rom. 5:15, 17). In Adam, we were imputed with death, but in Christ Jesus, we are imputed with righteousness (*one cancels out the other, scripture* states). Christ's priestly works canceled Adam's eternal sinful mess. The apostle Paul expressed a central doctrine of God the Holy Spirit's teachings, writing:

> But [the] God [BEING] clearly shows and proves His own love for us, by the fact that while we were still sinners, Christ died for us. Therefore, since we have now been justified [declared free of the guilt of sin] by His blood [how much more certain is it that] we will be saved from the wrath *of God* through Him.

These words show how the apostles theology prepares us from their (*God*) given eschatology (Rom. 5:8–9). The faith of grace by the word of God (*that is, by the merits of Christ's priestly works*) clearly keeps us saved from the first Adam's sin and all our contracted sins, which are forgiven by exempting us from God's wrath. The sins committed in the past are atoned in the present through our prayer/faith stand (*by the anointing of the blood/spirit*) and terminating future sins (*if we continue in His faith*) by our praying for our tomorrow, today (*is a faith practice/priestly chore*). God Jesus took a body like ours—He didn't have to but He did—and proved how He loves us (*as our human comrade, brother, best friend up in heaven*), and we needed an Adam (*High Priest*) like Him to be in our side even though we did not deserve anything from our Creator. God the Father testifies to us in scripture:

> God made you alive together with Christ, having [freely] forgiven us all our sins [*handwritten note acknowledging a debt*] having canceled out the certificate of debt consisting of legal demands [which were in force] against us and which were hostile to us. And this certificate He has set aside *and* completely removed by nailing it to the cross.

Our faith rests on His priestly works by His merits (Col. 2:13–14). Scripture shows that these legal demands are the requirements of the Mosaic law, which were violated by all of us. The debt is an eternal punishment for all violator's sins. (*This is also why they are all forgiven, past, present and future; for if not, these verses would make no sense.*) Gentiles were never directly liable to the Mosaic law, but as the apostle Paul explains, God holds the Gentiles also responsible for violating the principles of His law, regardless (Rom. 2:12–16). This is in God's nature as He is the *"Absolute"* (*Fabric of Existence*) and *cannot deny Himself.* Then His *absolute justice* demanded an eternal judgment for all those who rebel against His *absolute authority.* This we cannot take lightly as we begin to know and understand the God BEING's nature. These whole angels and human problems (*its cause and effect*) is about His awesome nature. This is why:

> **It pleased the *Father* for all the fullness [of deity—the sum total of His essence, all His perfection, powers, and attributes] to dwell [permanently] in Him (the Son), [His Word] and through [the intervention of] the Son to reconcile all things to Himself, making peace [with believers] through the blood of His cross; through Him, [I say,] whether things on earth or things in heaven.**

The lector noticed that this sinful problem started up in heaven, but God Jesus's priestly work covered all the heavens and the earth's eternal disorder (Col. 1:19–20). Now scripture states as a doctrinal position, a closing up of His word redemption, saying, **"For by the one offering He has perfected forever *and* completely cleansed those who are being sanctified [bringing each believer to spiritual completion and maturity]."** This is a (*teaching*) doctrine we must research: **"And in Him you have been made complete."** All scripture testifies to this (Col. 2:10) and adds a powerful witness:

And the Holy Spirit also adds His testimony to us [in confirmation of this]; for after having said, "This is the covenant that I will make with them after those days, says the Lord: I will imprint My laws upon their heart, And on their mind I will inscribe them [producing an inward change]." (*This is by His blood anointing*) *He* *then says* [*and remember, God is omnipresent; He includes all*], "And their sins and their lawless acts I will remember no more [no longer holding their sins against them]." Now where there is [absolute] forgiveness *and* complete cancellation of the penalty of these things, there is no longer any offering [to be made to atone] for sin.

The God BEING acts as the God BEING's nature is. This is how we read what the God BEING is communicating through His absolutes, attributes, and character. They are what backs up the word we read of Him. We are complete, He said, and it would make no sense if it were just about forgiving our yesterday's sins knowing that we live in a fallen nature. Paul, being saved, said, "O wretched man that I am! Who will deliver me from this body of death? I thank God—through Jesus Christ our Lord! [...*and*] There is now no condemnation [no guilty verdict, no punishment] for those who are in Christ Jesus [who believe in Him as personal Lord and Savior]." It is by the faith/hope in Christ's merits that we stand right before God (Rom. 7:24–25). Scripture states:

Therefore, believers, since we have confidence [*faith*] *and* full freedom to enter the Holy Place [the place where God dwells] by [means of] the blood of Jesus, by this new and living way which *He* [*the Father*] initiated *and* opened for us through the veil [as in the Holy of Holies], that is, through His [*Son's*] flesh, and since we have a great and wonderful Priest [Who rules] over the house of God [*Christ Jesus*] let us approach [the God BEING] with a true and sincere heart in unqualified assurance of faith, having had our hearts sprinkled clean from an evil conscience and our bodies washed with pure water [*this is all the work of our High Priest God Jesus*]. **Let us seize** [*meaning, to confiscate, captured, appropriate, and retake an opportunity or initiative eagerly and decisively*] *and* **hold tightly the confession of our hope without wavering, for He who promised is reliable** *and* **trustworthy** *and* **faithful [to His word].** (Heb. 10:14–22)

Therefore, as His priest (*of His temple, our body*), let us keep it always clean, washing our feet every day as He had said.

The Last Priestly Work for the Church on Earth

Then as we come to the end of this Bible study, we must affirm to all of those who have believed by the faith produced by the written word of God that it is His act of justifying us and His work of sanctifying us that brought us to His salvation (*as we recognize the sin and stop it on track*). Therefore, to affirm and declare the church that Christ *bought with His blood* is going to go through the great tribulation is to challenge (*impugn*) dismissing the doctrine of justification by faith. It is written:

Therefore, since we have been justified [that is, acquitted of sin, declared blameless before God] by faith, [let us grasp the fact that] we have peace [*from His last judgment*] with God [and the joy of reconciliation with Him] through our Lord Jesus Christ (the Messiah, the Anointed).

Scripture is saying that we don't owe God anything in Christ Jesus other than worship (Rom. 5:1 AMP). The apostles' theology assures us, as it prepares us, for all of which is about to happen. The author explained in his first published book how these doctrines came to be in *The Apostles Methodology to Interpret Scriptures*. This new book is a continuation to the realization that **"For God has not destined us to [incur His] wrath [that is, He did not select us to condemn us], but to obtain salvation through our Lord Jesus Christ"** (1 Thess. 5:9). The last act/agenda of God Jesus as judge, high priest, and son of God is written in scripture (*Paul said it, and as an author, I say the same:* **"It is no trouble for me to write the same things to you again, and it will help you to be more ready"** *[Phil. 3:1].*) for us to have a systematic process of scripture, saying,

After that, comes the end (completion), when He hands over the kingdom to God the Father, after He has made inoperative and abolished every ruler and every authority and power. For Christ must reign [as King] until He has put all His enemies under His feet. The last enemy to be abolished and put to an end is death [*she came into existence when Adam sinned*]. **For He (the Father) has put all things in subjection under His (Christ's) feet. But when He says, "All things have been put in subjection [under Christ]," it is clear that He (the Father) who put all things in subjection to Him (Christ) is accepted [since the Father is not in subjection to His own Son]. However, when all things are subjected**

to Him (Christ), then the Son Himself will also be subjected to the One (the Father) who put all things under Him, so that[the]God [BEING]may be all in all [manifesting His glory without any opposition, the supreme indwelling and controlling factor of life].

This is the last agenda of God Jesus, which They had in mind at Their first divine, heavenly summit (1 Cor. 15:24–28). Let us break these verses down to understand their sequence and bring the whole realization of the scripture revelation to light. God Jesus has made inoperative the principalities, powers, rulers, and every authority and power that dominates this evil age. The Messiah priestly works have giving the church the victory over these mentioned: **"I will build My church, and the gates of Hades shall not prevail against it"** (Matt. 16:18).

In our first book, we mentioned that Jesus of Nazareth came to earth and to take no advantage over the fallen creature called Satan. He left all His divinity by the Father's throne (*at the right hand of God*) and came as the firstborn over all creation, for the first Adam was created, so this means the Second Adam, Jesus-El-Emanuel, was like Adam in his first condition (*stamina*)—that is, without sin in a perfectly born body(firstborn of all creation). As a human, He fulfilled the demands of the Mosaic law requirement and became a sacrifice for our sins atone. Our enemy did not understand the God BEING's covenant with humanity, for he is a creature from another realm/creation (*he doesn't have like us God's image and likeness*), and scripture states in this reality: "*The wage of sin is death.*" The enemy used his lying power over humanity to take the blood of an innocent man, hanging Him in a wooden cross after beating Him to death, but that activated an inquiry in the courts of heavens.

As the Second Adam, a holy man/God (High Priest), Jesus went to heaven for a heavenly trial, for it is said, "**And just as it is appointed *and* destined for all men to die once and after this [comes certain] judgment**" (Heb. 9:27). Christ appeared up in the courts of heavens for "**everything is uncovered and laid bare before the eyes of him to whom we must give account**," and a judgment about this holy man/god and high priest had to take place by the Ancient of Days (Heb. 4:13). Daniel in a vision saw this (*for it was predestined by the Father*) and wrote: "**I was watching in the night visions, And behold, *One* like the Son of Man, coming with the clouds of heaven! He came to the Ancient of Days, and they brought Him near before Him.**"

In this King James Version, we must catch the words "*brought Him near,*" for a judgment had first to be made (Dan. 7:13). We then see this judgment in the words of the prophet Zachariah, saying, "**Then he showed me Joshua** [*which means Jesus in Hebrew and in Greek, a metaphor (symbolism)*] **the high priest standing before the Angel of the Lord, and Satan standing at his right hand to oppose him.**" This was a judgment at the courts of heaven, and the sentence was, "**And the Lord said to Satan, "The LORD rebuke you, Satan! The Lord who has chosen Jerusalem rebukes you! *Is* this not a brand plucked from the fire?**" (Zech. 3:1). Then to Christ, after His innocence was proven, for all things are naked to the eyes of whom we must give account. It was said,

> **Then to Him was given dominion and glory and a kingdom, that all peoples, nations, and languages should serve Him. His dominion *is* an everlasting dominion, which shall not pass away, and His kingdom *the one* which shall not be destroyed.**

For two thousand years, God Jesus has built His church of believers, His special treasure (Dan. 7:14). The apostle John was given to write about this revelation, for he saw Messiah at the throne of the Ancient of Days, and wrote:

> "Behold, the Lion of the tribe of Judah, the Root of David [*titles (as adjectives) given for the lector to know who this was*] has prevailed to open the scroll and to loosen its seven seals." And I looked, and behold, in the midst of the throne, and of the four living creatures, and in the midst of the elders, stood a Lamb as though it had been slain [*...Messiah*] Then He came and took the scroll out of the right hand of Him who sat on the throne. (Rev. 5:5–7)

In that same vision, God Jesus told John: "I am He who lives, and was dead, and behold, I am alive forevermore. Amen. And I have the keys of Hades and of Death" (Rev. 1:18). And this, many years before (*in this predestined context*) because the God BEING is not bound by temporal time. He appeared to His disciples and said, "All authority has been given to Me in heaven and on earth," meaning all power (Matt. 28:18). The Pauline perspective shows the militant power of our Lord and God Jesus (*the Christ*), saying,

> When He [the Father] raised Him from the dead and seated *Him* at His right hand in the heavenly *places*, far above all principality and power and might and dominion, and every name that is named, not only in this age but also in that which is to come. And He put all *things* under His feet and gave Him *to be* head over all *things* to the church, which is His body, the fullness of Him who fills all in all.

This is also why, "**And you are complete in Him, who is the head of all principality and power** [*of every fallen angelic and earthly demons' power*]" (Eph. 1:20–23; Col. 2:10). In other words, God the Father made God Jesus the head of all principalities and powers (*with us in Him*); therefore, Christ went to the evil one's headquarters and told him, "*Get out, this is not your office any longer!*" The Hebrew writer said God Jesus came to destroy the devil and wrote: "**Through death He might destroy him who had the power of death, that is, to say, the devil.**" Destroy here means dethrone, as to put to an end, demolish, wipe out, obliterate. The devil, as was then, has been destroyed, to reign no more (Heb. 2:14). The church of Christ has been elevated over the top and has been placed with Christ Jesus from everlasting to everlasting, He said so.

Christ Atonement Also Brought Destruction

The destruction of the devil has made a big ripple across the known heavens. All powers and principal dominions have been destroyed together with the evil one. The fallen angels were tied in chains of darkness on the last judgment day, and this has been recorded: "**And the angels who did not keep their proper domain, but left their own abode, He has reserved in everlasting chains under darkness for the judgment of the great day**" and also, "**Then He will also say to those on the left hand** [*tare/goats*] '**Depart from Me, you cursed, into the everlasting fire prepared for the devil and his angels.**'" The devil will burn with all of his followers (Jude 1:6; Matt. 25:41). Their defeat has been paraded. Paul wrote: "**Having disarmed principalities and powers, He made a public spectacle of** them, triumphing over them," at the cross of all places (Col. 2:15). Therefore, the prophets and psalmist as the Pauline and Johannian perspective, including those of the Hebrew writer, are similar about God Jesus's victory and new position of glory:

> He is the image of the invisible God, the firstborn over all creation. For by Him all things were created that are in heaven and that are on earth. [...] All things were created through Him and for Him. And He is before all things, and in Him all things consist of [*are held together*]. And He is the head of the body, the church, He is the beginning, the firstborn from the dead, that in all things He may have the preeminence.

God Jesus is more than meets the eye, and He lives in a body of *flesh and bones*. The Hebrew writer says about this:

> *His* Son, whom He [*the Father*] has appointed heir of all things, through whom also He made the universe [*through the Word*]; who being the brightness of *His* glory and the express image of His person and upholding all things by the word of His power, when He had by Himself purged our sins, sat down at the right hand of the Majesty on high, having become so much better than the angels, as He has by inheritance obtained a more excellent name than they. (Col. 1:15–18)

The prophet wrote of His gospel:

> He was wounded and bruised for our sins. He was beaten that we might have peace; he was lashed—and [so] we were healed! *We*—every one of us—have [*gone*] strayed away like sheep! *We,* who left God's paths to follow our own. Yet God laid on *him* the guilt and sins of every one of us! He was oppressed and he was afflicted, yet he never said a word. He was brought as a lamb to the slaughter; and as a sheep before her shearers is dumb, so he stood silent before the ones condemning him. From prison and trial, they led him away to his death. But who among the people of that day realized it was their sins that he was dying for—that he was suffering their punishment? [...] But he had done no wrong and had never spoken an evil word. But it was the Lord's good plan to bruise him and fill him with grief. However, when his Soul has been made an offering for sin, then he shall have a multitude of children, [converts/born again] many heirs. He shall live again, [resurrect] and God's program shall prosper in his hands. And when he sees all that is accomplished by the anguish of his Soul, he shall be satisfied; and because of what he has experienced, my righteous Servant shall make many to be counted righteous before God [as High Priest], for he shall bear all their sins. Therefore, I will give him the honors of one who is mighty and great because he has poured out his *Soul* unto death. He was counted as a sinner, and he bore the sins of many, and he pleaded with God for sinners.

An Omni-God works (Isa. 53). Therefore, the dragon, his fallen angels, the tares and goats (*demons*) are going to be thrown in the lake of fire for all eternity for what they've done. The one-third of the fallen angels were tied up by the God BEING for this purpose. They followed a loser, and they are bound to him for all eternity in death and the lake of fire.

Now the last enemy to be defeated is death, and it has already been subdued, for Christ has *the keys to Hades and death*. In the book of Revelation (*chapter 12*), the rest of the spectacle made of the devil and his followers is shown. Christ Jesus destroyed him out of office. Then Michael, the archangel, is about to kick him out of heaven; and he finalizes, being knocked out by an angel (*for we are sure he will put up a fight*), his lips Ziploced and tied up with a chain and thrown in hell for one thousand years. This is a fast version of God's predestined future. We are about to experience the snatching of the church of Christ, an almighty event by God Jesus, and no one will stop this from happening. It will begin by a war, which will break up in the heavens as the church is taken up to the City of Lights. At that moment (*already predestined*), it is said:

> **And war broke out in heaven: Michael and his angels fought with the dragon; and the dragon and his angels fought, but they did not prevail, nor was a place found for them in heaven any longer. So, the great dragon was cast out, that serpent of old, called the Devil and Satan, who deceives the whole world; he was cast to the earth, and his angels were cast out with him.**

In that very moment the enemy forces will fall into mystery Babylon (*as prophesied*) and the earth's expanse will be shaken like a blanket when it's shaken and pushed straight. It will roar, and ripples of a shock wave will explode throughout the earth. It is said of this event: "**And every mountain and island was moved out of its place**" (Rev. 6:14). An angel will "**cry mightily with a loud** voice, saying, 'Babylon the great is fallen, is fallen, and has become a dwelling place of demons, a prison for every foul spirit, and a cage for every unclean and hated bird!'" But this is for another book called *Terminal Damage* (Rev. 18:2). Every building will collapse, supermarkets, banks, gas stations, and all the streets as every highway and bridges will crumble, leaving a massacre of dead people all around the world. The world as we know it will cease to exist, and all the people left will incur the wrath of God and His great tribulation of seven years. And this has nothing to do with a nuclear holocaust; it's the wrath of God. The prophet Zephaniah wrote that God told him: "I will completely consume *and* sweep away all *things* from the face of the earth [in judgment]" (Zeph. 1:2). And "then I heard a loud voice saying in heaven, 'Now salvation, and strength, and the kingdom of our God, and the power of His Christ have come, for the accuser of our brethren, who accused them before our God, day and night, has been cast down'" (Rev. 12:8–10). The apostle's eschatology speaks about the deep wrath of God over the fallen earth. It is about to happen, and the only thing that can save you from God's wrath is the preparedness through the apostles' theology. *Why won't you listen?*

The Prophecy of the Rapemiur Is about to Happen

Jesus Christ's return is not what the church is waiting for but the snatching away of past and present believers. The people of (*Old Testament*) the first century and those of this last century are expecting Messiah's return like the Israelites of the first century were expecting Him to appear. Many false predictions have been made, and the faith/love of many because of evil has grown wax cold. It has been said since long ago: **"Where is the promise of His coming [what has become of it]? For ever since the fathers [*apostles*] fell asleep [in death], all things have continued [exactly] as they did from the beginning of creation."**

And the answer was, **"Nevertheless, do not let this one *fact* escape your notice, beloved, that with the Lord one day is like a thousand years, and a thousand years is like one day. The Lord does not delay [as though He were unable to act] *and* is not slow about His promise, as some count slowness, but is [extraordinarily] patient toward you, not wishing for any to perish but for all to come to repentance,"** all of the elect (2 Pet. 3:4, 8–9; Eph. 1:4). This statement seems to show that reality is just happening and not predestined, but scripture teaches otherwise. To us, it is happening now, but to God, it has been predestined as we go. He has edited it, His way. The God BEING is in control of all things. This is also why it has been written:

> **For by Him all things were created in heaven and on earth [...] all things were created *and* exist through Him [that is, by His activity] and for Him. And He Himself existed *and* is before all things, and in Him all things hold together. [His is the controlling, cohesive force of the universe].**

This is looking at reality through the eyes of God, in accordance with His word (Col. 1:16–17). This is what changes us to live a powerful life for Him. But let us make it clear: **"The day of the Lord will come like a thief [*and the unprepared*: "*none of the wicked shall understand*" *(Dan. 12:10)*] and then the heavens will vanish with a [mighty and thunderous] roar"** (2 Pet. 3:10). The apostle Peter accommodated his words to let us understand this mystery by saying, "Nevertheless, do not let this one *fact* escape your notice, beloved, that with the Lord one day is like a thousand years, and a thousand years is like one day." This must be looked up as a clue to determine this prophecy (2 Pet. 3:8).

The apostle Peter got this from Moses in psalm 90, saying, "For a thousand years in Your sight Are like yesterday when it is past." What was understood by the ancient rabbis to mean a "*thousand years*" is literally only one day (Ps. 90:4). We have another prophet who took this riddle from Moses and prophesied the day we are to expect the coming of the Lord, and this is where we get to understand the times as Moses declared of them, "So teach us to number our days, that we may cultivate *and* bring to You a heart of wisdom" (Ps. 90:12). God told Moses:

> The Lord also said to Moses [*first Messiah*], "Go to the people and consecrate them today and tomorrow [that is, prepare them for My sacred purpose], and have them wash their clothes [*today Christians by the sound doctrine*] and be ready by the third day, because on the third day the Lord will come down on Mount Sinai [in the cloud] in the sight of all the people."

We must add that Moses was a figure type to Messiah, the prophet like him to come (Exod. 19:10–11). Moses said, "The Lord your God will raise up for you a Prophet like me from your midst, from your brethren. Him you shall hear." We must understand this well: Hosea's prophecy and the information about the clue Moses and Peter meant for us to see (Deut. 18:15). The prophet Hosea wrote: "After two days He will revive us; On the third day He will raise us up, That we may live in His sight" (Hos. 6:2), and this adding that the same one thousand years is like a day. God Jesus is about to sound the trumpet. He started the countdown when He began to "*revive us*" or heal us (*which is the context of this word*), and this started two thousand years ago at Pentecost after His resurrection. The Lord started to revive us when He poured out the Holy Spirit on the day of Pentecost to the church, His body that became alive.

This birthday is written like this: "**When the day of Pentecost had come, they were all together in one place, and suddenly a sound came from heaven like a rushing violent wind, and it filled the whole house where they were sitting**" (Acts 2:1). Notice how this was the solemn feast of Leviticus 23 and was called Pentecost (*Feast of Weeks*). It was observed at the time of the grain harvest and the offering of the first fruits.

Pentecost is one of the three great annual Jewish festivals, after the Passover and before the Feast of Tabernacles (*Booths*). Just as Jesus's sacrifice was the fulfillment of Passover, fifty days later (Pente *means "fifth" or "fiftieth" in Greek*), the coming of the Holy Spirit was the fulfillment of Pentecost. There is no secret here; we are just following scriptures. It was at Pentecost (*fifty days after Passover*) that the church was born and God Jesus, the apostle Peter said, "**God raised this Jesus [bodily from the dead], and of that [fact] we are all witnesses. Therefore, having been exalted to the right hand of God, and having received from the Father the promise of the Holy Spirit, He has poured out this [blessing] which you both see and hear.**" He is the one healing/reviving people to be born again and seal/baptize with the Holy Spirit of the promise (Acts 2:32–33). Peter mentioned this other prophecy to them about what had happened at Pentecost from Joel (2:28), who said, "**It shall come about after this, that I shall pour out My Spirit on all mankind.**" This was not a secret to the Jews of Peter's days as he mentioned it to them. Then we must understand a holy man/God comes to the holy God the Father of heaven and earth and makes an exchange of His human blood for the promise Holy Spirit, which He poured to those in the upper room on the day of Pentecost as promised in prophecy.

Now what this all boils down to is that the church's birthday was fifty days after Passover, or after God Jesus resurrected from the dead. Some say that this happened in the year 28, 30, and/or even the year 33; and she is meant to be active on earth for two thousand years, meaning that we are at the end of the church age. The prophecy of Hosea states that, "*On the third day He will raise us up.*" Therefore, the snatching away of the church must be on the anniversary of the two thousand years of the church's birthday. If we add two thousand years after the Lord had resurrected (*year 28, 30, or 33?*) and fifty days after Passover of that year, then we have a near proximity of the rapture/snatching away of the body of Christ. This is what will trigger the great tribulation (*Jacob's troubles*) or the last week of Daniel's prophecy, before the second coming. We must be mindful that "**of that [exact] day and hour no one knows, not even the angels of heaven, nor the Son [in His humanity], but the Father alone.**" What we must do is to be watchful as prescribed in scripture: "**So be alert [give strict attention, be cautious and active in faith], for you do not know which day [whether near or far] your Lord is coming**" (Matt. 24:36, 42).

Luke wrote that Christ said, "**Watch therefore and pray** [*the faith of the elect*] **always that you may be counted worthy to escape all these things** [*pray for your tomorrow today*] **that will come to pass, and to stand before the Son of Man.**" This is the reason we advise repeating prayer for your tomorrow today (Luke 21:36). The prophet Isaiah said it best, showing two things we must do: "**Depart, depart, go out from there [the lands of exile** (*the world's evil age*)**], touch no unclean thing; go out of the midst of her (Babylon), purify yourselves, You who carry the articles of the Lord** (*the sound doctrine*) **[on your journey from there].**" First, we must follow the apostles' theology on their sound doctrine so that the anointing will always be in our life as a temple of God the Holy Spirit, and that is through prayers.

Then "For you will not go out in a hurry [as when you left Egypt], nor will you go in flight [fleeing, as you did from the Egyptians]; for the Lord will go before you, and the God of Israel will be your rear guard." The prophet was writing to people who did not know the God of Israel, in other words, Gentile Christians (Isa. 52:11–12). The apostle Paul explained how quickly this will be. He said, "Listen, I tell you a mystery: We will not all sleep, but we will all be changed—in a flash, in the twinkling of an eye, at the last trumpet" (1 Cor. 15:51). There is no need to be frightened, for we are assured this will be a fast and smooth transition, and the prophet Isaiah was assuring the born-again Gentiles that "*the God of Israel will be your rear guard,*" because why tell the Israelites "*the God of Israel,*" for they knew Him. Therefore, we close this book in prayer, for the God BEING lives in your personal future. And so we pray for our tomorrow today.

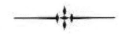

Answer the questions from this chapter to interact with others in a book club:

1. When Jesus of Nazareth walked the earth, was He a complete man in our condition?

2. Can it be said that reality has been ordained and predestined by the God BEING?
   Prove it.

3. Can you say that looking at reality through the eyes of God, according to His word, is a worldview for the born-again believer?

EPILOGUE

Summarizing Systematic Theology from This Book's Perspective

This book has brought the lector to a meditative state and a realization from the revelation given by the written word whose contents are translated to our present reality. We have touched this book's topic, *God in Flesh and Bones*, through a different venue, using the structure of systematic theology to interest the reader on the topic, and bring forth by our thematic the living meaning of our High Priest. No one can declare their own theological view of scripture without studying and assimilating what has been established throughout the church's history and its many collaborators to its knowledge. Feeling so grateful to God that this knowledge reached me, I want to give thanks to those professors who instructed me to follow this path.

They've collaborated, opening my spirit/soul into understanding theology in a different light. Thank you, Dr. Norman Wise and Dr. John Stevenson (Presbyterians), Dr. James Tino (Lutheran), and Dr. Ralph Curtin (Baptist) for all of you were very thorough and dedicated professors at Trinity International University in South Florida; and I want to give honor to whom honor is due.

The study of theology is the fuel that ignites our worship because the word of God provokes us to believe in Him. It is by looking at reality through the eyes of God, according to His written word, that the ultimate experience of our life is reached; and anyone looking elsewhere is missing out on the only truth that matters (*there is no light in darkness and its false doctrines*). A theist believer accepts that the Creator of this universe is a personal God (*with His creation*) and His written word carries His attribute of unchangeableness (*immutability*) **"in which it is impossible for God to lie."** She does not change, for He is behind every one of its precepts and concepts. God (*the I AM*) is unchanging in His character, will, and covenantal promises. *God* is *Spirit* whose BEING is wisdom, power, holiness, justice, goodness, infinite, truth, absolute, eternal, indescribable, and unchangeable. Therefore, we must know that our life consciousness (*this reality*) is intercepted and overlapped by God's conscious reality, and He is the one conceding the very moment in time and existence (*this created reality*) we are all experiencing right here and now (*in Him all things hold together*).

After being called/touched by the power of His word into a born-again spirit-filled status/condition, the word of God opens our eyes to see reality by the light she imparts radiantly throughout. This is so because God is light, and He is not hiding any part of Himself—that is, those we can understand by our fragile existence. What is known about God is evident within our inner consciousness (*sensorial spirit/soul reality*) for God has made it evident, (*He has placed eternity in our hearts*). This has been so;

for since the creation of the world, His invisible attributes, His eternal power and divine nature, have been clearly seen, being understood through His workmanship over all His creation (*God is sovereign*), the wonderful things He has made. Look around at all the abundance.

So those who fail to believe (*the abundance, perceive by our sensorial abundance*), trusting Him, are without excuse *and* without defense at His presence. We are the center (*piece/point*) physical creation, for we are God's word activated/manifested (*in His image and likeness [spirit/soul]*) to express ourselves in the rest of what has been created in heaven and earth. The God who created all things has revealed that there is no other God/Rock, for He has not found any other god. He is the only God BEING (the Eternal), and we use these terms to tie up all that He is in one thought (*the LORD, our God the Lord, is One*). He is a BEING, and we are His creation (*angels and humans alike*). We (*humanity*) have a beginning, and we have an end while He has always been and will always *be* the Eternal, the only God BEING. Understanding Him must be through what He has revealed of Himself in His written word (*in reaction to our death sentence*).

He has explained, "**The LORD your God the Lord is One**," but that is just the beginning knowledge of His (*invisible*) reality into our dead reality, for He lives in a reality of invisibility (*His own universe*), which is an attribute of His BEING because all the heavens created cannot withstand His glorious BEING. The Lord says, "Heaven is my throne, and the earth is my footstool." His reality is infinite/eternal from north to south and east to west, *His holy of holies.*

City of Gold, City of God, City of Light

We have been called to appear into that reality of invisibility (*to be caught up to His third heaven*) soon. This will be in a transformed body (*for flesh and blood cannot inherit the kingdom of God*) to the likeness of Christ (*we shall be like Him, for we shall see Him as He is*) in flesh and bones(*for this perishable must clothe itself with the imperishable, and this mortal with immortality*). He lives in a reality where inexpressible words are heard, which it is not lawful for a (*dead*) man to utter. We have been called to come to Mount Zion (*God's invisible reality and His throne*) into the city of the living God, the heavenly Jerusalem (*City of Gold, City of Light*). Scripture reveals of this city:

> He carried me away in the Spirit to a mountain great and high [*Mount Zion*] and showed me the Holy City, Jerusalem. It shone with the glory of God, and its brilliance was like that of a very precious jewel, like a jasper, clear as crystal. It had a great, high wall with twelve gates, and with twelve angels at the gates. On the gates were written the names of the twelve tribes of Israel [*earthlings*]. There were three gates on the east, three on the north, three on the south and three on the west. The wall of the city had twelve foundations, and on them were the names of the twelve apostles of the Lamb [*the City is meant for physical people*]. The wall was made of jasper, and the city of pure gold, as pure as glass. The foundations of the city walls were decorated with every kind of precious stone. The first foundation was jasper, the second sapphire, the third agate, the fourth emerald, the fifth onyx, the sixth ruby, the seventh chrysolite, the eighth beryl, the ninth topaz, the tenth turquoise, the eleventh jacinth, and the twelfth amethyst. The twelve gates were twelve pearls, each gate

made of a single pearl. The great street of the city was of gold, as pure as transparent glass. Then the angel showed me the river of the water of life, as clear as crystal, flowing from the throne of God and of the Lamb down the middle of the great street of the city [*they are the fabric of life*]. On each side of the river stood the tree of life, bearing twelve crops of fruit, yielding its fruit every month. And the leaves of the tree are for the healing of the nations. The city does not need the sun or the moon to shine on it, for the glory of God gives it light, and the Lamb is its lamp. The nations will walk by its light, and the kings of the earth [*the church*] will bring their splendor into it. On no day will its gates ever be shut, for there will be no night there. I saw no temple in it, for the Lord God Almighty [*the omnipotent, the Ruler of all*] and the Lamb are its temple. The glory and honor of the nations will be brought into it. The throne of God and of the Lamb will be in the city.

It is into this city we are called to appear to an innumerable company of angels (*millions of millions*); to the general assembly (*the Ancient of Days administration, thousands of thousands*) and church of the firstborn *who are* registered in heaven(*innumerable*); to God, the judge of all; to the spirits of just men made perfect; to Jesus, the mediator of the new covenant; and to the blood of sprinkling that speaks better things than *that of* Abel (*who was in a fallen nature*). In God's invisible reality, there is no need of lamps (*or today's electric light*) nor light of the sun, for the Lord God gives it His eternal light. There is no temple in it (*the city*) for the Lord God Almighty and the Lamb is its temple. (*They are the door to Their invisible reality.*)

The throne of God and of the Lamb will be in the city, and his servants will serve Him (*thousands of thousands*). God Jesus said to the church, "*I will make them a pillar in the temple of My God, and they shall go out no more*" and "*In My Father's house are many mansions; if it were not so, I would have told you. I go to prepare a place for you.*" God's invisible reality is eternally infinite (*as it is in light*) toward the north, south, east, and west. (*He will be our Temple and we will be part of it*). The city had no need of the sun or of the moon to shine in it, for the glory of God would illuminate it. The Lamb *is* its light, who alone has immortality (*He became a mortal*) and now dwells in unapproachable light, whom no (*dead*) man has seen or can see. (*He is the image of the invisible God, the firstborn over all creation.*) And they (*the church*) are members of the body of Christ. This is a known mystery (*secret*) revealed to us; for we are members of His body, of His flesh, and of His bones.

And it is written: "For this reason, a man shall leave his father and mother and be joined to his wife, and the two shall become one flesh. This is a great mystery, but I speak concerning Christ and the church." He said they shall reign forever and ever, for He has made us kings and priests to God the Father. Those overcoming will reign on the new heaven and earth (*which will be an infinite expanse, "Also, there was no more sea"*) He has promised to create for us a new plan. Then He who sat on the throne and said, "Behold, I make all things new." And He said, "It is done! I am the Alpha and the Omega, the Beginning and the End [*words of Christ/Messiah speaking as the Father*]. I will give of the fountain of the water of life freely to him who thirsts. He who overcomes (*by the imparted word* faith/hope) shall inherit all things, and I will be his God and he shall be My son [*by the God* BEING *will*]."

The Eternal, the God BEING, by His living Word/Verb has promised/prophesied all these things once He finishes all the works in this death time zone. It has been written:

Then comes the end, when He [Christ/Messiah] delivers the kingdom to God the Father, and He puts an end to all rule and all authority and power [*rebellion*]. For He must reign till He has put all enemies under His feet. The last enemy that will be destroyed is death [*brought to existence by Adam*]. For He has put all things under His feet. But when He says, "All things are put under Him," it is evident that He who put all things under Him [God the Father] is exempted. Now when all things are made subject to Him, then the Son Himself will also be subject to Him who put all things under Him, that He, the God BEING, the Eternal, may be all in all [*forever, Amen!*].

Behold the Hand, Behold the Nail (Yнvн)

At one point, God Jesus asked His disciples, "Who do people say that the Son of Man is?" and they answered, "Some say John the Baptist; others, Elijah; and still others, Jeremiah, or [just] one of the prophets." Then God Jesus turned around and asked them, "But who do you say that I am?" Simon Peter replied, "You are the Christ (the Messiah, the Anointed), the Son of the living God." To our corrupted understanding, we must remember it is God who reveals His godly BEING unto us, for we were born dead by sin and death. God Jesus told (Peter) as unto them, "Blessed are you [...] for flesh and blood has not revealed *this* to you, but My Father who is in heaven." Those of us who have received this special revelation of being born again must understand that the power of the Word (*which is spirit and is alive*) has given us the greatest riches in the whole eternal universe of God, and we must cultivate it each day.

The God BEING wants that "the one who boasts, boast in this, that he *understands* and *knows* Me [and acknowledges Me and honors Me as God and recognizes without any doubt], that I am the Lord who practices loving-kindness, justice, and righteousness on the earth, for in these things I delight." This is what God Jesus came to reveal to us about the Father, and we must acknowledge that the Father uses His written word as the testimony He gives of His Son, who is the Word, King, Messiah. God's name (YHVH) in the Hebrew language (*words*) is *Yod-Hey-Vav-Hey*, and it means "*Behold the Hand, Behold the Nail.*" This is the testimony of the Father, and He never meant for His name to be unpronounceable, for it is the testimony He is giving of His Son (*God is Light*). The revelation of Himself unto us has always been there, but our *dead-man-walking* attitude has blinded the motive of our Creator. As we begin to know Him (*through His illuminating word*), we capture that He is in the office/function of redeeming us from sin and death—that is, from this *death time zone* that we are living in.

God Jesus has created from the ashes of a burned civilization, a people: a chosen race, a royal priesthood, a consecrated nation, a(special) people for *God's* own possession so that we may proclaim the excellencies (the wonderful deeds and virtues and perfections) of Him who called you out of darkness into His marvelous light [*Scripture says*]. The God BEING has sat us together with Messiah/Christ, which is above all things (in every realm), in subjection under Christ's feet and appointed Him (*God in flesh and bones*) as (supreme and authoritative) head over all things in the church, which is His body (*who has the feet*) the fullness of Him who fills *and* completes all things in all (*His believers*). For His intent was that now, through the church, the manifold wisdom of God should be made known to the rulers and authorities (*powers and principalities of darkness*) in the heavenly realms. This is saying so much of God's motive for His chosen nation and royal priesthood.

Once the believer *knows* the God BEING by His living word, they would come to *understand* that God the Father has been (so very) rich in mercy, because of His great and wonderful love with which He loved us (*before the foundation of the world*) even when we were (spiritually) dead *and* separated from Him because of our sins. He made us (spiritually) alive together with Christ (for by His grace—His undeserved favor and mercy—we have been saved from God's judgment). And He raised us up together with Him (when we believed) and seated us with Him in the heavenly *places*, in Christ Jesus (and He did this), so that in the ages to come (*these last two thousand years*), He might (clearly) show the immeasurable *and* unsurpassed riches of His grace in (His) kindness toward us in Christ Jesus (by providing for our redemption).

For it is by grace (God's remarkable compassion and favor drawing you to Christ) that you have been saved (actually, delivered from judgment and given eternal life) through faith. And this (salvation) is not of yourselves (not through your own effort); but it is the (undeserved, gracious) gift of God (*God's gifts are irrevocable; salvation falls into that category as a gift*), not as a result of (your) works (nor your attempts to keep the law), so that no one will (be able to) boast *or* take credit in any way (for his salvation). This is the testimony that the Father has given of His Son and whoever does not believe it will stand corrected at judgment day with no excuses to Him, in front of whom all things are naked and we must give account. In the courts of earth, one is innocent until proven guilty, but in the courts of heaven, guilty as charged and a payment is due. The only perfectly acceptable payment is the one the God BEING has provided for our fallen race (*Behold the Hand, Behold the Nail*).

High Priest According to the Order of Melchizedek

The apostle's theology (*tradition*) is what prepares the believer to being found worthy to escape the apostle's eschatology (*God's wrath*). Their theology is the continuation of God Jesus's priestly work for the church on earth, through the ages. God Jesus established a new covenant under better promises with the Father for us. He said, "Here I am, I have come to do your will," (*which was a horrendous death*). He sets aside the first (*covenant*) to establish the second (*and acquire the third, the transformation*). And by that will, we have been made holy through the sacrifice of the body of Jesus Christ once and for all (*by His merits*). For by one sacrifice, he has made perfect forever those who are being made holy (*that is complete*).

Therefore, He is also able to save forever those who come to God through Him since He always lives to make intercession for them (*as high priest of a new priesthood order*). He, having offered one sacrifice for sins for all time (*His own blood*), sat down at the right hand of God, waiting from that time onward until His enemies are made a footstool for His feet. For by one offering, He has perfected for all time those who are sanctified. Therefore, brothers *and sisters*, since we have confidence to enter the holy place by the blood of Jesus, by a new and living way which He inaugurated for us through the veil, that is, *through* His flesh, and since *we have* a great priest over the house of God (*in the priesthood order of Melchizedek*), let's approach the God BEING with a sincere heart, in full assurance of faith, having our hearts sprinkled *clean* from an evil conscience (*through the faith/hope of His word*), and our bodies washed with pure water. Let's hold firmly to the confession of our hope without wavering, for He who promised is faithful. Scriptures are soaking wet with the holy blood of God Jesus's sacrifice, and it changes the believer within and without. Show me your faith without works, and I will tell you that is not the faith produced by the omnipotent word of God, for she produces the works. Therefore, we pray for our tomorrow today and watch the powerful force of our living God preparing us for that moment of death or snatching away at the trumpet sound.

Jesus of Nazareth, our God and King, has fulfilled all the requirements of the covenant of the law; and that's confirmed in scripture. He completed the Passover and went to the temple of heaven (*which was not made by human hands*) and offered His holy blood, interchanging with the Father, to receive the promised Holy Spirit. He is our high priest by the Father and lives in a body of flesh and bones to let us know this covenant is from everlasting to everlasting. He has three more solemn festivities to complete the full cycle of His priestly works and then comes the end when He turns all things unto Himself and become once more the God BEING He has always been.

My first publish book, *The Apostles Methodology to Interpret Scriptures*, was set apart from other Christian books as it was pointing to a path, not a conclusion, while this book, *God in Flesh and Bones*, is bringing the lector into a firm realization that this reality of God is about to be busted open for those who He has called from generation to generation, and I am so thankful of Him for letting me be part of this great activity approximating through the work of these books. Thank you, my Savior, and I pray that all those who read these words become edified profoundly by the work and collaboration of your gospel, my Lord.

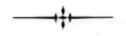

About the Author

Marcelino Esquilin was born in Rio Piedras, Puerto Rico in July of 1955 and as of today he is sixty-seven years young. While writing this book his pursuing a master's degree in theology at Knox Seminary. He has been married now for 42 years with Sofia de la Rosa. They met as church youth. They procreated four wonderful sons and daughters and are grandparents to three beautiful grandkids (*and waiting for more*). Marxel as he rather be call is the author of three published books, he is also a Christian song writer/singer. He has worked in the pass as missionary, evangelist, Sunday school teacher, church musician, and pastor, but prefers being a Sunday school teacher. At one time, Marxel explains, that he made a prayer to the Lord because of a revelation he was shown and ask if he could be part of that great activity approximating. The Lord has answered his prayers through these personal achievements. Marcelino's belief has always been of a Pentecostal orientation and as the Apostle Paul taught, the snatching away from this existence to the heavenly reality onto the City of Light, City of God. If in the process of getting there he can edified someone, his goal and prayers have been achieved. One of his favorite biblical passages by Paul is: "Brothers and sisters, look at what you were when God called you. Not many of you were wise in the way the world judge's wisdom. Not many of you had great influence. Not many of you came from important families. But God chose the foolish things of the world to shame the wise, and he chose the weak things of the world to shame the strong. He chose what the world thinks is unimportant and what the world looks down on and thinks is nothing in order to destroy what the world thinks is important. God did this so that no one can brag in his presence. Because of God you are in Christ Jesus, who has become for us wisdom from God. In Christ we are put right with God, and have been made holy, and have been set free from sin. So, as the Scripture says, "If people want to brag, they should brag only about the Lord." When the Lord saved Marxel he was twenty-two years of age, had just came out of the Vietnam-era, was locked up in a mental ward, suicidal but the Lord had other plans for his life and in resurrection day, Sunday, April 10, 1977, looking for death, life found him in an evangelistic campaign by Yiye Avila, a Puerto Rican evangelist. He was healed from chronic depression, Hepatitis-C, and three packs of cigarettes per day. All the glory of any achievement he gives to the Lord, and if any glory or honor by his work is reached, it must be given onto the Lord, God Jesus our Messiah and High Priest who is about to come for us all. Thank you for acquiring my books. I will be eternally grateful and remember our relationships are eternal.